AF327640

EDUCATING FOR SOCIAL JUSTICE IN EARLY CHILDHOOD

Bringing together scholarship and examples from practice, this book explores ways in which early childhood curriculum – including classroom practices and community contexts – can more actively engage with a range of social justice issues, democratic principles and anti-oppressive practices.

Featuring a stellar list of expert contributors, the chapters in this volume present a cross-section of contemporary issues in childhood education. The text highlights the voices of children, teachers and families as they reflect on everyday experiences related to issues of social justice, inclusion and oppression, as well as ways young children and their teachers engage in activism. Chapters explore curriculum and programs that address justice issues, particularly educating for democracy, and culminate in a focus on the future, offering examples of resistance and visions of hope and possibility.

Designed for practitioners, graduate students and researchers in early childhood, this book challenges readers to explore the ways in which early childhood education is – and can be – engaging with social justice and democratic practices.

Shirley A. Kessler is a retired Professor of Early Childhood Education at National-Louis University, USA.

Beth Blue Swadener is Professor of Justice Studies and Social and Cultural Pedagogy at Arizona State University, USA.

CHANGING IMAGES OF EARLY CHILDHOOD

Series Editor: Nicola Yelland

Books in this forward-thinking series challenge existing practices in early childhood education and reflect the changing images of the field. The series enables readers to engage with contemporary ideas and practices of alternative perspectives which deviate from those theories traditionally associated with the education of young children and their families. Not only do these books make complex theory accessible, they provide early childhood educators with the tools to ensure their practices are backed by appropriate theoretical frameworks and strong empirical evidence.

Titles in the *Changing Images of Early Childhood* series include:

Childhood and Postcolonization: Power, Education, and Contemporary Practice
by Gaile S. Cannella and Radhika Viruru

Rethinking Parent and Child Conflict
by Susan Grieshaber

Rethinking Early Literacies: Reading and Rewriting Worlds
by Mariana Souto-Manning and Haeny S. Yoon

Meaning Making in Early Childhood Research: Pedagogies and the Personal
edited by Will Parnell and Jeanne Marie Iorio

Found in Translation: Connecting Reconceptualist Thinking with Early Childhood Education Practices
edited by Nicola Yelland and Dana Frantz Bentley

Educating for Social Justice in Early Childhood
edited by Shirley A. Kessler and Beth Blue Swadener

EDUCATING FOR SOCIAL JUSTICE IN EARLY CHILDHOOD

*Edited by Shirley A. Kessler
and Beth Blue Swadener*

Routledge
Taylor & Francis Group

NEW YORK AND LONDON

First published 2020
by Routledge
52 Vanderbilt Avenue, New York, NY 10017

and by Routledge
2 Park Square, Milton Park, Abingdon, Oxon OX14 4RN

Routledge is an imprint of the Taylor & Francis Group, an informa business

© 2020 Taylor & Francis

The right of Shirley A. Kessler and Beth Blue Swadener to be identified as the authors of the editorial material, and of the authors for their individual chapters, has been asserted in accordance with sections 77 and 78 of the Copyright, Designs and Patents Act 1988.

All rights reserved. No part of this book may be reprinted or reproduced or utilised in any form or by any electronic, mechanical, or other means, now known or hereafter invented, including photocopying and recording, or in any information storage or retrieval system, without permission in writing from the publishers.

Trademark notice: Product or corporate names may be trademarks or registered trademarks, and are used only for identification and explanation without intent to infringe.

Library of Congress Cataloging-in-Publication Data
A catalog record for this title has been requested

ISBN: 978-0-367-24698-3 (hbk)
ISBN: 978-0-367-24699-0 (pbk)
ISBN: 978-0-429-28397-0 (ebk)

Typeset in Bembo
by Taylor & Francis Books

We dedicate this book to scholars and early childhood educators who are imagining and working for a more just world – and to their powerful partners, young activists.

CONTENTS

PART II
Social Justice in the Classroom: Democratic and Anti-bias Practices

PART III
Way Forward: Stories of Hope and Possibility

ILLUSTRATIONS

CONTRIBUTORS

William Ayers is a Distinguished Professor of Education at the University of Illinois at Chicago who writes about social justice and democracy, education and the cultural contexts of schooling, and teaching as an essentially intellectual, ethical and political enterprise. His books include *A Kind and Just Parent; Teaching toward Freedom; To Teach: The Journey, in Comics*; and *Demand the Impossible!*

Dana Frantz Bentley is an Assistant Professor in the Early Childhood Program at Lesley University and a PreK teacher at Buckingham Browne and Nichols School in Cambridge, Massachusetts. She has been an early childhood teacher for 17 years, working in a wide range of urban classroom settings in Boston and New York City. Dana positions herself as a critical practitioner, wondering with and through her experiences with children. Her research is primarily focused on anti-bias work with young children, exploring how these early experiences frame children as empowered, political individuals. Her recent publications include "An idea is in your body": "Technology" and transformation in the early childhood classroom; Toward inclusive understandings of marriage in an early childhood classroom: Negotiating (un)readiness, community, and vulnerability through a critical reading of King and King; and a co-edited book, *Found in Translation: Connecting Reconceptualist Thinking with Early Childhood Practices*.

Marianne (Mimi) Bloch is Professor Emerita in the Department of Curriculum and Instruction and the Department of Gender and Women's Studies at the University of Wisconsin-Madison. She is a founding member of the international reconceptualizing early childhood education conference. Her research and writing include a variety of books, chapters and articles, including the (2018) co-edited volume: Block, M.N., Swadener, B.B. & Cannella, G.S. (Eds.)

Reconceptualizing Early Childhood Care and Education – A reader, Critical Questions, New Imaginaries and Social Activism (New York: Peter Lang). She is a member of the recently started *receactivism* group and of the International Consortium for Critical Childhood Policy.

Gail Buffalo is an Ed.D. candidate in Interdisciplinary Studies at Teachers College, Columbia University. Her dissertation research seeks to center the certification experiences of intersectionally minoritized early childhood teachers using a critical race narrative approach. She has authored/coauthored book chapters on critical pedagogy, including "Henry Giroux and the 'Crisis' of 21st Century Education" (Russell-Buffalo, 2014), "Pedagogy of reinvention: Paulo Freire in 20th and 21st Century Education" (Russell-Buffalo & Stanford, 2014), as well as articles on teacher education, including "Taking a cross-country journey with a world map: Examining the construction of practitioner identities through one case study" (Vetter & Russell, 2011). Buffalo is also an instructor at Teachers College, Columbia University.

Betty Chan is an educator who is inspired by the constructivist approach to listening to and learning with children. She has worked primarily with preschool aged children utilizing Reggio inspired approaches in her work. Currently she is teaching PreK at Buckingham Browne and Nichols School in Cambridge, Massachusetts. Prior to that she worked at the Boulder Journey School in Boulder, Colorado learning and working alongside others who are also inspired by the works of educators in Reggio Emilia.

Jeanne Marie Iorio is a senior lecturer in early childhood education at the University of Melbourne. Prior to her move to Australia she worked as an assistant and associate professor at the University of Hawaii, West Oahu. Her research, training and writing focus on disrupting and rethinking accepted early childhood practices, particularly in relationship to the image of the child as capable. Her publications (with co-editor Will Parnell) include *Rethinking Readiness in Early Childhood Education: Implications for Policy and Practice* (2015); *Disrupting Early Childhood Education Research: Imagining New Possibilities* (2016); and *Making Meaning in Early Childhood Research: Pedagogies and the Personal* (2018).

Shirley A. Kessler is a retired Professor of Early Childhood Education at National-Louis University, Wheeling, IL. Her research interests include classroom research, curriculum theory, and history of the kindergarten and the kindergarten curriculum. She was a founding member of the groups, Reconceptualizing Early Childhood Education and the Special Interest Group within the American Educational Research Association, Critical Perspectives on Early Childhood Education. Major publications include an edited collection with Beth Blue Swadener (1992), *Reconceptualizing the Early Childhood Curriculum: Beginning the Dialogue* and

Kessler (2018), "Reconceptualizing the early childhood curriculum: An unaddressed topic", in M. Bloch, B.B. Swadener & G. Cannella (Eds.) (2nd ed.), *Reconceptualizing early care & education: Critical questions, new imaginaries and social activism.*

Casey Khaleesi has been an educator in Arizona for 30 years and an advocate for listening to and learning from children and youth. She currently teaches special education and has worked with all levels of education. She recently completed her MA in Social and Cultural pedagogy at Arizona State University. Her thesis examined middle school children's embodied experiences of high stakes testing.

Angeles Maldonado is a mother and human rights scholar activist studying race, migration, discourse and social movements in Arizona. She is the CEO for Ybarra Maldonado Law Group and the Founder and Executive Director of the Institute for Border Crit Theory, whose mission is to foreground the voices and experiences of people of color living in the borderlands through social justice education and pedagogy, borderland research and the publication of counter-narratives of resistance. Dr. Maldonado believes strongly that migration is a fundamental human right and all borders must be resisted.

Rebecca New is a retired Associate Professor of Education at the University of North Carolina-Chapel Hill, where she has taught undergraduate and graduate courses on culture, child development and early childhood education. Current research in the US utilizes her training as a psychological anthropologist, as Principal Investigator of a longitudinal ethnographic study of Chinese and Latino/a immigrant families' cultural models of parenting during children's early transitions from home to preschool, kindergarten and first grade. Publications include *Diversity and Developmentally Appropriate Practices* (1994; co-edited with Bruce Mallory); a 4-volume *Early Childhood Education: An International Encyclopedia* (2007; co-edited with Mon Cochran); and *Anthropology and Child Development* (2008; co-edited with Robert A. LeVine). Current book projects include one long in the making – *Approaching Reggio Emilia: The 100 Languages of Early Childhood Education*; and an historic review of *Cultural Images of Children and Teachers: A Century of U.S. Early Childhood Education.*

Michelle Salazar Pérez is the J. Paul Taylor Endowed Professor and Associate Professor of Early Childhood Education at New Mexico State University. She uses women of color feminisms to examine dominant constructions of childhood/s, particularly how they influence public policy and subjugate the lived experiences of marginalized people/s and communities. She is co-editor of the book *Critical examinations of quality in childhood education and care: Regulation, disqualification, and erasure* and a special issue in the *Global Studies of Childhood* journal that centers global south onto epistemologies in childhood studies. Her work has been published in *Teachers College Record, Equity & Excellence in Education*, the *Journal of Early Childhood Teacher Education* and *Review of Research in Education*.

Lacey Peters is an Assistant Professor of early childhood education at Hunter College of the City University of New York. Her research interests include the examination of the viewpoints, and decision-making processes of parents and family members, as well as early childhood professionals. She is currently working on a project that foregrounds Universal PreKindergarten teachers' perspectives on using authentic assessment systems. Her publications focus on discourses and policy issues in quality improvement and rating scales, children's rights and perspectives on early education and social engagement, and constructions of readiness.

Ayesha Rabadi-Raol, M.A. in Early Childhood Education and Special Education, is a doctoral research fellow at Teachers College, Columbia University, New York. Her research focuses on issues of equity and justice in early childhood education and teacher education. Specifically, her work questions how immigrant and transnational students and teachers of color have been positioned by educational institutions in the US. Rabadi-Raol is also an instructor in the department of Curriculum and Teaching at Teachers College, Columbia University, where she teaches preservice teachers about multicultural education and the teaching of reading and writing in the primary grades with an equity and justice perspective. She has authored/coauthored articles and book chapters, including the 2018 *Review of Research in Education* article entitled "(Re)Centering Quality in Early Childhood Education: Toward Intersectional Justice for Minoritized Children" (with Mariana Souto-Manning).

Kia S. Rideaux is a Curriculum and Instruction Doctoral Candidate at the University of North Texas. Over the last 14 years as an early childhood educator, she has served in the roles of classroom teacher and EC-6 teacher educator. Her research interests center marginalized feminist perspectives and utilize critical qualitative methodologies to address issues of equity and diversity in early childhood education. She has published several chapters and journal articles about teacher educators of color, African American girls and lensing childhood studies with women of color theoretical perspectives.

Cinthya M. Saavedra is Associate Professor and Academic Program Director of Mexican American Studies at The University of Texas Rio Grande Valley. Her research centers Chicana/Latina feminist epistemology in education research. In addition, her scholarship addresses critical methodologies such as testimonios, pláticas and critical reflexivity. Her work is published in *Review of Research in*

Education, Equity & Excellence in Education, the *International Journal of Qualitative Studies in Education* and *TESOL Quarterly*.

Mara Sapon-Shevin is Professor of Inclusive Education in the Teaching and Leadership Department of the School of Education at Syracuse University. Mara presents frequently on inclusive education, anti-bullying strategies, cooperative learning, social justice education, differentiated instruction, friendship, community building, school reform and teaching for diversity. The author of over 150 books, book chapters and articles, Mara writes extensively about the fields of full inclusion, cooperative learning, social justice education and teaching for diversity. Mara's books include *Widening the Circle: The Power of Inclusive Classrooms, Because We Can Change the World: A Practical Guide for Building Cooperative, Inclusive Classroom Communities, Educational Courage: Resisting the Ambush of Public* and *Condition Critical: Key Principles for Equitable and Inclusive Education*.

Kylie Smith is an Associate Professor at Melbourne Graduate School of Education, University of Melbourne and has worked in early childhood services for over 30 years. She has published extensively in children's rights-based research and anti-bias perspectives, and is interested in young children's performances of identity and is currently exploring how respectful relationships programs might look in early childhood spaces. She has served as Associate Dean for Research in the Melbourne Graduate School of Education and has led funded projects, including working with municipalities, focused on young children's perspectives and experiences.

Mariana Souto-Manning is a Professor of Early Childhood Education and Teacher Education at Teachers College, Columbia University, and holds additional academic appointments at the University of Iceland and King's College London. She is Founding Co-Director of the Center for Innovation in Teacher Education and Development (CITED). From a critical perspective, Professor Souto-Manning's research examines inequities and injustices in early childhood teaching and teacher education, critically (re)centering methodologies and pedagogies on the lives, values and experiences of intersectionally minoritized people of color. Souto-Manning regularly collaborates with teachers and engages in community-based research. She has published nine books, including the 2016 winner of the American Educational Studies Association Critics' Choice Award, *Reading, Writing, and Talk: Inclusive Teaching Strategies for Diverse Learners, K-2* (with Jessica Martell), and a number of peer-reviewed articles in journals such as the *Journal of Teacher Education, Research in the Teaching of English, Teaching and Teacher Education* and *Teachers College Record*. Souto-Manning has received the 2011 American Educational Research Association (AERA) Division K Innovations in Research on

Diversity in Teacher Education Award, the 2017 AERA Teaching and Teacher Education Mid-Career Award and other research awards issued by professional organizations such as AERA, AESA and NAECTE.

Beth Blue Swadener is Professor of Justice Studies and Social and Cultural Pedagogy at Arizona State University. Her research focuses on childhood studies, internationally comparative social policy, with focus on sub-Saharan Africa, and children's rights and voices. She has published over 80 articles and book chapters and co-edited and authored 14 books, including *Children and Families "At Promise"*; *Power and Voice in Research with Children*; *Does the Village Still Raise the Child?*; *Decolonizing Research in Cross-Cultural Context*; *Children's Rights and Education*; and *Reconceptualizing Early Childhood Care and Education: A Reader*. Swadener is also a founding member of Reconceptualizing Early Childhood Education, Local to Global Justice, the Jirani Project, and Friends of the Girl Child Network.

Clifton Tanabe is Dean and Professor in the College of Education at the University of Texas, El Paso. Prior to his move to Texas, he served in a variety of different roles at the University of Hawaii, Mānoa, including Special Assistant to the Chancellor for Institutional Transformation and Executive Assistant-Chief of Staff. He was also a faculty member in the College of Education and lecturer in law in the William S. Richardson, School of Law. Dr. Tanabe was a co-founder and director of the Research Center for Cultural Diversity and Community Renewal at the University of Wisconsin, La Cross and earned his PhD in Educational Policy Studies and a Law Degree both at the University of Wisconsin, Madison. His scholarly interests are in equity, access and innovation in higher and K-12 education practice and policy.

FOREWORD

I write the foreword for this book from the south Texas US/Mexico borderlands or, as Gloria Anzaldúa so fittingly described the borderlands as, "*una herida abierta*, where the Third World grates against the first and bleeds" (2012, p. 25). This open wound, Anzaldúa observes, keeps bleeding never having a chance to heal. The borderlands are contentious yet home to many. Anzaldúa (2012, p. 25). poignantly writes,

> This is my home
> this thin edge of
> barbwire.

Often the borderlands are being renewed with new bodies that cross the border to find new opportunities, fleeing violence and seeking hope. Yet many, including children, are met with rejection or worse, incarceration. I write this in a time when children of all ages are being held in cages, separated from their loved one; some may never see their families again. Several of these very young children who speak other languages than English are being asked to represent themselves in court often without counsel. The crime? Crossing borders. Borders that are artificial and arbitrary. They are part of 500 years of coloniality of power in the Americas (Quijano, 2007). The coloniality of power permeates many aspects of our lives. It leads to tragedies such as the caging of children (Merchant, 2018). Living in south Texas, this tragedy is too close. I can't help but think of my own privilege crossing when I came to this country with my family. Unlike the fate of many young children now, I was able to be with my family and seek a less violent existence – violence including civil war in Nicaragua partly funded by the United States. That is all many trying to cross are seeking, a less violent existence.

This is why *Education for Social Justice in Early Childhood Education* is such an important book that builds on the work of scholars who have been engaged in social justice work for a long time – many of whom are authors in this volume. This book is a reminder and plea that we need to think of early childhood education from epistemologies of liberation and epistemologies from the margins that can offer a different possible present and future. Often, people think of early childhood as busy playgrounds, playdough and happy children. Though that image sooths us, we must realize that children are with us in this world, a world full of complexity, nuance, tragedy, and wrapped in a Euro-American and colonialist understanding of the world while adhering to neoliberal ordering of the world. Early childhood education then is another important component of social justice. Working with and for children is just as critical as other social justice projects and should not be relegated to the margins of social justice movements.

In my personal narrative, the consequences of war and the selfish interest of "first worlds" in other "third world" countries impacted my childhood and my family in many ways – trauma, economic hardships and cultural dissonance, to name a few. Thus, children have stories to tell, experiences to unpack and deserve an education that takes into account their full selves. Young children engage in this world in powerful ways making sense of inequalities, their gender and race, multiple languages and cultures and have imaginative and creative answers to problems if we hear them. We only have to stop and listen and we will see and experience these examples transpiring in the everyday interactions found inside and outside classrooms. Teaching bilingual third grade children in Texas taught me one thing, children can contemplate the world around them. They can make sense of colonialism, colorism and injustices, to name a few.

The authors in this volume also remind us that early childhood education is more than the education of children. It is also about the adults surrounding children, such as teachers, parents, families, communities and the sociopolitical and historical moment in which all of us find ourselves in. As I've worked with immigrant families with young children, I have developed different perspectives of their world. Families, often the *mujeres*, are struggling with multiple layers of racism, sexism, abuse and economic hardships. Yet women are navigating and surviving beyond the expected. These important lessons in navigation are being passed down to children. That's why when we think of social justice in early childhood education all these lives are important in the journey to transform early childhood education. We must pay attention with intersectional lenses to early childhood teacher education and the communities in which children and families live. Social justice must take on the project of examining critically the marginalized bodies that have been disciplined through white lenses. Authors in this volume challenge all of us to think deeply about the experiences of teachers, people and communities of color.

I appreciate the authors in this volume whose work in reshaping the curriculum of early childhood make it a point to make pedagogy an issue of social justice. Our work to ensure that we create spaces and moments where democracy is not taken as an easily defined concept but constantly reworked, rethought is necessary. What better space than the early childhood classroom, where children can contribute and help us reimagine these taken-for-granted concepts. Rethinking our pedagogy through anti-bias curriculum and teaching becomes an essential strategy in the struggle for social justice as well. How can we be more intentional and mindful in our pedagogy with children? It may not always be smooth or perfect but that's where the magic happens – magic that appears through love and hope as we build relationships with children, families and communities. After all, we cannot have a social justice movement in early childhood education if we can't center love and hope. What this book is pushing us to do is to reimagine early childhood education as a place of transformation, hope and liberation and full of possibilities, resilience, agency and love in all aspects of what we do. We can't forget that every day there are stories, moments and spaces of resistance, hope and possibilities. Let's capture them like the authors in this volume have.

Cinthya Saavedra 0000-0002-2311-1972

References

Anzaldúa, G. E. (2012). *Borderlands/La frontera: The new mestiza*. San Francisco, CA: Aunt Lute Books.

Merchant, N. (2018). Immigrant kids seen held in fenced cages at border facility. *Associated Press news.com*, June. Retrieved from https://apnews.com/6e04c6ee01dd46669eddba 9d3333f6d5.

Quijano, A. (2007) Coloniality and modern/rationality. *Cultural Studies*, 21, 168–178.

ACKNOWLEDGEMENTS

We acknowledge our long-time mentors who have helped us focus on issues of social justice and continue to inspire us – Mimi Bloch, Carl Grant, Michael Apple, Clarence Karier, Herbert Kliebard. We also acknowledge the scholar activists – both colleagues and graduate students – who have impacted our work in numerous ways. We deeply appreciate the scholarship, community and classroom engagement, and contributions to this volume of the chapter authors.

We also acknowledge Grethel Ochoa Bobadilla, graduate editorial assistant at Arizona State University, Misha Kydd, Helen Strain, Olivia Powers and Katie Paton of Routledge/Taylor and Francis, and Sarah Fish for their support in completing this book.

Finally, we acknowledge Nicola Yelland for including this volume in her book series, Changing Images of Early Childhood and our families for their ongoing support.

CHANGING IMAGES OF EARLY CHILDHOOD

The books in *Changing Images of Early Childhood* consider contemporary and alternative theoretical perspectives in the domain of early childhood education. The aim of the books is to introduce the reader to new and diverse theoretical perspectives and to make them accessible so that their relevance to everyday practices is highlighted. The topics span classroom, family and community settings and provide readers with *rich* descriptions of everyday lives in global contexts. The books in the series enable us to engage in meaningful conversations around the personal and complex sets of interactions that we experience in the early childhood years. Our focus centers on their relevance to the lived experiences and everyday practices of adults who interact with young children in a myriad of environs, thus enabling educators to create learning environments which are underpinned by a respect for all participants, equity and social justice.

The *Changing Images of Early Childhood* books challenge and confront educators with a wide range of topics. They reflect the *complex* nature of our lives in a postmodern world where issues around globalism, capitalism, democracy and the multifaceted nature of our contemporary experiences are not easily resolved but need to be confronted. They have been created to bring to the forefront the issues faced by marginalized groups so that they might be interrogated with *respect* and from perspectives that are relevant to the nature and culture of those groups and individuals. Additionally, we want to share the innovate practices of educators who are at the forefront of thinking dynamically about the challenges inherent to living in the 21st century.

This volume, *Education for Social Justice in Early Childhood*, edited by Shirley Kessler and Beth Swadener, is timely and significant. It is published at a critical juncture of democratic life across the globe.... at a time when actions of governments threaten the stability of our political systems and our daily lives, as we seek to build communities and contribute to societies that are strong and fair. As the editors state in their opening line in the introduction, *This is a book about justice, written at a time when a range of injustices are directly affecting young children, families, communities and nations.*

The authors in this volume originate from diverse locales and perspectives, yet have a common theme in their quest for social justice for young children and their families. Their chapters highlight the diverse ways in which our work in early childhood environments, which encompass classrooms, communities and working with families, can serve to create places in which social, environmental and other forms of justice and well-being are recognized and inculcated. The authors of the chapters in this book recognize and highlight in their work the many ways that we can contribute to working for social justice. Their experiences illustrate the myriad of actions that we can instigate to achieve these goals, with a variety of experiences, approaches and standpoints as we interact on a daily basis with young people, their families and teachers.

At the core of this book is the critique that 'contemporary threats to democracy and civil rights must be seen within the context of neoliberal political theory.' The central premises of neo-liberal ideology have long had a significant impact on the lives of young children and their families. Those who are the most vulnerable, including single mothers, children in poverty and many in minoritized communities are characterized as being responsible for their circumstances, while external, social, political and economic factors work to manifest their disadvantage. Systems have been set up to control, document and assess their lives, and put in the domain of private enterprise which profit from provision of 'services.' Government support for families in need is frequently diminished or removed.

The authors in this volume strive for social justice as recognition, as redistributive and as representative. Thus, social justice means that we value social and cultural diversity and respect and honor all human beings. This book makes a major contribution to extending our knowledge of the salient issues regarding social justice and provides early childhood educators with practical ways in which we can all work towards these dignified ideals.

Nicola Yelland

INTRODUCTION

This is a book about justice, written at a time when a range of injustices are directly affecting young children, families, communities and nations. The authors in this volume frame some of the many ways in which our practices and pedagogy in early childhood contexts, including classrooms and communities, can counter social, environmental and other forms of injustice. Recognizing that there are many ways to work for social justice, as well as many definitions, we intentionally invited authors who bring an array of experiences, approaches and standpoints in work with young people, their families and teachers.

The numerous injustices we document occur at a time when democracy is under threat in the US and around the world. Guarantees of free and fair elections, the rights of marginalized people including migrants and refugees, freedom of the press and the rule of law are all under attack (Abramowitz, 2018; Levitsky & Ziblatt, 2018). US leadership now advocates an "America first" nationalistic ideology, retreating from commitments to treaties that aim to secure peace in the Middle East and from agreements that address the serious issue of global warming and climate change. The use of racist terminology and obscene language to denigrate people of color and women is increasingly common, resulting in extreme partisanship and divisions within the government and society, a common characteristic of failing democracies (Levitsky & Ziblatt, 2018). The efforts to arrest, detain and deport undocumented immigrants and asylum seekers have led to chaos and fear even death among many families in the US, as well as Australia, and have been instrumental in separating children from their parents.

We argue that these threats to democracy and civil rights must be seen within the context of neoliberal political theory, a term coined at a meeting in Paris in 1938 when social democracy, represented by Roosevelt's New Deal, was viewed by some as a manifestation of a collectivism that was on a continuum with Nazism and communism (The Guardian, 2016). Friedrich Hayek, an Austrian economist and leader of this new kind of liberalism, argued in 1944 that government planning would lead inexorably to totalitarian control. Neoliberal ideology, dominant in the US since the 1980s when it became fully realized under the administrations of Ronald Reagan in the United States and Margaret Thatcher in Britain, emphasizes the value of free market, most commonly associated with laissez-faire economics, minimal state intervention in economic and social affairs, and commitment to freedom of trade and capital (Springer, 2016). As Chesney put it,

> Neoliberal initiatives are characterized as free market politics that encourage private enterprise and consumer choice, reward personal responsibility and entrepreneurial initiative, and undermine the dead hand of incompetent, bureaucratic and parasitic government, that can never do good even if well intended which it rarely is.
>
> *(Apple 2001, p. 17).*

Mike Segar (2016) summarized neoliberal principles that include:

- Lower corporate and personal taxation;
- A thinning of the welfare net;
- The weakening of trade unions;
- Deregulation of the business community and
- The privatization of publicly owned industries and companies (p. 2).

We add the privatization of public education to this list. An emphasis on personal responsibility is also a hallmark of neoliberal ideology, as reflected in a range of work requirements and naming of welfare reform laws emphasizing both work and personal responsibility. In this framework, children and families considered "at risk" (Swadener & Lubeck, 1995) have largely themselves to blame and not larger structural factors or systems of oppression. Naomi Klein argued that under the neoliberal policies of deregulating, privatization, austerity and corporate trade, the living standards of many people have declined precipitously (Klein, 2016).

Impacts of neoliberal policy on the real lives of children and families has long been documented (e.g., Polakow, 1993; 2007), including impacts of "ending welfare as we know it" early in the Clinton administration and the impacts on "other" children and families, including single mothers, children in poverty and many in minoritized communities. From pathologizing discourse about single mothers and poor children, to policies that made material conditions of childrearing and child care challenging, neoliberal policies have damaged families and young children. More recently, neoliberal policies have tended to emphasize quality rating, investing public funds in "high scoring" early childhood centers, often at the expense of investment in programs with greater economic need (Nakagawa, Peters & Swadener, 2012).

The influences of neoliberal policies more broadly on education are numerous. Business models have been adopted where schools are run like business (Apple, 2001); the bottom line is student achievement, measured by tests in early childhood that lack validity and reliability (Urban and Swadener, 2016). Competition between schools is regarded as necessary to progress. Voucher plans, where parents are given vouchers to pay for their child's education when parents choose what they believe is the best school for their child, highlight "freedom of individual choice" that is emphasized by neoliberal economists and those bankrolling such policies (e.g., the Koch brothers). Charter schools, affiliated with school districts but not governed in the same ways as public schools, use public moneys and typically operate for profit (Apple, 2001). "Underlying neoliberal views in education is a vision of students as human capital … students as future workers … who must be given the requisite skills and dispositions to compete efficiently and effectively" (Apple, 2001, p. 38).

Neoliberal governing policies have also had a tremendous influence on school practice and a curriculum planning process that excludes the voices of parents and children, and thus inhibits a democratic education (Gutmann, 1987), although marginalization of "public interests" in education is not a new phenomenon as Tyack and Cuban wrote in 1984 (Tyack & Cuban, 1995). Since then, however, the control of education has been further removed from local interests with the publication in the US of the widely influential report by the National Commission on Excellence in Education (NCEE, 1984), *A nation at risk: The imperative for educational reforms.* The report asserted that because of the supposed decline in student achievement, the nation was no longer a leader in industry, science and innovation, and this decline threatened its position as a world leader unable to compete in a world economy (Berliner & Biddle, 1995). The NCEE report led school leaders and policy makers to plan and implement a series of school reforms. However, efforts to improve students' achievement as measured on the National Assessment of Educational Progress (NAEP) indicate students have little or no improvement. In 2017 schools earned grades between a C-minus and a C-plus (Education Week, 2017).

It is within the context of neoliberal political theory that threats to public education and social justice in education must be viewed. The US Secretary of Education at the time of this writing is a strong advocate of school choice/privatization, threatening the very notion of public education. Her policies have rolled back regulations on campus sexual assault and for-profit colleges, scaled back investigations into the civil right violations of transgender students and rescinded guidance outlines for students with disabilities (Reilly, 2017). Furthermore, US schools are not safe places for children to learn. For example, next to the water dispenser at North Western High School in Flint Michigan reads a sign, "Do Not Drink Until Further Notice," because the water is contaminated with lead.

No less important is the number of unspeakable tragedies that have occurred because of mass school shootings that have taken place since the first one at Columbine High School in Colorado in 1999. At the time of this writing 122 children and young students have been murdered in schools (Basu, 2018), and according to a 2018 survey by the Pew Research Center, 53% of students surveyed are "very worried" or "somewhat worried" that a shooting will take place in their school (Pew Research Center, 2018). This fear is especially prominent among low-income parents. At the same time legislators who receive contributions from the National Rifle Association refuse to enact gun laws that require the elimination of assault rifles and more stringent background checks required of gun purchasers.

In this volume, we highlight specific threats to social justice in early childhood education and approaches and tactics to counter these threats. In doing so we align ourselves with what others have called "public intellectuals" or "radical educators." Our responsibility is to develop counter-hegemonic educational programs in schools as well as in community, state and federal governments. That is, we must understand and interrupt those forces that produce social difference at all levels which requires an activist role on the part of educators. As public intellectuals we must bear witness to ideas and practices that produce inequalities. In addition, we must show "spaces of possibility" where our work can interrupt and create alternative visions of collective living and democratic education. Further, we must "act as critical secretaries" of cultural realities that illuminate opportunities of understanding and action (Apple, 2018, p. 4). Finally, as radical educators we must mobilize to work against oppressive structures and policies as politically active citizens. Possible allies in this struggle are social movements from below, teacher unions, activist educators, student activists, progressive governments and some school board members (Apple, 2018, p. 5). We write this at a time of unprecedented public-school teacher activism in many US states, with the "Red for Ed" and other movements calling attention to the low pay, lack of resources for public education and underfunding of education in general. Early childhood educators have been part of this movement.

The term social justice has wide ranging meanings and interpretations. One way to address social justice topics in early education and care is to consider the framework put forth by Nancy Fraser and others. Fraser sees social justice as three-dimensional: social justices as "recognition," social justice as "redistributive" and social justice as "representative," though these concepts overlap (Woods, Mackenzie & Wong, 2013). We draw upon two of these orientations. Social justice as recognition values social and cultural diversity. This approach to research makes visible "the values, languages and experiences of cultural and social backgrounds that are relevant to communities" in early childhood settings (p. 286). Similarly, Hytten and Bettez (2011) point out that among the several strands included in education for social justice is an ethnographic/narrative strand that portrays injustice as well as narratives about personal experiences of lived injustice; and a theoretically specific strand, such as Whiteness and anti-oppressive studies. Redistributive justice refers "to the equitable distribution, or redistribution, of resources, including those valued knowledges, skills and practices of the dominant culture, to all" (Woods et al., 2013, p. 286).

We likewise see the concept of representative justice pertinent to the collective work represented in this book. Representative justice refers to the right of all members of a community to participate in decisions regarding the education of their children. We include children as members of a community whose input into the curriculum is vital for the realization of democratic education. This view of justice corresponds to what Hytten and Bettez (2011) term the "democratically" grounded strand in education for social justice that includes studies of visions of what it means to be an educated person in a democracy and curriculum as well as practices developed to achieve this vision. We also honor and respect children's rights, including a right to childhood, and to participation, provision and protection.

In addition, among many discourses educators draw upon when claiming a social justice orientation are anti-oppressive education, feminism, and critical race theory, to name a few (Hytten & Bettez, 2011, p. 9). We include environmental justice (Pelo, 2008; Swadener & O'Brien, 2008) as well as early childhood scholarship on the "more than human" (Taylor, 2017; Taylor & Pacini-Ketchabaw, 2015; Braidotti, 2013) in social justice education.

Organization of the Book

With so many issues related to broad framings of social justice in early childhood, we sought to organize the book into chapters that serve to highlight key areas as we view social justice, voice, inclusion, democracy, embodied practices, love, activism and other themes. The book is divided into three parts. The chapters in Part I foreground voices of children, families and teachers confronting issues of social justice including immigration and threats of deportation, persistent color-blindness or muting in early childhood education through the experiences of Black teachers, and voices of both children and feminist teachers confronting gender-based violence. Raising a few of the many issues confronting young children, their families, advocates and teachers, this section is meant to offer a window into the everyday lives and experiences of those at the center of early years care and education.

Part II includes chapters that provide specific historical and contemporary examples of social justice in early childhood contexts, particularly in the classroom or care setting, but also in the community. Emphasizing the potential for early childhood curriculum (formal and informal) in promoting democratic and anti-bias practices, authors in this section unpack the contributions of specific approaches (e.g., Reggio Emilio in Italy) as well as in social justice movements, including the 19th century kindergarten movement and, more recently, in the 1960s civil rights movement and contemporary social movements.

The writings in Part III are intended to create spaces for hope, resistance and possibility in order to reclaim a just vision of the future that is inclusive of all children. Contributors to this section critique and resist re-production of racial and cultural injustice as well as whiteness, dominant forces and policies in early education and the lack of embodiment and touch in early childhood. The book ends with an historical example that is intended to point a way forward in organizing for social justice in early childhood.

Part I: Voices of Children, Teachers and Families

Central to issues of social justice are dynamics of power and voice. Those who are most affected by issues of oppression, exclusion and marginalization, for example, are not typically the voices or perspectives that are widely considered – or given due weight – when decisions that affect them are made. A theme from the disability rights movement, "nothing about us without us" (Charlton, 2000), comes to mind when considering issues affecting young children, their parents and teachers.

A trend in early childhood and children's studies research in the past two decades has been greater recognition of children's rights-based research that consults with children versus studying them. Such scholarship often draws specifically from the United Nations Committee's General Comment No. 12, *The right of the child to be heard* (UNCRC, 2009), which emphasized children's right to participate in decisions affecting them and to have their views taken seriously: "The views expressed by children may add relevant perspectives and experiences and should be considered in decision-making, policy-making and preparation of laws and/or measures as well as their evaluation" (p. 5).

Dominant views about children/youth are primarily centered on the notion that they are "pre-adult becomings" or "deferred citizens" (Cheney, 2007), meaning, they have little agency to influence change until they are older or reach an age of majority. Furthermore, because youth is commonly defined by the teenage years, children younger than 12 are often distanced from participatory or political involvement because they are seen variously as being inferior, dependent on older people or need to be shielded from more complex social issues. Alternatively, young children included in political activity are at times utilized as props to incite empathy from observers, situated as tools of persuasion in advocacy without regard of how the process may affect them.

Similarly, voices of teachers and parents of color have all too often been marginalized or ignored (e.g., Delpit, 1995; Ladson-Billings & Tate, 1995; Ladson-Billings, 2005). Critical race theory (CRT) (Ladson-Billings & Tate, 1995 and others) and related theories, including Tribal CRT (Brayboy, 2005) and Border CRT (Maldonado, 2013) have provided important frameworks for better understanding the experiences, forms of resistance and alternatives for those in liminal spaces in the US and beyond. Contemporary early childhood scholarship demonstrates ways that racial and cultural inequities are reproduced through an array of policies, including high stakes testing and teacher credentialing (e.g., Souto-Manning & Rabadi-Raol, 2018; Souto-Manning & Cheruvu, 2016), that reinforce Whiteness (Sleeter, 2017). Black and Chicana feminist scholarship, such as the work of Perez and Saavedra (2012), has also enriched writing and thinking about early childhood education. Such work is associated with research that advocates for social justice and more democratic and inclusive practices in a range of early childhood contexts.

Angeles Maldonado, Beth Blue Swadener and Casey Khaleesi's chapter seeks to understand the everyday life experiences of children in immigrant families growing up in the Borderlands of the US Southwest. A primary aim of this chapter is to go deeper into what it means to consult with young children on matters affecting their daily lives, with focus on children's engagement with social issues affecting their families and ways in which they express agency.

In the second chapter, Kia Rideaux and Michelle Salazar Pérez challenge color-blindness in early childhood through narratives of Black early childhood teachers. Their narratives reveal discrete forms of cultural erasure and racism and provide insights regarding educational approaches that disrupt color-blindness and reimagine more socially just pedagogical practices.

In Chapter 3, Kylie Smith examines the effects of emergent and child centered approaches to promote social justice and particularly gender equity in early childhood classrooms. Research evidence clearly shows that children construct their gendered identities at a young age and that children as young as two years are developing stereotyped values, attitudes and relationships. Smith examines the ways in which educators listen to children's views and opinions and, drawing on feminist politics, endeavor to create activist classrooms that consider prevention and intervention pedagogy to create collective communities that challenge and change social and structural gender norms and behaviors.

Finally, in Chapter 4, Marianna Souto-Manning, Gail Buffalo and Ayesha Rabadi-Rao analyze and critique ways that Eurocentric definitions of quality in early childhood education reproduce racial and cultural inequities and serve to perpetuate the overwhelming Whiteness present in teaching and teacher education. They conclude with offering ways to implications reconceptualize early childhood teacher certification in ways that interrupt injustice and foster justice, drawing from the voices and experiences of early childhood educators of color.

Part II: Democratic Education and Pedagogy

There are numerous and conflicting approaches to educating children to participate in democratic processes and to be aware of democratic institutions and their functions. Historically speaking, teaching the young to be good citizens was one of primary purposes of education in the Colonial Era (Kaestle, 1983). During this time citizenship meant that men should keep informed of the issues and vote intelligently (Curti, 1971). Women who did not have the franchise were expected to train their sons to acquire a sound moral character (Kaestle, 1983). Though our Founding Fathers had rejected monarchy and an aristocracy, they nonetheless feared chaos and anarchy without authoritarian leadership. Thus, they advocated a democratic form of government where the public would be educated according to the values articulated by the elite, who understood what was required to maintain social stability and economic prosperity. As Kaestle put it the elite, "...pinned their hopes on the creation of a republic, a representative form of government in which the general will would be refined and articulated by the best men" (Kaestle, 1983, p 4).

George Wood (1998) describes this view as democracy in the "weak" sense, whereby democratic politics is seen as a process of simply choosing those who will be making the important decisions that will affect their lives. Democracy in the "strong" sense focuses on the need for public participation in deliberation and action based on their interests and what they see as the "common good." Similarly, Apple (2018) describes two different understandings of democracy: "thin" versus "thick." Thin understandings of democracy foster a market-oriented version, that includes consumer choice, possessive individualism and an education that aims to address economic needs of the nation as defined by the powerful (p. 4), characteristic of neoliberalism. Thick understandings of "democracy" fosters collective participation in search of the common good in the development of "critical citizens." Thus, there are many conflicting and contrasting views as to what a "democracy" should look like and the best ways to realize that vision through education. As Apple (2018) put it, "The struggle for democracy in education has been and still is exactly that – a *struggle*" (p. 4).

In the United States the principles and practices of democratic living are typically taught in the "social studies," a term adopted in 1916 by the National Education Association Committee on the Social Studies and the American Historical Association (Kessler, 2001). Before that, what we think of as the social studies was a collection of separate disciplines – history, geography and civics. At the same time, these committees stated that the primary purpose of the social studies was to teach the skills and attitudes necessary for good citizenship. Topics to be taught in early childhood were listed as the following: Kindergarten - Self, School, Community, Home; Grade 1 - Families; Grade 2 - Neighborhoods; Grade 3 - Communities, in later grades to include States, US history, etc. – the "expanding environments approach."

Seventy years later, these same topics appeared in most curriculum guides, textbooks and other materials used between 1955 and 1975 (Gehrke, Knapp & Sirotnik, 1992). Further, the most common approach identified in 1992 was called "conservative cultural continuity," that is, social studies as the transmission of citizenship-related information with an emphasis on the inculcation of traditional values (p. 18). Larry Cuban writes that only in the progressive era in the United States, roughly between 1915 and 1957, did policy elites and members of the general public expect the public schools to promote democratic principles and the practice of citizenship in the public schools (Cuban, 2015). But, as Gehrke, Knapp, and Sirotnik (1992) point out, there is little consensus among educators as to what should be taught to make one a good citizen. For example, Parker (2003) and Derman-Sparks (1989) argue multicultural and anti-bias education are vital components of a democratic curriculum if the potential of democracy is to be realized.

In 2010 the National Council for the Social Studies (NCSS) revised its standards for elementary and secondary social studies (NCSS, 2010) that clarified to some extent "good citizenship." The stated purpose of the social studies is "help young people make informed and reasoned decisions for the public good as citizens of a culturally diverse, democratic society in an interdependent world." The NCSS "emphasizes the importance of educating students who are committed to the ideas and values of democracy."

Statements such as the proclamation of the NCSS seem to have had little effect on students' understandings and participation in democratic living, with a few exceptions. We note that the instructional model, "action civics," aims to teach students about government and to harness that knowledge to launch them into collective action on issues they care about (e.g. Gewertz, 2019). Ample evidence documents the poor state of civic literacy among students in the US, including low levels of K-12 proficiency on civics tests, and the inability of most adults to identify basic civics facts (Rebel, 2018). Perhaps lack of understanding basic civics is related to the fact that only 17 states require students to take a civics test and only eight states require students to earn a passing score to receive a high school diploma upon graduation (Education Commission of the States, 2017). Clearly, it is past time for educators to advocate for social justice by calling for a radical change in social studies education based on "strong," or "thick," understandings of what democracy means. The chapters in this section reflect that perspective.

Shirley Kessler elaborates on the history of democratic education in early childhood, beginning with the opening of the first English-speaking kindergarten in 1860 by Elizabeth Peabody and later in the Kindergarten and Workingmen's school in 1878. The first program exemplifies a concept of democracy in the strong or thick sense, while the later represents a weak sense or thin understandings of democracy. Kessler then describes current programs that teach democratic behaviors and a democratic curriculum.

tIn Chapter 6, Dana Frantz-Bentley with Betty Chan narrate classroom processes in Dana's early childhood classroom as she endeavors to teach an anti-bias curriculum. She describes the classroom "circle" where the curriculum takes shape and becomes a "space of transformation." Franz-Bentley points out the delicate balance between teacher facilitation and child leadership in creating spaces for children to learn and practice a democratic curriculum.

Lacey Peters writes in Chapter 7 that the results of the 2016 election in the US have (re)ignited activism as more and more people show an increased interest or responsibility in acting to confront socio-political injustices. Acknowledging children as social agents and contributing members of society is vital to strengthening children's advocacy efforts. This chapter explores children's participation in social justice movements, and shares insights on ways in which adults can work *with* children to engage in social action.

In Chapter 8, Rebecca New describes the educational program for young children in the town of Regio Emilia in northern Italy, known worldwide for its municipal early childhood services. The conceptual framework of cultural models is used to illustrate Reggio Emilia's radical role during key events in Italy's complex political history and the influence of that history on the city's commitment to social justice and equity vis-à-vis a pedagogy of home-school-community relationships characterized by conflict, inquiry and collaboration. The chapter concludes by highlighting Reggio Emilia's responses to immigrant and refugee families, guided by a conceptualization of democracy as dynamic, deliberative, negotiated and evolving.

Part III: Way Forward: Stories of Resistance, Hope and Possibility

The final part is intended to raise further issues of countering oppression, framing resistance and providing more embodied strategies in early childhood contexts – anchored in pedagogies of hope (Freire, 1994), love and possibility.

In Chapter 9, Jeanne Iorio and Clifton Tanabe employ a "practice of hope" to counter hegemonies of efficiency and control in working toward social justice. The chapter draws from an early childhood research project focused in a coastal town in Victoria, Australia that supports the building of relationships between children *with* place as a means of building a relationship between humans and the earth. This research seeks to understand how teachers support children in learning from relationships in their 'common' worlds with the human and the more-than-human.

Mara Sapon-Shevin writes in Chapter 10 about ways in which touch can be part of fostering loving citizenship in early childhood education. She argues that although physical touch is widely acknowledged as critical to young children's growth and development, current policies and practices often reduce opportunities and support for both physical activity and physical interaction with others. Sapon-Shevin envisions what early childhood education would be like if children's bodies (individually and collectively) were at the center of education.

In Chapter 11, focusing on meanings of social justice and representation in early childhood education and child care, Mimi Bloch reflects on 25 years of resisting dominant pedagogies in early education, as well as examples from contrasting programs in which she has recently volunteered. She finds reasons for hope with small political and pedagogical successes reflected in shifts in thinking as well as actions. Bloch provides a renewed vision for imagining different possibilities for the field.

In the final chapter, Shirley Kessler draws from the organizing efforts of faculty at Teachers College in the 1930s to serve as a model for what educational organizations and associations could do to counter current efforts to standardize curriculum development and education evaluation undertaken by the Organization for Economic Cooperation and Development. Kessler calls for direct political action by educators based on an articulated political platform developed to serve the interests of children and communities in the current political and economic contexts.

It is our intention that this volume speak to many audiences concerned with trends in early childhood that have moved the field further from a space for democracy, cultural relevance, inclusion and social justice.

References

Abramowitz, M. J. (2018). Freedom in the world 2018: Democracy in crisis. Retrieved from http://freedomhouse.org/report/freedom-world/freeom-world-2018

Apple, M.W. (2001). *Educating the "right" way: Markets, standards, god, and inequality*. New York: Routledge.

Apple, M.W. (2018). The struggle for democracy in education. In M. Apple (Ed.) with L. A. Gandin, L. Shuning, S. Meshulam, & E. Schirmer, *The struggle for democracy in education* (pp. 1–19). New York: Routledge.

Basu, Z. (2018). 122 Killed in mass school shootings since Columbine. February 15. Retrieved from http://www.axios.com/122-killed-in-mass-schootings-since-columbine

Berliner, C.C., & Biddle, B.J. (1995). *The manufactured crisis: Myths, fraud, and the attack on America's public schools*. New York: Basic Books.

Braidotti, R. (2013). *The posthuman*. Cambridge: Polity.

Charlton, J. I. (2000). *Nothing about us without us: Disability oppression and empowerment*. Berkeley: University of California Press.

Brayboy, B. M. (2005). Toward a tribal critical race theory in education. *The Urban Review*, 37(5), 425–446. doi:10.1007/s11256–11005–0018-y

Cheney, K.E. (2007). *Pillars of the nation: Child citizens and Ugandan nation development*. Chicago: University of Chicago Press.

Cuban, L. (2015). Federal education policy and democracy. *Teachers College Record*, 17, 1–7.

Curti, M. (1971). *The social ideas of American educators*. Totowa, NJ: Littlefield, Adams & Co.

Delpit, L. (1995). *Other people's children: Cultural conflict in the classroom*. New York: The New Press.

Derman-Sparks, L. (1989). *Anti-bias curriculum: Tools for empowering young children*. New York: National Association for the Education of Young Children.

Education Commission of the States (2017). Education trends. Retrieved from https://wwwecs.org/wp-content/uploads/The-Civics-Education-Initiative-2015-2017.pdf

Education Week (2017). U.S. education in 2017 in 10 charts. Retrieved from https://www.edweek.org/ew/section/multimedia/us-eduation-in-2017-in-10-charts.html?cmp=eml-enl-eu-mostpop&M=58329786&U=1810990

Freire, P. (1994). *Pedagogy of hope: Reliving pedagogy of the oppressed*. New York: Bloomsbury Press.

Gehrke, N.J., Knapp, M. D., & Sirotnik, K. (1992). In search of the school curriculum. *Review of Research in Education*, 18(1), 51–110.

Gewertz, C. (2019). "Action civics" enlists students in hands-on democracy. *Education Week*, March 20.

Gutmann, A. (1987). *Democratic education*. Princeton: Princeton University Press.

Hytten, K., & Bettez, S.C. (2011). Understanding education for social justice. *Educational Foundations*, 25(2), 7–24.

Kaestle, C.F. (1983). *Pillars of the republic: Common schools and American society 1780–1860*. New York: Hill & Wang.

Kessler, S. (2001). Critical perspectives on social studies in early childhood education. In J. Jipson & J. Johnson (Eds.), *Resistance & representation: Rethinking childhood education* (pp. 128–149). New York: Peter Lang.

Klein, N. (2016). It was the democrat's embrace of neoliberalism that won it for Trump. *The Guardian*, November 9.

Ladson-Billings, G.J. (2005). The evolving role of critical race theory in educational scholarship. *Race, Ethnicity, and Education*, 8(1), 115–119.

Ladson-Billings, G., & Tate IV, W. (1995). Toward a critical race theory of education. *Teachers College Record*, 97(1), 47–68.

Levitsky, S., & Ziblatt, D. (2018). *How democracies die.* New York: Crown.

Maldonado, A. (2013). *Raids, Race, and lessons of fear and resistance: Narratives and discourse in the immigration movement in Arizona.* (Doctoral dissertation). Retrieved from Arizona State University, ProQuest Dissertations and Theses database. (UMI 3590934)

Nagasawa, M., Peters, L. & Swadener, B.B. (2012). The costs of putting quality first: Neoliberalism, (in)equality, (un)affordability, and (in)accessibility? In M. Bloch, B.B. Swadener, & G. Cannella (Eds.) *Reconceptualizing Early Childhood Care and Education: Critical Questions, New Imaginaries and Social Activism* (pp. 279–290). New York: Peter Lang.

National Commission on Excellence in Education (NCEE) (1984). *A nation at risk: The imperatives for educational reform.* Washington, DC: US Department of Education.

National Council for the Social Studies (NCSS) (2010). National Curriculum Standards for Social Studies. Retrieved from http://www.socialstudies.org/standards

Parker, W.C. (2003). *Teaching democracy: Unity and diversity public life.* New York: Teachers College Press.

Pelo, A. (2008). Introduction: Embracing social justice in early childhood education. In A. Pelo (Ed.), *Rethinking early childhood education* (pp. ix–xii). Milwaukee, WI: Rethinking Schools.

Perez, M.S. & Saavedra, C. M. (2012). Chicana and black feminisms: *Testimonios* of Theory, identity, and multiculturalism. *Equity and Excellence in Education*, 45(3), 430–443.

Pew Research Center (2018). *A majority of U.S. teens fear a shooting could happen at their school, and most parents share their concern.* Retrieved from http://www.pewresearch.org/fact-tank/2018/04/a-maority-of-u-s-teens-fear-a-shootig-could-hapen-at-their-school-and-most-parents-share-their-concern

Polakow, V. (1993). *Lives on the edge: Single mothers and their children in the other America.* Chicago: University of Chicago Press.

Polakow, V. (2007). *Who cares for our children? The child care crisis in the other America.* New York: Teachers College Press.

Rebel, M.A. (2018). *Flunking democracy: Schools, courts, and civic participation.* Chicago: University of Chicago Press.

Reilly, K. (2017) The biggest controversies from Betsy DeVos' first year. December 14. Retrieved from http://time.com//5053007/betsy-devos-education-secretary-2017-controversies

Segar, M. (2016). Democratic primaries in the shadow of neoliberalism. *The Huffington Post*, May 16.

Sleeter, C. (2017). Critical race theory and the whiteness of teacher education. *Urban Education*, 52(2), 155–169.

Souto-Manning, M., & Cheruvu, R. (2016). Challenging and appropriating discourses of power: Listening to and learning from early career early childhood teachers of color. *Equity & Excellence in Education*, 49(1), 9–26.

Souto-Manning, M., & Rabadi-Raol, A. (2018). (Re)Centering quality in early childhood education: Toward intersectional justice for minoritized children. *Review of Research in Education*, 42.

Springer, S. (2016). *The discourse of neoliberalism: An anatomy of a powerful idea.* Maryland: Rowman & Littlefield.

Swadener, B.B., & Lubeck, S. (1995). *Children and families "at promise": Deconstructing the discourse of risk.* Albany: State University of New York Press.

Swadener, B. B., & O'Brien, L. M. (2008). Social responsibility and teaching young children: An education for living in ethical and caring ways. In J. Andrzejewski & L. Symcox (Eds.), *Social justice, peace, and environmental education: Transformative standards* (pp. 121–135). New York: Routledge.

The Guardian (2016). Neoliberalism – the ideology at the root of all our problems. Retrieved from www.theguardian.com

Taylor, A. (2017). Beyond stewardship: Common world pedagogies for the Anthropocene. *Environmental Education Research*, 23(10), 1448–1461.

Taylor, A., & Pacini-Ketchabaw, V. (2015). Learning with children, ants, and worms in the Anthropocene: Towards a common world pedagogy of multispecies vulnerability. *Pedagogy, Culture & Society*, 23(4), 507–529.

Tyack, D., & Cuban, L. (1995). *Tinkering toward utopia: A century of public school reform.* Cambridge, MA: Harvard University Press.

United Nations Convention on the Rights of the Child (UNCRC) (2009). Comment on Article 12 – The Right of the Child to be Heard. Retrieved from https://www2.ohchr.org/english/bodies/crc/docs/AdvanceVersions/CRC-C-GC-12.pdf

Urban, M., & Swadener, B.B. (2016). Democratic accountability and contextualized systemic evaluation. *International Critical Childhood Policy Studies*. Retrieved from www.receinternational.orgupdateVol.

Wood, G.H. (1998). Democracy and curriculum. In L. Beyer and M. Apple (Eds.), *The curriculum: Problems, politics and possibilities* (2nd ed.) (pp. 177–198). New York: State University of New York Press.

Woods, A., Mackenzie, N.M., & Wong, S. (2013). Social justice in early years education: Practices and understanding. *Contemporary Issues in Early Childhood*, 14(4), 285–289.

PART I

Voices of Children, Teachers and Families

1

IMMIGRANT CHILDREN IN ARIZONA

Social Justice Implications for Education in the Borderlands

Angeles Maldonado, Beth Blue Swadener and Casey Khaleesi

Introduction

Arizona has long seen anti-immigrant policies that violate civil and human rights, including orchestrated tactics to generate a public spectacle and symbolic war against "illegal immigration." One outcome of this hostile environment has been a vulnerable and criminalized community, traumatized under the incessant and real threat of deportation. Through public community resistance, we are aware that anti-immigrant policies have been and continue to affect immigrant families and children in serious ways. We are concerned and vigilant of changes in federal immigration laws and policies, deportation priorities, the separation of migrant children at the border, the conditions of deportation centers, and the treatment of newly arrived asylum seekers. We fear the increased militarization of the border and how nationally widespread nativist discourse is impacting children living in the borderlands. Our chapter draws from interviews with immigrant children in Arizona and situates their perspectives in Border Crit Theory. We discuss children's trans-border identities, language, family, safety, visions for the future, and views of schooling. We conclude with concrete recommendations for supporting the well-being and education of immigrant children.

Living in the Borderlands: Background

I came to the United States at the age of eight. I left my home, my friends, my cousins, my grandparents, my aunts, my uncles, and my dog, Chiquitillo. My parents, like many immigrant families, wanted to provide their daughters with a future that they did not see available for us in Mexico. Growing up as an immigrant child, however, was far from easy. I often found myself questioning my identity, trying to make sense of my new geography but never quite feeling like it was home. This experience of straddling borders is the impetus for my interest in immigration. Living and growing up in Arizona provided me with an informal education about what it means to be an American, and what it means to belong or be seen in many ways as an outsider. "It is like living in a home without foundation, *sin tierra para plantar nuestras raices*" (Maldonado, 2013). Immigrant children continue to grow up straddling borders both through their physical bodies and through their language and culture; their identities can remain in liminality, which can impact their sense of agency in the world.

(Angeles Maldonado)

The border is a highly politicized geographical space in which the violation of human rights is justified and rationalized under the fabricated knowledge that the border is a place of danger. It delineates through walls and policies who gets to belong by strategically attacking the identities of those it seeks to exclude. It is imperative to understand the political climate of the borderlands as well as its geographical history, as it sheds light on the ways in which this context impacts people who live there. Historically, Arizona, for example, straddled two countries and is on indigenous land. Arizona was part of the state of Sonora, Mexico until 1848, when the United States took possession through the Treaty of Guadalupe Hidalgo. It is ironic, therefore, that many regard Mexican migrants as outsiders. Still, the border region has been made to be a space of indistinction, where policies and laws exist and are intentionally designed to delineate and demarcate the land through the systemic criminalization and racialization of people of color while safeguarding White Supremacy.

The United States is experiencing an identity crisis. President Trump ran a campaign with the promise of building "a giant beautiful wall" and "Making America Great Again." Beyond this problematic divisive nativist discourse, a series of laws and immigration policies, under the lie of concerns for public safety, have had the direct result of inciting fear (Toomey et al., 2014) and the deportation of families who have resided in Arizona for many years. Police and immigration agents target and criminalize migrant communities in the name of safety; yet immigrant families are the ones whose safety becomes jeopardized. The trauma inflicted upon families has only escalated during the Trump administration. On April 8, 2018, Attorney General Jeff Sessions announced a "zero-tolerance policy," calling for the prosecution of all individuals who entered the United States "illegally." This strict criminalization of migration resulted in heinous acts by the Immigration and Customs Enforcement (ICE) agency, including the unforgivable practice of separating children from their parents upon apprehension at the US/Mexico border. Immigrant families detained are crowded into cells known as *hieleras* (ice chests) due to intentionally set extremely cold temperatures. Children, some as young as three months old, are detained in facilities for children, some of which were discovered to be unlicensed, and reports of child neglect and physical and sexual abuse within these sites have been reported.

Living undocumented in the borderlands can also mean living in over-policed neighborhoods, where racial profiling and discrimination, criminalization, transient employment, low wage jobs, long work hours, employment insecurity, under-payment, underfunded schools, a lack of access to health-care and insurance, working under the table, and a heightened risk for injuries, health hazards, due to exposure to chemicals, and poor or dangerous working conditions exist (Panikkar et al., 2015). People may fear calling the police, where the police and other agencies are known to actively collaborate with ICE and may also restrict seeking public assistance or inter-acting with governmental agencies for other reasons (Toomey et al., 2014).

Another policy that directly affects immigrant children in Arizona is the Structured English Immersion (SEI) model, requiring all instruction, text, and work produced by students be in English only. This model has received backlash as to its validity regarding its effectiveness (Krashen, Rolstad, & MacSwan, 2007). The model has been criticized for its infringement on children's civil rights (Rios-Auguilar, Gonza-lez-Canche & Moll, 2010) via linguistic imperialism (Jimenez-Silva, Bernstein & Baca, 2016): an attempt "to capture the way one language dominates another, with Anglo centricity and professionalism ... within a structure in which unequal power and resource allocation is affected and legitimated" (Phillipson, 1992, p. 54). The SEI model, as compared to bilingual models, strips away one of the most prevalent cul-tural identifiers immigrant children have, their native language.

Our Research

What does it mean to be an immigrant child in Arizona? How are identities and imagined futures impacted? What are the implications for social justice practices in early childhood contexts? These are questions our research sought to address. We conducted activity based conversational interviews with 23 children living in Arizona, examining their views and experiences on home, school, and community. We ana-lyzed the interviews by applying Border Crit Theory (Maldonado, 2013), an emergent critical theory for understanding and contextualizing the experiences of people of color living in the borderlands. Our interviews underscored the significance of consulting and talking with children in immigrant families on issues that affect their lives. Themes of our conversations included discussions about identity, migration, notions of home, belonging, race, citizenship, status, bilingualism, family, community, neighborhood, education, schooling, friendship, and altruistic desires for the future.

Our work is also situated in a children's rights-based framework, and we draw specifically from the United Nations Convention on the Rights of the Child Committee's General Comment No. 12, "The Child's Right to be Heard" (United Nations, 2009), which emphasized children's right to partici-pate in decisions affecting them and to have their views taken seriously: "The views expressed by children may add relevant perspectives and experiences and should be considered in decision-making, policy-making and preparation of laws and/or measures as well as their evaluation" (p. 5). We build on research that foregrounds younger people's views (e.g. Pérez, Medellin & Rideaux, 2016; Lundy & Swadener, 2015; Soto & Swadener, 2005; Swadener, Peters & Gaches, 2012; MacNaughton, Hughes & Smith, 2008) that highlight the ways young children tell adults about their lives and experiences and the concerns that they have for people close to them and for their immediate environment. Here children are "rights bearers" and adults are "duty bearers" who are required to help children build the capacity to express views on issues affecting them.

Theoretical Framework

Critical Race Theory (CRT) was founded in response to Critical Legal Studies (CLS) and maintains that race and racism is endemic to everyday life (Delgado & Stefancic, 2000). Border Crit is inspired by CRT, and other critical theories such as Tribal Critical Race Theory (Tribal Crit) which sees colonization as endemic to everyday life (Brayboy, 2005) and Latino/a Critical Race Theory (Lat Crit) which "emphasizes issues that affect Latina/o people in everyday life" (Delgado Bernal, 2002; Espinoza & Harris, 1997; Hernandez-Truyol, 1997; Villalpando, 2003). Thus, Border Crit (Maldonado, 2013) maintains and recognizes not only race and colonization but also borders as endemic to everyday life and focuses on issues that directly impact and concern border communities. Border Crit recognizes the borderlands as a space that is historically, ideologically, and politically different than the rest of the country. Border Crit theory scholars seek to expose and name the racial ideologies behind the symbolic parade of laws and immigration enforcement practices that dominate the borderlands and foreground the voices of people of color living there. We see narratives and stories of border communities as legitimate though frequently undervalued sources of knowledge and maintain a social justice commitment to the communities we represent in research.

Conversations with Children

We conducted 23 activity-based conversational interviews (Tay-Lim & Lim, 2013) with children ages 5 to 9 years old in an elementary school, in their homes, and in a community center. We offered art supplies and paper and asked children to do a drawing of their home, school, or community. The interviews were approximately 30 minutes in length. All interviews were digitally recorded and transcribed. We began with questions such as, "Tell me about your family," or "How do you help at home?" We also asked about a typical day at school and about their teachers and classes. As we continued the interviews, we found ourselves rewording questions and providing examples. We used open-coding, a process of examining data and developing categories of information and interconnecting them (Strauss & Corbin, 1990), based on our research questions and discussed and analyzed the data collectively. We apply Border Crit Theory to analyze and unpack possible deeper meanings of children's responses based on what we know in the literature about immigrant families, our existing knowledge of movements and communities, and through our own cultural understandings and experiences.

Trans-border Identities

Most children drew pictures of their families first. While they drew and colored, they discussed where their family was from, indicating a sense of multiple identities including family on both sides of the US/Mexico border. For example, one eight-year-old child reflected:

INTERVIEWER: Do you play outside? ... Since you mentioned you don't really have a neighborhood?

CHILD: ... um ... mostly when my cousins come from different places we usually play ...

INTERVIEWER: Where are they coming from?

CHILD: I think we all come from Mexico, but we were born here ... so we are Mexican slash American.

It seemed this boy had an understanding that though he was not physically born in Mexico, he still was theoretically born there. In stating, "We all come from Mexico," it seems he is redefining identity to translate not only to where one is born but to where one shares connections. He went on to share with us about his grandparents:

INTERVIEWER: But your grandparents live in Mexico.

CHILD: Yeah, and my mom and dad lived in Mexico.

INTERVIEWER: Do you get to go down and see your grandparents very often?

CHILD: Nnno. Um, mostly we're going to see one of 'em cuz I only have grandpas. I don't have any grandmas. I've never seen any of 'em, and one of em, um, died when ... and one of em died I think before I was born.

We observed that his identity was also connected to where one's family is from and his desire to physically connect one day. Other children we talked to also expressed wanting to see missing family living in Mexico.

On Safety

Another dimension of children's awareness of the border and their families' precarious immigration status is their expression of fear and/or concerns over their families' safety. One seven-year-old girl described worrying about her mother, when talking about the future:

INTERVIEWER: Is there anything that worries you?

CHILD: Uhuh.

INTERVIEWER: What?

CHILD: I worry in the night because I'm afraid that my mom's gonna die. *Y a veces, um, um, y a veces, um, um, y a veces lloro.* (And sometimes, um, um, and sometimes, I cry)

INTERVIEWER: *A veces lloras? Oh. Porque lloras?* (You cry sometimes? Oh, why do you cry?)

CHILD: *Porque extraño mi papa.* (because I miss my dad)

We learned in this interview that her father had been arrested and was being held in an immigration detention facility in Eloy, Arizona. We know that visiting these centers is challenging for families in mixed immigration status. Her younger sister, age five, reflected with the following when asked about her hopes for the future:

CHILD: I wish that there wasn't laws and I wish that the man that's mean, he wasn't real …

INTERVIEWER: Which man?

CHILD: The man that Puente doesn't like that they are fighting about him …

INTERVIEWER: The president?

CHILD: uh huh and also this other guy, I forget his name.

INTERVIEWER: Arpaio?

CHILD: Yes, I wish they weren't real because their laws are horrible.

INTERVIEWER: What laws?

CHILD: I don't like [the laws] about the Mexicans and I don't like about um Arpaio that he steals things from people. I feel sad about those two because they are not doing anything nice to the world, they are hurting the people, they are hurting their families.

Our experiences working with impacted immigrant families inform us that children living in the border have a hyper awareness of laws and the possibility of deportation. This awareness is reflected in the response above. She discusses and connects the ways laws and the people who enforce them are impacting not just her family but families in general. She expresses a desire for the laws to not "be real." She goes on to express missing her father who was detained at the time of the interview and seems anxious about her mom's health.

Despite the reality that police carry out many anti-immigrant policies and hurt communities of color, through systemic racial profiling and excessive use of force, some of the children in this study spoke positively about the police. For example:

INTERVIEWER: Do you know what you want to be when you grow up?

CHILD: Mmmm, when I grow up I want to be a police.

INTERVIEWER: You want to be a police? Okay. Do you know anybody else who's a police?

CHILD: Um, a police came my school and showed me a dog police.

INTERVIEWER: Oh …

CHILD: Like, he, he like, if you're lost and stuff, he will look, and find you.

INTERVIEWER: Oh. And so, why do you want to be a police? You want to look for kids?

CHILD: Yeah, if they're lost.

The reasonings for wanting to be a police officer varied but reflected children's altruistic desires to provide safety. We know that schools teach children to view the police in a positive light, as community helpers and may bring in police officers and firefighters to present or speak.

It is also becoming more frequent and concerning to have School Resource Officers (SROs) in schools; sworn law enforcement officers "responsible for safety and crime prevention." According to the ACLU's 2017 report, *Bullies in Blue: Origins and Consequences of School Policing*, the role of police can be linked to increased mass incarceration and the criminalization of typical youth behavior; "students are arrested in schools, places meant to provide safe haven, for behavior that is noncriminal in any other venue …" (ACLU, 2017). We are concerned for the safety of students, particularly minorities, with the presence of SROs on campus.

Children also raised concerns about safety in their neighborhoods. When asking them about where they live, this is what one child said:

Child: It's scary at night…That's why I don't go outside.

This child went on to say he was afraid of being kidnapped and that his mother told him to not play outside. We met this child in an afterschool program in a community center in Maryvale, Arizona. Another child, who lived in a rural community, stated:

Child: I wish I had a neighborhood …

Immigrant families who experience poverty can have limited housing options and often live in remote areas or in communities with high crime rates. Some children did not feel safe about moving to new neighborhoods, for example:

Child: Neighbors loved me. I miss them since we left the trailer. They cared for me when my mom went to the emergency place.

Children were clear about the lack of access to safe spaces to play, such as parks, or more home space such as not having a backyard. Some expressed this as, "I want a park," or "I wish we had a place to swim." We also were amused by the creativity and resiliency of children. One child told us that he and his brothers would play hide and seek with a cup; they would hide the cup since they did not have space to hide themselves. Such quotes reflected a child's right to play (Peters & Swadener, 2018).

Language and Bilingualism

Language was a significant topic in our interviews. We began each conversation asking children if they preferred that we do the interview in English or Spanish. At times there were children who would choose Spanish, but then switch to responding in English, or vice versa. This led us to ask about language directly. We asked what they enjoyed about being bilingual and what language they spoke at home. It became evident that children were straddling not only geographic borders, but also linguistic ones. When asked about what they like about being bilingual, one six-year-old child mentions that his parents do not speak English. He also related that his mom gets mad at his siblings when they do not speak in Spanish. For example;

INTERVIEWER: What do you like about being bilingual?
CHILD: Um. It's good. Cuz, you know why? Cuz my brother's talking English but they don't. My mom gets mad at them cuz they, they want em to talk in Spanish.

In contrast, another child, age six, discusses how her mom wants her to learn English, and in fact does not speak with them in Spanish even though she's bilingual, because she wants her to learn English.

INTERVIEWER: And what language does your mom speak?
CHILD: English and Spanish. But she don't want to talk in English to us. Wait. Not English, Spanish, because we are, we need to know how to speak English.

Another child expressed that he understood that, "You make more money if you are bilingual." We observed the ways in which immigrant children code switch and have learned to understand the contexts and spaces in which to use English and Spanish. In an English-only state with limited bilingual programs, children have learned that English is the language of schooling, yet when offered the opportunity many chose to continue the conversation in their mother tongue.

Schooling and Immigrant Children

I have been an educator for almost 30 years. I was drawn to the teaching profession because of two experiences I had at a very young age that had a profound effect on me. My second-grade teacher left an imprint of love for school and education; my third-grade teacher left an imprint of fingernails on my forearms. Through the years I drew on both experiences to remind me that as a teacher I too have the capability of having a profound effect on children's lives. The effect I had the most concern for was not how much I could teach them but about how I treated them. Over my nearly three decades of working in public education it was becoming increasingly more difficult for me to observe how our system was continually invoking its neoliberal agenda by implementing such policies as No Child Left Behind (NCLB) and Structured English Immersion (SEI). The system's push to maintain the status quo and to value capitalism over compassion was the crux that had me step out of the classroom as an instructor and into the classroom to be instructed. I graduated from the Social and Cultural Pedagogy Master's program at ASU with the intention of working on educational policy reform.

(Casey Khaleesi)

Even in this neoliberal and anti-immigrant political climate, children in this study expressed having positive experiences in school. Many described what their day looked like, telling us in detail about their daily schedule. We got the sense that they liked knowing the structure and routine of their school day. A number of children had positive views of their school experience, for example:

Child: School makes me so happy!
Child: I like everything there.
Child: I like everything!

We also asked whether there was anything they wished to change at school, and many responded, "No." When the question was reworded to "What would you change if you were principal?", children were more willing to share their ideas. One child stated:

Child: That, that, the teachers learn how the kids can learn.

Another child, discussed what he would change he referred to discipline practices of the school:

Child: That when I am a principal, I would … that they all let their kids be on green. That the teachers let the kids to, to always be on green

He referred to the popular trend in behavior management, the "positive discipline" approach, that involves cards representing stoplight colors. Teachers assign a color to each student's name depending on his/her behavior that day. Green means the student is following directions; yellow means the child has been warned regarding a behavior; red means a child has reached a point where a consequence is meted out for bad behavior (Khaleesi, 2018).

Other suggested changes by children had to do with the physical appearance of the school and its environment. A nine-year-old boy describes:

Child: It's pretty weird, but I'd add a waterslide and a pool.

Creating better spaces to play, such as soccer fields and pools, were among some suggested improvements.

While immigrant children in this study expressed "being happy," there were some who described challenging situations at school, such as being new, making new friends, and being bullied by other students. One six-year-old girl described being labeled by her teacher in a derogatory way:

Child: Sometimes she call me "Ranch" … because she thinks I'm Ranch.

She seemed upset because to be labeled ranch or *del rancho* implies being from the outskirts of society and considered "less" civilized. This incident illustrates the need for culturally sensitive educators for all children.

What We Learned from Children and Know from Migrant Communities

And I suppose our migration story never leaves us … it becomes part of our identity, and resurfaces in our everyday understandings of self, amidst a world that feels distant. We become either foreign to this land or foreign to the people who birthed us. We belong to two worlds and we exist reading between the lines, making sense of the in between. When volunteering with family reunification efforts recently, I watched tears fall off of a migrant child's cheek … and in that moment, I saw myself … still healing, still making sense of the loss and nostalgia of walking away from the land that loved me, but couldn't care for me and into a land that denounces all that I represent.

(*Angeles Maldonado*)

We want to complicate the often-simplified rationalization of injustice. Border Crit denounces the neutrality of law and government and seeks to unveil its contradictions through counter stories. Border Crit Theory research demands that we consider the significance of context and place. The border is a contested space, and so as we examine what children told us we want to also complicate their narrative and integrate what we know from direct experiences with impacted communities organizing for migrant rights. What we are seeing is a direct and intentional attack on the transborder identity. Although our interviews took place prior to development of recent immigration policies, we know immigrant communities have experienced trauma and injustice for many years. It's important that we continue conversing with impacted children, not only for research purposes, but as a tool for social justice advocacy. The children in this pilot study shared narratives that illustrate safety concerns and struggles, but mainly resiliency. Despite the borders in the immigrant childhood experience, we do not see migrant children as victims, but rather we observed enthusiasm and powerful hopes for their own futures.

Gloria Anzaldúa (1987) describes her yearning for family in Mexico as the "Transborder Family Imaginary." Many of the children we interviewed displayed an understanding of their identity as transborder. Children referred to themselves and their families as belonging to both Mexico and the United States, despite the fact that many were not even born in Mexico and some may have never even visited. Their yearning for family became even more prevalent in their responses about their hopes for the future, and many described wanting to be with family in Mexico or visit relatives.

When we speak about the transborder identity, we hope to convey the constant juggling of meaning and the recreation of new meanings. Having a transborder identity can often require a person to entertain two seemingly contradictory ideas. The external world of the migrant child is often colored with the imposition of meanings that may not relate to one's direct experience or that may impact one's family or home life in a distinct way. Children are therefore required to juggle the meaning of a term and decide what meaning to apply. Therefore, code switching is not limited to language but is also consistently required when children belong to two social contexts and therefore meaning constructs.

As child advocates, it is painfully obvious that the family separation policy that Trump invoked at the time of this writing not only carries immediate consequences, but will undoubtedly carry long lasting impacts on children and those who know them. Just in educational ramifications alone, children who are experiencing the unimaginably stressful and highly toxic situations at the border will most likely experience physical and mental health issues, PTSD, and "developmental issues due to reduced neural connections to important areas of the brain. Toxic stress is associated with damage to the area of the brain responsible for learning and memory" (Kaiser, 2018).

The Southern Poverty Law Center's Teaching Tolerance (SPLC, 2016) project reported that fear and anxiety levels among children of color had escalated significantly since Trump's presidential campaign and his heightened anti-immigration rhetoric and unjust policies. Teachers reported an increase in racial tensions, intimidation, and bullying towards Mexican and Muslim students associated with ways in which Trump targeted them during his campaign that emboldened white students to act on their prejudices.

One student's desire for everyone to be "on green" speaks to school discipline that invokes punitive consequences for behaviors labeled as undesirable. Zero tolerance policies have exacerbated the situation leading to a disproportionate number of students of color being suspended multiple times and/or expelled. These policies usually leads to the students' first contact with the juvenile detention system which often leads to adult incarceration and the "school to prison pipeline" (Nelson & Lind, 2015).

Migrant families, particularly those that left their countries of origin fleeing poverty or violence, often arrive with very little resources and experience a myriad of financial and legal hardships. These challenges directly impact children's well-being and sense of safety. Children spoke about safety for themselves or their families, concerns over parents working late, and not having access to parks. One child explained that he had no neighbors, and he was very afraid of snakes (the child was living in a rural area in West Phoenix). Another boy said that he was not allowed to play outside because his mom was afraid of the traffic around their house. Others spoke about not going out at night for fear of being shot. Fears about death also were expressed, such as knowing of family who had been killed or had died. Another child was afraid of her mother dying. Some children referenced Trump and Arpaio, and offered reflections about missing a parent who was in immigration custody, as described in the quote above, *"Porque extrano a mi papa"* (because I miss my dad).

In the next section, we express the importance of creating caring borderless spaces to counteract the pervasive injustice that exists in the outer terrain.

Implications and Discussion: Creating Borderless Educational Spaces

> My passion for social justice goes back to childhood and being what now might be labeled "high empathy." With a mother engaged with community work, who died when I was 10, and a father teaching government and bringing me to City Council meetings and with my early friendships with children with disabilities, I often thought about what was unfair or unjust and organized clubs that focused in part on neighborhood "service" projects. Coming of age in the late 60s, I was an activist by the 70s, focused on gender, civil rights, stopping war, and disability rights. I also knew by high school that a deep interest was in young children – how they think, feel and come to understand and impact the world.
>
> This interest has grown to include 30 years of work in primarily early childhood contexts in sub-Saharan Africa, work with children in urban US settings, as well as work with educators and community leaders in indigenous communities. Concern for more nuanced understandings of children's rights has also shaped my work, and I have collaborated on several projects that foreground children's views. I have long considered children to be theorists of their lives, as we take up in this section.
>
> *(Beth Swadener)*

The idea of children as theorists is not new, yet we seldom regard them as creators or holders of knowledge. As we engaged with children, it was evident that they had their own clear ideas and explanations about how the world ought to be. We began our research seeking to explore and foreground children's "views and voices" but what we found was not just opinions and perspectives, but rather their theories about their worlds and how to resolve identified problems.

Educators and practitioners not only have a social responsibility and an opportunity to play a role in becoming "supporting advocates" and accomplices to ensure the academic success of migrant students, but more importantly to caring about them as children, which must entail their social, psychological, and emotional development. Education scholars have long documented the role that schools play in reproducing the values of the nation state and in indoctrinating children to be "good" citizens (e.g., Apple, 1979). Critical education scholars, including Paulo Freire (1970) and bell hooks (1994), affirm the need to transform education to become a practice for liberation. There are many ways to begin this work; we offer some recommendations for educators.

Reading Between the Lines

Border Crit theory urges us to also be border crossers; to be transborder advocates we must learn to "read between the lines" and understand the lives and education of migrant children within the context of their migration story and within the geographical political landscape in which their lives are situated. We also learned that we cannot isolate children's experiences from their relationships with their families. Thus, a child's difficulty with reading or having a low math score is no longer seen in isolation. Student misbehavior is no longer a sign of a problem with them, but rather an opportunity to look beyond the surface and seek to understand what other challenges that child is facing or managing and what systems are in place to disable or could be in place to enable children of color to be successful. This understanding can empower educators with the ideas and tact necessary to create classrooms and schools that are not only inclusive, but educational settings that are sensitive to the experiences of the children that inhabit the classroom. We need healing and safe spaces that encourage creativity, flexibility, and love.

Listen to Children

Empathy and listening are imperative. Children are resilient vital actors; asking them about their lives matters. As Soto (2002) documented, young bilingual children are altruistic and care deeply about their families and communities. Creating classrooms that reflect altruism and caring practices further support all children. If we look at education as a space for promoting social justice, we must listen to what children are telling us. Are we asking questions that matter? Are we creating spaces that are situated within a child-rights based framework that preserve the rights of children to participate in telling their own stories?

Understanding and respecting children's funds of knowledge (González, Wyman & O'Connor, 2011) goes far in creating a caring and inclusive environment. Challenging social and political landscapes and regimes of power are (re) shaping people's lived experiences – and their search to be at "home" in their life-worlds. In much discourse, views about younger people are primarily centered on the notion that children are "pre-adult becomings" (Holloway & Valentine, 2000) or "deferred citizens" (Cheney, 2007), as they have little agency to influence change until they are older or reach an age of majority. Children and youth are resilient contributors to action, advocacy, and activism.

Creating Intentional Mindful Spaces

Educators should interrogate the physical space of their classroom and ask, "What symbols are made visible or suppressed?" Awareness about what a child brings to the classroom must be met with a concerted effort to make the classroom a welcoming place. When children are experiencing separation from their homeland, culture, language, and sometimes even their parents, school should not be a place that exacerbates a loss of identity. Teachers should ensure that children see themselves in the curriculum and classroom environment, and feel supported in their identity, language and culture. Children should be able to look around their classroom and see that they belong.

Districts should also be intentional about hiring practices and actively recruit culturally sensitive and passionate educators of color, and bi- and multilingual staff. We need educators that are unapologetically pro-migrant, pro-black, pro-woman, pro-queer, and pro-humanity. Representation in the classroom matters. Educators are the first filter through which children are learning about themselves and about the world. Hiring educators that not only value diversity, but that understand marginalized communities, or have a track record of working with minoritized communities, is imperative in creating borderless educational environments.

Finally, children value play. The importance of play has long been recognized in the early childhood field, yet has been threatened by a growing academic readiness emphasis in early years education. We must recognize that children are holistic beings with more than cognitive needs and modes of development. Children have the right to move their bodies without restriction, regulation, and control. Children of color, in particular, are disciplined for the ways in which they use their bodies and may be seen as a threat. We need safe spaces that embrace and promote play and movement.

Using Culturally Relevant Curriculum

The implementation of culturally relevant curriculum is paramount to creating a borderless educational classroom. Interrogating what children are learning and the format in which it is presented is critical. Schools and early childhood programs need to encourage the practice of using stories and learning components to develop curriculum that is relevant to children and their families. Educators must be cognizant of the "lived" experiences of students by using children's literature that reflects similar experiences and creating learning environments that reflect the cultures of students, instead of the materials that reflect a white middle-class bias that persists in most learning materials. This approach should not be confined to the classroom, but should be visible throughout the school or child care setting.

Borders in the classroom can take multiple forms, including language, culture (home versus school) and curriculum itself. For example, if children cannot relate to the curriculum, bridging to children's experiences with examples and materials from daily life can increase relevance and connections. Being sensitive to the identities of children and using oral storytelling, offering tactile experiences and opportunities for physical play can increase children's comfort, engagement and sense of belonging. Providing love, caring, seeing the promise in all children can help create a more inclusive borderless classroom community.

Conclusion

Our Arizona study represents a small part of an emerging global network involving research that focuses on enacting children's participatory rights to share their lived experiences. We explored children's perspectives amidst a tense and polarizing socio-political landscape. We believe children must be taken seriously in decision-making and the process of creating policies and laws that impact them and their families. We anchor our research alongside migrant communities and in solidarity with their struggle for human rights, dignity, and justice in these deeply challenging times.

References

ACLU (2017). *Bullies in blue*(White Paper). New York:American Civil Liberties Union (ACLU). https://www.aclu.org/issues/juvenile-justice/school-prison-pipeline/bullies-blue

Apple, M. (1979). *Ideology and curriculum*. New York: Routledge.

Anzaldúa, G. (1987). *Borderlands: La frontera*. San Francisco: Aunt Lute Books.

Brayboy, B. (2005). Toward a tribal critical race theory in education. *Urban Review*, 37(5), 425–446. doi:10.1007/s11256-005-0018-y

Cheney, K.E. (2007). *Pillars of the nation: Child citizens and Ugandan national development*. Chicago: University of Chicago Press.

Delgado, R., & Stefancic, J. (2000). Introduction. In R. Delgado, & J. Stefancic (Eds.), *Critical Race Theory: The cutting edge* (2nd ed., pp. xv–xix). Philadelphia: Temple University Press.

Delgado Bernal, D. (2002). Critical race theory, Latcrit theory, and critical raced gendered epistemologies: Recognizing students of color as holders and creators of knowledge. *Qualitative Inquiry*, 8(1), 105–126.

Espinoza, L., & Harris, A. (1997). Embracing the tar-baby: LatCrit theory and the sticky mess of race. *La Raza Law Journal*, 10(1), 499–559.

Freire, P. (1970). *Pedagogy of the oppressed*. New York: Continuum.

González, N., Wyman, L., & O'Connor, B. (2011). The past, present, and future of "funds of knowledge. In *A Companion to the Anthropology of Education* (pp. 479–494). Hoboken, NJ: Wiley-Blackwell. doi:10.1002/9781444396713.ch28

Hernandez-Truyol, B.E. (1997). Borders (en)gendered – Normativities, Latinas, and a LatCrit paradigm. *NYU. Law Review*, 72, 882–927.

Holloway, S.L., & G. Valentine (2000) Children's geographies and the new social studies of childhood. In S.L. Holloway and G. Valentine (Eds.), *Children's geographies: Playing, living, learning* (pp. 1–26). London: Routledge.

hooks, bell (1994). *Teaching to transgress: Education as the practice of freedom.* New York: Routledge.

Jimenez-Silva, M., Bernstein, K.A., & Baca, E.C. (2016). An analysis of how restrictive language policies are interpreted by Arizona's Department of Education and three individual school districts' websites. *Education Policy Analysis Archives,* 24(105).

Kaiser, H. (2018). Henry J. Kaiser Family Foundation (KFF). Key health implications of separation of families at the border (as of June 27. 2018). Retrieved from: https://www. kff.org/disparities-policy/fact-sheet/key-health-implications-of-separation-of-families-a t-the-border/

Khaleesi, C. (2018). "It makes me sad because I think… I can never be good enough.": What students are saying about high-stakes testing. (Masters thesis). Retrieved from Arizona State University, ProQuest Dissertations and Theses database.

Krashen, S., Rolstad, K., & MacSwan, J. (2012). Review of "Research summary and bibliography for structured English immersion programs" of the Arizona English Language Learners Task Force. In C. Faltis & B. Arias (Eds.) *English learners in Arizona,*(pp. 107–118). Bristol, UK: Multilingual Matters.

Lundy, L., & Swadener, B.B. (2015). Engaging with young children as co-researchers: A child rights-based approach. In O. Saracho (Ed.), *Handbook of research methods in early childhood education, Volume II* (pp. 657–676). Charlotte, NC: Information Age Publishing.

MacNaughton, G., Hughes, P., & Smith, K. (Eds.) (2008). *Young children as active citizens: Principles, policies and pedagogies.* Newcastle, UK: Cambridge Scholars Publishing.

Maldonado, A. (2013). *Raids, race, and lessons of fear and resistance: Narratives and discourse in the immigration movement in Arizona.* (Doctoral dissertation). Retrieved from Arizona State University, ProQuest Dissertations and Theses database. (UMI 3590934)

Nelson, L., & Lind, D. (2015) The school-to-prison pipeline, explained; Police officers in the classrooms are just the tip of the iceberg. Retrieved from https://www.vox.com/ 2015/2/24/8101289/school-discipline-race

Panikkar, B., Brugge, D., Gute, D.M., & Hyatt, R.R. (2015). "They see us as machines:" The experience of recent immigrant women in the low wage informal labor sector. *PLoS ONE* 10(11), e0142686. doi:10.1371/journal.pone.0142686.

Perez, M.S., Medellin, K., & Rideaux, K.S. (2016). Repositioning childhood lived experiences within adult contexts: A Black feminist analysis of childhood/s regulation in early childhood care and education. *Global Studies of Childhood,* 6(1), 67–79.

Peters, L.E., & Swadener, B.B. (2018). The right to childhood and the ethos of play. In P. K. Smith & J. Roopnarine (Eds.), *The Cambridge handbook on play: Developmental and disciplinary perspectives* (pp. 722–742). London: Cambridge University Press.

Phillipson, R. (1992). *Linguistic imperialism.* Oxford, England: Oxford University Press.

Rios-Aguilar, C., Gonzalez-Canche, M., & Moll, L. (2010). Implementing structured English immersion (SEI) in Arizona: Benefits, costs, challenges, and opportunities. The Civil Rights Project/Proyecto Derechos Civiles. Retrieved from https://www.civil rightsproject.ucla.edu/research/k-12-education/language-minority-students/implementi ng-structured-english-immersion-sei-in-arizona-benefits-costs-challenges-and-opportu nities?searchterm=implementing+sei

Soto, L.D. (2002). Young bilingual children's perceptions of bilingualism and biliteracy: Altruistic possibilities. *Bilingual Research Journal,* 26(3), 599–610.

Soto, L.D., & Swadener, B.B. (Eds.). (2005). *Power and voice in research with children.* New York, NY: Peter Lang.

Southern Poverty Law Center SPLC (2016). The Trump effect: The impact of the presidential campaign on our nation's schools. Retrieved from https://www.splcenter.org/20160413/trump-effect-impact-presidential-campaign-our-nations-schools

Strauss, A.L., & Corbin, J.M. (1990). *Basics of qualitative research: Grounded theory procedures and techniques.* Newbury Park, CA: Sage Publications.

Swadener, B.B., Peters, L., & Gaches, S. (2012). Taking children's rights and participation seriously: Cross-national perspectives and possibilities. In V. Pacini-Ketchabaw & L. Prochner (Eds.), *Resituating Canadian early childhood education.* New York: Peter Lang, 189–210.

Tay-Lim, J., & Lim, S. (2013). Privileging younger children's voices in research: Use of drawings and a co-construction process. *International Journal of Qualitative Methods*, 12, 65–83.

Toomey, R.B., Umaña-Taylor, A.J., Williams, D.R., Harvey-Mendoza, E., Jahromi, L.B., & Updegraff, K.A. (2014). Impact of Arizona's SB 1070 immigration law on utilization of health care and public assistance among Mexican-origin adolescent mothers and their mother figures. *American Journal of Public Health*, 104(Suppl 1), S28–S34. doi:10.2105/AJPH.2013.301655

United Nations (1989). *UN Convention on the Rights of the Child.* Geneva: United Nations.

United Nations (2009). *Convention on the Rights of the Child Committee's General Comment No. 12.* Geneva: United Nations.

Villalpando, O. (2003). Self-segregation or self-preservation? A critical race theory and Latina/o critical theory analysis of a study of Chicana/o college students. *International Journal of Qualitative Studies in Education*, 5, 619–646.

2

COUNTERING COLOR-BLINDNESS IN EARLY CHILDHOOD EDUCATION

Elevating the Embodied Experiences, Perspectives and Voices of Black Women Educators

Kia S. Rideaux and Michelle Salazar Pérez

Introduction

Social injustice can manifest in young children's social worlds in myriad ways. Children of color, for instance, with rich family and cultural experiences, are often positioned as deficient in early years education, which too often universalizes White identities as the "standard" for developmental outcomes and academic achievement (Burman, 2008). Rather than honoring the cultural attributes that contribute to the brilliance of children of color, deficit and "at risk" labels persist (Delpit, 2012; Swadener & Lubeck, 1995). These racialized injustices have been foundational to "color-blindness" in early childhood education and care. With the diversity among us in the United States and globally, educators, schools, and care providers must be equipped to affirm all childhoods, especially those most marginalized (Delpit, 2006; Ladson-Billings, 1994; Souto-Manning, 2013). By challenging color-blindness, minoritized children's identities, histories, struggles, and legacies are acknowledged and honored. This moves early childhood education and care in the direction of social justice.

Theoretical Framework

What Is Color-Blindness and How Is It a Social Justice Issue for Early Childhood Education?

Color-blindness is the misguided notion that one should treat people as "equals" by ignoring, and thereby erasing, Black, Brown, and Other racialized identities. Some assert that being color-blind is helpful in countering injustice; however, color-blindness exacerbates oppression through non-recognition and devaluation of distinct and historically marginalized identities. Delpit (2007) explains that Paley's (2000) book, *White Teacher*, has been helpful for teacher candidates to understand that "to say you don't see color is to say you don't see children" (Delpit, 2007, p. 159). This powerful message resonates with us as authors, educators, and educational researchers who are concerned with the ways in which color-blindness continues to exist in early childhood contexts (and beyond) despite the vast literature and educational materials available that have problematized color-blindness and have offered ways to counter it through anti-bias and anti-racist education (Boutte, Lopez-Robertson, & Costello, 2011; Derman-Sparks, LeeKeenan, & Nimmo, 2015; Doucet & Adair, 2013; Farago, Murray, & Swadener, 2017; Husband Jr., 2012; Pacini-Ketchabaw, Berikoff, Elliot, & Tucker, 2007). Noteworthy is that while efforts have been made to inform and offer social justice oriented alternatives to educators, much of the research has focused on the experiences of White educators (Souto-Manning & Cheruvu, 2016).

To offer a different perspective, we seek to elevate the embodied experiences of three Black women educators who have grappled with color-blindness in first, second, and third grade classrooms in suburban schools with predominately White teaching faculties and administrations. The purpose of the research is to contribute to social justice education. To us, as educators, social justice education means affirming and illuminating all school experiences. As women of color, this informs our research by emboldening us to engage critically with and pursue narratives that challenge the cultural hegemony present in our early childhood school communities. To document these re-narrativizations, we align our inquiry with Hytten and Bettez (2011) who describe one of many strands of social justice education as ethnographic and narrative. They suggest:

> Writings in this strand tend to be passionate and evocative. As opposed to creating categories and definitions, or offering broad principles for just practices, the primary focus of these works is to capture more vividly some lived consequences of injustice and to offer rich images of more just social and educational practices.
>
> *(p. 14)*

By sharing the lived experiences of Black women educators and their encounters with color-blindness in early childhood contexts, discrete forms of cultural erasure and racism are revealed, as well as insights into ways to disrupt color-blindness and reimagine more socially just early childhood professional and educational spaces.

Black Feminisms

The research shared in this chapter utilizes Black feminisms, which have been theorized through the everyday lived experiences of Black women and include analyses of their daily and systemic encounters with racism, sexism, classism, and heteronormativity that have become part of the realities of women of color living in the margins (Collins, 2000; Lorde, 1984). hooks (1999) constructs marginality "as much more than a site of deprivation"; she views it as "a radical possibility, a space of resistance … [and] as a central location for the production of counter-hegemonic[1] discourse that is not just found in words but in habits of being and the way one lives" (p. 149). As such, the margins can incite social justice through empowerment, resistance, and transformation of color-blind discourses[2] in educational spaces and beyond. By reclaiming and shifting dominant narratives, Black feminisms can foster a critical consciousness that reveals and dismantles systems of domination[3] and encourages the formation of collective sisterhoods in the struggle against inequities and injustice.

The central tenets of Black feminisms can be found in the powerful narratives and experiences that the educators share throughout this chapter. Their connections with cultural knowledge inform their loving support of children of color with whom they work, in addition to challenging the color-blindness they see and experience as professionals working in predominately White schools and classroom spaces.

Research Description

The collaborators in the research were three Black women educators teaching in grades one, two, and three in two elementary schools. The two schools were in a suburban district (within a larger urban context in Texas) with a majority White teaching faculty and administration. One school is classified as Title I, with 49% of the children having Latinx and low-income identities. The other school served mostly White and Asian, middle-class students. Interestingly, the three educators in both of these schools had mostly White students in their classrooms.

The research began with interviews in which the educators shared their general awareness of and experiences with color-blindness. The educators were then asked to engage in photovoice, a critical, feminist, participatory research approach, where participants take photographic images to explain and discuss social issues they are facing within a particular context (Mejia, Quiroz, Morales, Ponce, Chávez, & Oliviera y Torre, 2013; Wang & Burris, 1997). For this project, the educators were asked to take photographs that represented color-blindness at their schools and the ways in which they countered color-blindness in their curriculum, pedagogy, and professional school settings. The research was framed and analyzed with a Black feminist lens (Collins, 2000), and therefore, power dynamics, oppression, and empowerment were central to theorizing the educators' experiences with color-blindness in their school contexts.

Research Phase I: Embodied Color-Blind Experiences

The forthcoming moments were shared during initial interviews. The educators were asked to reflect on their everyday encounters with children, colleagues, and parents, and the ways in which their isolation as women of color in predominately White spaces shaped their professional and personal lives. Throughout the interview conversations, the educators revealed incidents of challenge and tension, as well as stories of empowerment and resistance. Several themes emerged from the interviews, two of which include acts of "affirmation" and "protection" in color-blind spaces and encounters.

Affirming Young Black Girls

The educators shared that they found it necessary to affirm the experiences and livelihoods of Black children and Other children of color in their classrooms. As an example, Ms. Truth explained:

> I knew why she [a young Black girl in my class] was wearing a hood. She didn't like how her hair looked naturally. I let her wear it for a while and then I called [her] over and I said, "Why do you have your hood on?" She said, "I'm cold." I said, "It's pretty warm." She said, "I'm freezing, Ms. Truth." I was like, "Okay." I let her do that all day. She came in the next day, [and] had her hood on. I said [to myself], "I'm not going to let it go." I pulled her aside, not in front of the classroom. I pulled her into the room. I said, "I think I know why you have your hood on." She just cried. I mean tears streaming down her face … "I want you to take your hood off. You are beautiful inside and out. You don't need to worry about what these people think about you, or that your hair looks different. You are gorgeous."
>
> *(H. Truth, January 23, 2017)*

In this private exchange between Ms. Truth and her student, we are given a glimpse into the dynamic between a Black woman and young Black girl in a mostly White school space. One can witness the symbiosis of Black feminist thought, culturally relevant praxis, and social justice education in action as Ms. Truth communicates her capacity to discern why a young first grader would elect to conceal rather than reveal her natural hair. The historical discourse about Black hair has been one filled with negative consequences for Black women, who have been misunderstood, villainized, and/or eroticized (Thompson, 2009). For a young Black girl, early recognition of the threat her hair might pose illustrates how color-blind and discriminatory discourses resound even in spaces where racist acts are not explicit.

Relying on her own educational experiences as a young Black girl living in the rural south, Ms. Truth shared that she was able to interpret her students' desires to conceal and "fit in" as problematic, for the moment was reflective of her own childhood experiences with racism and color-blindness. As hooks (1996) shares in her memoirs of girlhood, *Bone Black*, the frailty of Black girls' confidence is often misunderstood and unknown as Black families often teach girls to be strong and articulate, at times rendering their pain invisible. Ms.

Truth's embodied knowing, however, empowered her to confront a young girl's attempt to conceal what she perceived to be a racial and cultural inadequacy, untangling its power. By affirming young Black girls and other students of color in her care, Ms. Truth recognized her positionality and role in enacting social justice education by creating a safe space for students of color, especially important in a predominately White school, where the student may not hear otherwise that she, too, is beautiful.

Protecting Embodied Ways of Being

Another theme that emerged was that the educators felt as if they had to protect their embodied ways of being. As an example, Ms. Walker explained:

> I was told my first year that the tone of my voice was harsh. I didn't know what that meant. That maybe my students could be, feel – that … it [my voice] comes off a little harsh and that maybe they (students, faculty, parents, and administrators) are feeling like, intimidated or threatened or misunderstood by [me], and I'm like "Well…what am I supposed to say?"
>
> *(T. Walker, February 17, 2017)*

Here, the oppressive narrative of the dangerous Black female body (inclusive of her "tone" and voice) labels Black women as threats to themselves and to others in their environments (Evans-Winters & Esposito, 2010; Evans-Winters & Girls for Gender Equity, 2017). Black women, like young Black girls and other girls of color, often find schools to be inhospitable spaces of surveillance, ultimately placing limits on their full potentials (Crenshaw, Ocen, & Nanda, 2015).

In this excerpt, Ms. Walker grapples with the dangers of misrecognition, in which stereotypes about Black women prevail. Harris-Perry (2011) illustrates how Black women challenge misrecognition by learning to stand straight in a "crooked room." That is, Black women have historically countered long-standing stereotypes and images used to shame them. Harris-Perry (2011) names recognition (or visibility) as a complex social interaction in which Black women seek social justice in color-blind spaces. In Ms. Walker's encounter, she shared how she eventually confronted the White school administrator who labeled her voice as "dangerous," and in doing so, "straightens out" the image of Black skin/women as threatening and needing to be controlled.

Research, Phase II: Countering Color-Blindness in Early Childhood Contexts

During the second phase of the study, the early childhood educators engaged in photovoice by taking pictures of images that demonstrated what it was like to be a Black educator in their schools. They focused on naming what was being ignored, illustrating examples of color-blindness and indicating how color-blindness could be challenged. With each image, the educators were asked to provide a description and context for what inspired them to capture it. In the following examples, the educators shared through their images their everyday experiences: 1) enacting silence as self-care and professionalism; 2) designing curriculum; and 3) using love as a tool to transcend color-blindness. The embodied experiences of Black womanhood and girlhood allowed each educator to recognize, react to, and critique the hegemonic control and invisibility created by color-blind discourses within their classrooms, among their colleagues, and in larger society. The educators' intentional efforts to foster visibility, acknowledgement of racism, and engage in resistance are all enactments of social justice education.

Silence as Self-Care and Professionalism

In the first image (see Figure 2.1) and following interview excerpt, Ms. Truth described an oppressive encounter with her White colleagues in the teachers' lounge, who often expressed their support for Trump and his political agenda in communal spaces at school. Ms. Truth shared:

> This is an EIE, Engineering and Education Design, where the students have to build a wall using their own recipe for mortar … and a really fun

FIGURE 2.1 Science based engineering activity

> lesson, but we [my student teacher and I] were sitting in the lounge when I said [to her], "Oh, gosh, we've got to get the walls built today."

Ms. Truth then explained that another educator in the lounge said, "Are you going to get the second graders to pay for it?" Ms. Truth continued:

> I didn't say anything. Then, another one [a White educator in the lounge] said, "Oh, no she's going to get the second graders to build it. No, to pay for it, but then they're not going to get to use it" … It was all this little behind the, underhanded jargon or conversation about the election and all of that. I didn't say anything the whole time. I just kind of sat and they kept talking about it. I was sitting there looking, and my student teacher didn't say anything either, so these three [White] teachers are kind of talking, and then one finally said, "I'm sure it's okay for us to talk about this because I know we're all the same."
>
> (H. Truth, February 17, 2017)

Ms. Truth explained that what the three educators meant by saying, "We're all the same" is that they were all White and supporters of the Republican Presidential candidate at the time, Donald Trump. Ms. Truth was astounded by the racist undertones. As a Black woman, she could relate to the injustice felt by Latinx peoples due to Trump's rhetoric of expanding the Mexican border wall and his dog-whistle politics.

The actions of Ms. Truth's fellow educators in this moment reveals how normalizing the erasure of racial difference, or color-blindness, allows White people to display their racial views in a "sanitized way" (Bonilla-Silva & Forman, 2000, p. 76). In deciding not to address her colleagues' potentially racist remarks, Ms. Truth's silence might at first glance appear to allow color-blind oppression to continue in this space. However, both children and adults alike struggle with the language needed to challenge racist discourses (Boutte, 2008; Tatum, 1997). For some educators of color, the demonstration of self-care, or preserving one's mental health, is more important for survival than fighting back and/or being labeled the "angry Black woman" (Collins, 2000; Lewis, Mendenhall, Harwood, & Huntt, 2016).

In this case, Ms. Truth's ability to discern the assault, yet maintain and model professionalism for a future Black early childhood educator (her student teacher), aligns with previous research that marginalized women are not only capable of surviving daily negative infractions, but can thrive despite acts of discrimination and erasure of their humanness (Edwards, McArthur, & Russell-Owens, 2016). Black women's pedagogy of self-care in hostile environments warrants consideration as a valued method to affirm and support social justice for not only women of color educators, but all early childhood educators who are often undervalued and unappreciated as educational professionals (Miller, Dalli, & Urban, 2012).

Designing a (Sub)Conscious Social Justice Curriculum

When describing the next photovoice picture (see Figure 2.2), Mrs. Cooper discussed a bulletin board she designed prior to the start of the study, featuring covers of books and teacher designed posters describing common themes found in children's literature. In the image, there is a cover of a children's book with a

FIGURE 2.2 Posters displayed to help children make "text to self" connections

young Black girl holding the hand of an adult, presented next to the themes "compassion," "acceptance," and "perseverance."

Mrs. Cooper shared:

> In this picture … it's a book jacket, and it's titled, *A Sweet Smell of Roses*. It takes place during the Civil Rights Movement … I was just trying to have different genres posted so that the kids could understand themes and messages of stories. I didn't realize that I had stapled this particular book jacket by the words compassion, and acceptance, and perseverance. I just thought, "Did I do that consciously? Or was it subconsciously?" When I think about it I feel like I did it subconsciously, because I hadn't noticed it before this project.

As Mrs. Cooper revealed, it wasn't until she was asked to identify moments that illustrate how color-blindness is challenged in her curriculum and pedagogy that she was able to see the intention behind her message. That is, Mrs. Cooper hoped to encourage acceptance and compassion towards children of color, and to illustrate the history of perseverance that children of color have embodied in the face of racism (one of the major themes of the book). Mrs. Cooper's realization of this curricular choice illustrates one way in which Black women's critical consciousness is formed and cultivated, and ultimately how Black women, whether consciously or subconsciously, find ways to enact social justice education by resisting color-blindness in early childhood settings.

Collins (2000) asserts that "racist and sexist ideologies permeate the social structure to such a degree that they become hegemonic, namely, seen as natural, normal, and inevitable" (p. 5). As such, those who advocate for social justice call for an elevated level of consciousness so that one can think critically and act against the cultural hegemony present in our early childhood school communities. Mrs. Cooper's critical reflection of self and her praxis provides insight into how color-blind hegemony can (sub)consciously be challenged within predominately White spaces.

"It's a Heart Thing": Love as Tool for Transcending Color-blindness

In another photovoice engagement, Ms. Walker discussed how her identity shifted from "teacher of Black children" in the center of a city metroplex, to a suburban educator of mostly White children. Ms. Walker drew upon her childhood experiences being raised in a majority Black metropolitan city (and later teaching in the same school system) to bring context to how she built connections with new students and families in her care. In the past, she used her positionality as a Black educator to enact social justice education by bringing attention to her students' racial identities, unique academic strengths, as well as providing context to understanding her students' home and community lives.

Describing her photovoice picture (see Figure 2.3), Ms. Walker explained how she continued the same practices in her new school setting.

FIGURE 2.3 Teacher desk displaying students' artwork

I save this area for their (e.g., students') art work that they give to me. It made me think of when I was teaching in [the] inner city … and really the area of my desk looks no different now than it did then, even though the face of my class has changed. The look of my class has changed (from mostly Black to mostly White). I was kind of thinking along those lines as okay, I could still show that love and that connection, and the relationship that's built between your teacher and the students that goes beyond color. It's just, it's a heart thing …

(T. Walker, April 21, 2017).

Although Ms. Walker struggled with and challenged the dominance of color-blindness in her new school setting, she understood the significance of tapping into her own cultural competence (Gay, 2010; Ladson-Billings, 1994) and why maintaining a sense of openness to diversity of all kinds has allowed her to build connections among the multiple aspects of her students, parents, and peers' identities. Employing her intersectional subjectivity as a Black woman, Ms. Walker's "pedagogy of heart" became a strategy to transcend color-blindness by highlighting the way she has valued the children in her classroom community. As hooks (2013) explains:

Love moves us beyond categories and therein lies its power to liberate. Free to love, we are free to be our authentic selves. We are free to take the path that leads us away from domination toward new lives of optimal well-being. We are free to think, to write, to dream, to live beyond race.

(p. 199)

Tapping into the transformative power of love to dismantle historical systems of oppression allowed Ms. Walker to not only see the students' racialized identities, but to know her students beyond skin tone alone. In *Writing beyond race: Living theory and practice*, hooks' (2013) urges that "to value ourselves rightly we are called to move beyond race. We are called to recognize that ethnicity, that skin color, are but one fragment of a holistic identity" (p. 198). Ms. Walker's commitment to remaining connected to her own personal narrative and pedagogy of love as a Black woman in a predominately White space allowed for a more socially just classroom where all students could feel accepted, connected, and visible (Delpit, 2006).

Concluding Thoughts

This chapter brings attention to and problematizes color-blindness in early childhood settings, articulated through the embodied experiences, perspectives, and voices of three Black women educators. Each of their narratives have centralized what are often marginalized viewpoints, opening sites for resistance, transformation, and social justice in early childhood education. Collins (2000) explains that a major "dimension of Black women's activism consists of struggles for institutional transformation" (p. 204). The early childhood educators' presence and embodied wisdom in White school spaces inspired them to take action that countered color-blindness in their pedagogy and work as early childhood professionals, clearly enacting educational transformation.

For early childhood educators of color, strategies for advancing a more inclusive school environment include maintaining a reflexive teaching practice by remembering their own school experiences and childhoods, using that knowledge to connect and nurture relationships with young children of color who are in their care, and validating themselves and others. For educators with dominant identities, learning the herstories of colleagues of color and ways to challenge oppressive thought and actions can foster collective and allied efforts. If one should find that color-blindness is not explicitly apparent, educators must be open to learning from those who have had first hand experiences with the oppressive ways in which color-blindness can manifest and influence curriculum, pedagogy, and professional relationships. Together, a transformative spirit can inspire each of us to work collectively to identify and counter color-blindness in early childhood education.

Implementing direct approaches to foster color consciousness and dialogue that challenges racialized discourses is essential for nurturing early childhood classrooms that are inclusive of all young children. Countering color-blindness can become "a critical site for not just fending off hegemonic ideas from dominant culture, but in crafting counter-hegemonic knowledge that fosters changed consciousness" (Collins, 2000, p. 285). Fostering a collective, changed consciousness allows us to reimagine early childhood education in ways that recognize, honor, and celebrate the wisdom of Black women educators and children of color.

Notes

1 Hegemony occurs when dominant and oppressive ideologies become universalized knowledge. A critical consciousness, or an understanding of how power produces and perpetuates social and institutional hierarchies (and subsequent inequities and injustices), can counter hegemony.
2 MacNaughton (2005) explains that "Foucault (1972) understood discourse as a body of thinking and writing that used shared language for talking about," understanding, and examining a topic, and "are found in everyday practices and decision-making" (p. 20).
3 A matrix of domination is "the overall organization of hierarchical power relations for any society" (Collins, 2000, p. 299). Matrices encompass intersecting race, class, gender, and sexuality oppressions (among others) and are enacted systematically through structural, hegemonic, disciplinary, and interpersonal power.

References

Bonilla-Silva, E., & Forman, T. A. (2000). "I am not a racist but …": Mapping White college students' racial ideology in the USA. *Discourse & Society*, 11(1), 50–85.
Boutte, G. S. (2008). Beyond the illusion of diversity: How early childhood teachers can promote social justice. *The Social Studies*, 99(4), 165–173.
Boutte, G. S., Lopez-Robertson, J., & Powers-Costello, E. (2011). Moving beyond color-blindness in early childhood classrooms. *Early Childhood Education Journal*, 39(5), 335–342.
Burman, E. (2008). *Deconstructing developmentally psychology* (2nd ed.). London: Routledge.
Collins, P. H. (2000). *Black feminist thought: Knowledge, consciousness, and the politics of Empowerment* (2nd ed.). New York: Routledge.
Crenshaw, K., Ocen, P., & Nanda, J. (2015). *Black girls matter: Pushed out, overpoliced, and underprotected*. New York: African American Policy Forum and Center for Intersectionality and Social Policy Studies. Retrieved from https://static1.squarespace.com/static/53f20d90e4b0b80451158d8c/t/54dcc1ece4b001c03e323448/1423753708557/AAPF_BlackGirlsMatterReport.pdf
Delpit, L. (2006). *Other people's children: Cultural conflict in the classroom* (2nd ed.). New York: The New Press.
Delpit, L. (2007). Seeing color. In W. Au, B. Bigelow, & S. Karp (Eds.), *Rethinking our classrooms: Teaching for equity and justice* (pp. 158–160). Milwaukee, WI: Rethinking Schools.
Delpit, L. (2012). *"Multiplication is for White people:" Raising expectations for other people's children*. New York: New Press.
Derman-Sparks, L., LeeKeenan, D., & Nimmo, J. (2015). *Leading anti-bias early childhood programs: A guide for change*. New York: Teachers College Press.
Doucet, F. &, Adair, J. K. (2013). Addressing race and inequity in the classroom. *Young Children*, 68(5), 88–97.

Edwards, E., McArthur, S. A., & Russell-Owens, L. (2016). Relationships, being-ness, and voice: Exploring multiple dimensions of humanizing work with Black girls. *Equity & Excellence in Education*, 49(4), 428–439.

Evans-Winters, V. E., & Esposito, J. (2010). Other people's daughters: Critical race feminisms and Black girls' education. *Educational Foundations*, 24(1–2), 11–24.

Evans-Winters, V. E., & Girls for Gender Equity (2017). Flipping the script: The dangerous bodies of girls of color. *Cultural Studies <=> Critical Methodologies*, 17(5), 415–423.

Farago, F., Murray, C., & Swadener, B. B. (2017). Confronting and countering bias and oppression through early childhood policy and practice: An introduction. *International Critical Childhood Policy Studies*, 6(1), 1–6.

Foucault, M. (1972). *The archeology of knowledge*. (A. M. S. Smith, Trans.). New York: Pantheon.

Gay, G. (2010). *Culturally responsive teaching: Theory, research, and practice* (2nd ed.). New York: Teachers College Press.

Harris-Perry, M. V. (2011). *Sister citizen: For colored girls who've considered politics when being strong isn't enough*. New Haven, CT: Yale University Press.

hooks, B. (1996). *Bone black: Memories of girlhood*. New York: Henry Holt.

hooks, B. (1999). *Yearning: Race, gender, and cultural politics*. Boston, MA: South End Press.

hooks, B. (2013). *Writing beyond race: Living theory and practice*. New York: Taylor & Francis.

HusbandJr., T. (2012). "I don't see color": Challenging the assumptions about discussing race with young children. *Early Childhood Education Journal*, 39(6), 365–371.

Hytten, K., & Bettez, S. C. (2011). Understanding education for social justice. *Educational Foundations*, 25(1–2), 7–24.

Ladson-Billings, G. (1994). *The dreamkeepers: Successful teachers of African American children*. San Francisco, CA: Jossey-Bass.

Lewis, J. A., Mendenhall, R., Harwood, S. A., & Huntt, M. B. (2016). "Ain't I a Woman": Perceived gendered racial microaggressions experienced by Black women. *The Counseling Psychologist*, 44(5), 758–780.

Lorde, A. (1984). *Sister outsider: Essays and speeches by Audre Lorde*. Berkeley, CA: Crossing Press.

MacNaughton, G. (2005). *Doing Foucault in early childhood studies: Applying post-structural ideas*. New York: Routledge.

Mejia, A. P., Quiroz, O., Morales, Y., Ponce, R., Chávez, G. L., & Oliviera y Torre, E. (2013). From mares to mujeristas: Latinas making change with photovoice. *Action Research*, 11(4), 301–321.

Miller, L., Dalli, C., & Urban, M. (Eds.). (2012). *Early childhood grows up: Towards a critical ecology of the profession*. Dordrecht, Netherlands: Springer Netherlands.

Pacini-Ketchabaw, V., Berikoff, A., Elliot, E., & Tucker, A. (2007) Anti-racism and post-colonialism in early childhood education. *The Early Childhood Educator*, 22(2), 30–33.

Paley, V. G. (2000). *White teacher* (3rd ed.). Boston, MA: Harvard University Press.

Souto-Manning, M. (2013). *Multicultural teaching in the early childhood classroom: Strategies, tools, and approaches, Preschool–2nd grade*. Washington, DC: Association for Childhood Education Rion International; New York: Teachers College Press.

Souto-Manning, M., & Cheruvu, R. (2016). Challenging and appropriating discourses of power: Listening to and learning from early career early childhood teachers of color. *Equity and Excellence in Education*, 49(1), 9–26.

Swadener, B. B., & Lubeck, S. (Eds.). (1995). *Children and families "at promise": Deconstructing the discourse of risk*. Albany, NY: State University of New York Press.

Tatum, B. D. (1997). *Why are all the Black kids sitting together in the cafeteria? And other conversations about race.* New York: Basic Books.

Thompson, C. (2009). Black women, beauty, and hair as a matter of being. *Woman's Studies, 38*(8), 831–856.

Wang, C. C., & Burris, M. A. (1997). Photovoice: Concept, methodology, and use for participatory needs assessment. *Health Education & Behavior, 24,* 369–387.

3

CHILDREN'S VOICES AND GENDER PEDAGOGIES FOR EQUITY IN AND OUT OF EARLY CHILDHOOD CLASSROOMS

Kylie Smith

Introduction: Thinking Back

I consciously began to explore ideas of gender equity and the early childhood classroom in 1989 while completing a Diploma in Children's Services at the University of Melbourne. Glenda MacNaughton (1995, 2000, 2005) introduced to one class the Anti-Bias Curriculum (Derman-Sparks and the ABC Task Force, 1989) wherein she presented and analyzed concepts of *identity, attitudes, prejudice, stereotyping, bias, power and empowerment.* This experience provided me with the language, research and literature to help me understand how young children develop biased attitudes and behaviors that mark people as inferior or superior based on gender, sexuality, race, ethnicity, ability and religion.

This chapter explores the possibilities of centering attention on gendered pedagogies to support gender identity development and equality in early childhood education within and through neoliberal policies in Australia. This chapter specifically draws attention to the ways in which gender-based violence prevention policies support new attention to gender equity in the early childhood classroom. In the past 10 years in Australia, due to public outcry supported through social media and the financial cost to government, attention has been drawn to the prevalence and effects of gender-based violence. Globally, the #MeToo and #TimesUp movements have fuelled this focus on gender equality and respectful relationships. In the past five years the role of early education in creating a generational shift in attitudes and behaviors in the prevention of gender-based violence has created opportunities for gender pedagogy to be authorized in the early childhood classroom.

I was particularly drawn to discussions and goals connected to gender identity. I grew up in a household where I was encouraged to play football, cricket, basketball, "chasey," climb fences, build with the Lego and race my Hot Wheel cars with my brothers and predominately male cousins which has influenced my feelings of connection to the issue of gender equity. Because of these experiences at home and in the classroom, I was drawn to the goal of helping to free children, "from constraining, stereotypic definitions of gender role so that no aspects of development will be closed off simply because of a child's sex" (Derman-Sparks and the ABC Task Force, 1989, p. 49). Did my lived experiences of digging holes in the backyard in one moment and then playing with my dolls and a tea set in another resonate with the goal, "to promote equality of development for both sexes by facilitating each child's participation in activities for physical, cognitive, emotional, and social growth" (Derman-Sparks and the ABC Task Force, 1989, p. 49)? When considering social justice and gender equity, I believe that my and others' lived experiences, family background, friends, social media, popular culture, socioeconomic class, gender, sexualities, ethnicity all color the way we understand what is fair and unfair and if we are silent or act when we are confronted with discrimination and bias against ourselves and others.

To enable me to address the goals I wanted to accomplish, I developed a pilot project that aimed to create "Respectful Relationships" in early childhood (Victorian Department of Education and Training, 2017b). This chapter also will analyze the benefits and risks when educators listen to children's views and opinions when drawing on feminist politics to create activist classrooms that consider prevention and intervention pedagogy. In this research project, teachers and staff were made aware of the need for girls and boys to develop healthy relationships as well as the social and emotional skills required to be resilient throughout life if/when they face bias behaviors directed towards themselves or others. In addition, this project explored ways that collective communities could challenge and change social and structural gender norms and behaviors and thus create more respectful gendered relationships.

Background for the Study

Over the past 30 years researchers, educators and others have explored gender and equity in early years education. Much of this research was pursued in the late 1990s and early 2000s. During this time early childhood feminist researchers argued that as children learn about gender, they learn sexist values, beliefs and attitudes, and relationships (Blaise, 2005; Davies, 2003a; Mac-Naughton, 1995, 2000, 2000, 2005; Robinson & Jones Diaz, 2006). Further, researchers reported that many children by the age of three had stereotypical views of what boys and girls should wear, who they could be friends with, what toys and materials were appropriate to play with, and the ways boys and girls should or could behave (Ärlemalm-Hagsér, 2010; Campbell, Alexander & Smith, 2017; Campbell, Smith & Alexander, 2017; Shutts, Kenward, Falk, Ivegran & Fawcett, 2017).

Shifts from a social welfare government funding model to privatization, marketization and competition between and among early education and care sectors has been seen in many countries (e.g. Penn, 2013). In Australia early concerns for social justice and gender equity as a social endeavor have shifted with government policies now perceiving equity as access, and now situating the achievement of success at the site of the individual – the good educator, good child and the good parent. Within these policy discourses, notions of quality drive illusions of an education system that is an even playing field for children and their families irrespective of gender, sexuality, class, culture, ethnicity, religion and ability (Campbell, Smith & Alexander, 2017; Smith, Tesar & Myers, 2016). It is thought that if educators work hard enough and provide a high-quality program, and children actively participate in the program, then children will grow up to be productive economic citizens of the nation and the world.

Reason for the Study

In Australia, at least one woman is killed by a partner or former partner every week (Bryant & Cussen, 2015), and one in four women have experienced at least one situation of violence with an intimate partner (Cox, 2016). Given the influence of government policy, attention has focused on the financial cost of domestic violence in terms of health, administration and welfare that altogether cost an estimated at $21.7 billion a year. Financial figures like these and community activism have been a driving force for change that resulted in the development of the Australian Federal Government's "National Plan to Reduce Violence against Women and their Children 2010–2022" (Council of Australian Governments, 2009). One initiative of the action plan was the development of a framework, along with resources, in a document called "Change the Story: A Shared Framework for the Primary Prevention of Violence Against Women and Their Children in Australia," released in November 2015, by Our Watch, ANROWS and VicHealth (2015).

"Change the Story …" identified the need to involve the youngest children, those in child care and early learning services (which are outside of the formal school environment), in working to end gender-based violence (Our Watch et al., 2015, p. 39). This need created opportunities for gender activist research and pedagogy to be introduced into early childhood settings. While research and pedagogy that supports the development of young children's gender identity development and gender equality is not new in early childhood education (e.g. Blaise, 2005; Davies, 2003a, 2003b; MacNaughton, 2000, 2005; Robinson & Jones Diaz, 2006), little of this work has made explicit connections between gender identity development, social and emotional learning, and gender-based violence prevention (Office of Preschool and Child Care, 1993).

Federal and state government funding for gender-based violence prevention programs began to filter into the education sector in 2009. Funding has been directed towards the development of a framework to support a school-wide approach to building respectful relationships. A school-wide approach is where every class incorporates gender equity in their curriculum, and the school policies and practices promote equity for students, staff, families and community. This has been extended to include the development of Respectful Relationships curriculum, resources and training for teachers (Victorian Department of Education and Training, 2017a, 2017b). The trickle down to early childhood has been slow and governments are unclear about how a whole-of-school approach can be implemented in a diverse early childhood sector characterized by different hours of operation, staff qualifications and employment. While there has been tension about what training for early childhood educators might look like, gender violence-prevention strategies align with key learning outcomes within Australian National Curriculum Frameworks. For example, in *Belonging, Being and Becoming: The Early Years Learning Framework for Australia* (DEEWR, 2009), under "Outcome 1: Children have a strong sense of identity, gender is identified as part of a child becoming."

Secondly, in 2016, a second edition of the *Victorian Early Years Learning and Development Framework* was released (Victorian Department of Education and Training, 2016). The revised framework includes "practice principles" that promote gender equality and respectful relationships. One practice principle – "Respectful relationships and responsive engagement" - asks early childhood professionals to "recognize and deepen their understandings about other people and how values and beliefs influence their own world view" (Victorian Department of Education and Training, 2016, p. 11). A focus in policy on national productivity and naming "gender work" within two curriculum frameworks authorizes spaces for (re)igniting and re-imagining gender pedagogies in the early childhood classroom. Some of this has begun through a pilot project called "Respectful Relationship Program for Early Childhood Settings" (Victorian Department of Education and Training, 2017b).

Approach to the Research

The research program described in this chapter was designed using action research methods that explore what a "whole-of-service" approach to violence prevention might look like in the early childhood sector. Action research is an approach to investigating a problem or question through a collaborative cycle of planning, acting, observing and reflecting (Smith, 2015). Action research is a participatory research approach where the researcher undertakes research *with* participants to create change in practice. Action research was used as a way to work with participants to produce learning relevant to them, rather than to produce data on/about their learning. The project was funded by a seed grant from the Melbourne Social Equity Institute at the University of Melbourne. Three child care services in Melbourne are taking part in the project, two long-day care services and a preschool. The experiences and learning of one of these three services indicates the ways in which researchers, educators and families worked within and through neoliberal policies to identify key issues regarding gender: violence prevention, existing practices and the ability to act collectively to change existing approaches to gender equality and safety.

Like others, I too have critiqued neoliberal policies and raised concerns about the effects of these discourses on opportunities to develop critical gender pedagogies (Campbell, Alexander, & Smith, 2017; Campbell, Smith, & Alexander, 2017). I have slipped into "modernist discourses" and have been implicated in the operation of binary debates of bad/good and right/wrong. This slippage has meant that I have been drawn to understandings of power as an entity or force that can be placed on or over people to control, silence, intimidate and/or oppress. This epistemological footprint reinforces the idea that power can be contained and controlled and given to or back to others.

The Study

Banksia Children's Center is a day care service in an inner Melbourne suburb in Australia that participated in the project from late November 2016 to June 2017. The Center is open Monday through Friday from 7:30 a.m. to 6:00 p.m. and provides education and care for children three months to five years of age. All educators at the service participated in the project. The educators had diverse qualifications, including Certificate III,[1] Diploma,[2] Bachelor and Masters and different years of experience. The educators answered a pre- and post-online questionnaire to gain insight into how their understandings of gender development and pedagogy and connections to prevention of gender-based violence changed over the course of the project. Each participant then took part in five one-hour workshops over a period of six months. The workshops occurred from 6:00 to 7:00 p.m., after the Center was closed so that all educators could participate. Educators at the Center gave up time normally used for staff meetings, so if there were urgent issues to discuss, they stayed until after 7:00 p.m. to discuss Center business. This fact necessitated a huge commitment by educators, particularly as people on an early shift may have started work at the Center at 7:30 a.m., resulting in a 12-hour working day for them.

Findings

Across the life of the project educators' ideas, theories and practices were documented through educators' reflections and my field notes. There were five key learnings that emerged during the project. These learnings were:

1. Missing gender literature;
2. The importance of time to stop, reflect and talk as a service;
3. The effects of a gender lens;
4. Intervention approach to gender pedagogy;
5. Time to bring theory and practice together in the everyday.

Missing Gender Literature

In the first workshop I introduced literature which reported that by the age of three to four years most children will have developed clear understandings of gender norms and behaviors and are able to perform and conform to these norms (Blaise, 2005; Davies, 2003a, 2003b; MacNaughton, 2000, 2005; Robinson & Jones Diaz, 2006). For all but one person in the group this finding was a surprise. When I discussed key early childhood gender researchers who have been prominent in Australia and internationally, most of the educators indicated that they had not had access to their work. My response was mixed because for me these authors have influenced my classroom pedagogy and my research agenda over a period of time. Over the course of the following five workshops, I brought in text books and journal articles for educators to explore. These texts were mixed theoretically and were a combination of research and practical materials For example, I made available several publications, such as *The Power of Mum* (MacNaughton, 1995); *Equal Play, Equal Work* (Office of Preschool and Child Care, 1993); *Innocence, Knowledge and the Construction of Childhood* (Robinson, 2013); and *Frogs and Snails and Feminist Tales* (Davies, 2003a). I was also surprised that many children's picture books which challenge gender norms and behaviors were new to most of the educators. These books included what I thought were relatively well-known books like *The Paper Bag Princess* (Munsch, 2006). At each workshop I brought new texts or resources to share with educators. These resources were passed around, examined, discussed and noted whether to purchase for themselves individually for the Center.

On reflection after the first workshop, I realized that it wasn't a surprise that the early childhood gender work which emerged in the late 1990s and early 2000s was now absent on the current early childhood educators' radar, their bookshelf or classroom. Neoliberal education policies during the past 20 years have driven literature, programs and professional development to focus on areas such as brain development, literacy and transition to school as a way to ensure future citizens that can compete and be productive citizens within a global market (Smith, Tesar & Myers, 2016). Neoliberal policies are also evident in the Australian early childhood "National Quality Standards Framework" (Australian Children's Education and Care Quality Authority (ACECQA), 2017) where the premise is that if a "quality" program is provided, then all children have equal access to education. In this context, issues of gender are irrelevant because all children have equal access to programs. If children fail, then the problem is at the site of the individual child or the family, rather than the effect of the reinforcement of gender norms and behaviors that exclude girls from accessing resources, storylines and opportunities. The effects of broader dominant patriarchal power dynamics in the social context revealed in feminist and feminist poststructural literature are neutralized or eliminated within and through the notion of quality.

The Importance of Time to Stop, Reflect and Talk as a Service

What was evident from the first workshop and continued across each of the workshops was the importance of time for educators to stop, reflect and talk with each other. There are limited opportunities in day care settings for educators to spend time together as a whole service, or to engage with critical reflection, debate ideas and (re)imagine pedagogy. The structure of the workshops created spaces for powerful conversations about gender norms, attitudes and behaviors, all of which disrupted developmental discourses of the young and innocent child by offering alternative gender lenses to explore identity "performances" in and outside the classroom.

The Effects of a Gender Lens

In the first workshop educators were asked to reflect on how they observe "performances of gender" in their classroom. The educators working with the children under three years of age reported that they didn't notice stereotypical behaviors in their room. They saw children as being too young to understand gender norms and hadn't considered the need for critical gender pedagogy with this age group. However, educators working with the children over three noticed gendered norms and reflected on how they would talk with children about being fair and sharing resources. The educators raised questions about how children learn and understand these gender norms and attitudes at a young age. Using a gender lens, we talked about and debated the role of popular culture and marketing corporations, such as experiences of going to the shop to buy a birthday present and being directed to the pink aisle of the toy section through gender markers of color. In the middle of this discussion a gasp came from the administrator at the Center. She turned to the Center director and said, "Oh no, we just sent an email to the families asking them to choose a toy or gift to be donated to the Father Bob Foundation for Christmas, and we asked them to label it to let us know if it is for a boy or a girl."

This conversation between staff grew in momentum and created cracks in people's views of how the world is gender marked, producing effects that reinforce gender norms, attitudes and behaviors, such as in clothing, toys, bedding, backpacks, drink bottles, storylines and characters in books and movies, birthday cards, wrapping paper … the list continued to grow. The educators in the rooms for younger children looked at each other and asked: "What about our children's backpacks? Their clothes? How are children taught gender norms and attitudes from a very young age through clothes and other childhood artifacts?" These reflections helped all educators consider how gender norms and behaviors are constructed and distributed throughout society and to acknowledge that children are in this space from birth.

Intervention Approach to Gender Pedagogy

Another key learning was that many of the practices for engagement with children in critical gender pedagogy came as a response or intervention as to how a child or adult had excluded someone from play or resources - for example, a child who stopped a boy from sitting next to her because she was saving the table for girls, or a parent who told their (male) child that he couldn't or shouldn't wear the sparkly skirt in the dress-up area because the skirt was for girls. The intervention approach to gender pedagogy became a repeated theme in examples and conversations between and with educators.

Ideas of child-centered and the emergent curriculum and children's interests and "voice" were common and were drawn upon by many educators as the reason a more preventative approach to gender pedagogy wasn't pursued. One educator noted that she only discussed gender fairness if children talked about it because she was "taking a child's rights approach to curriculum development." Over the past 20 years children's right to be heard in research, policy and pedagogy has been advocated for and taken up in practice in many children's settings. In Australia young children's right to be heard in early childhood has been endorsed and promoted through the Australian Early Years Learning Framework (DEEWR, 2009) and the Victorian Early Years Learning and Development Framework (Victorian Department of Education and Training, 2016). Many early childhood educators draw on child centered practice and the emergent curriculum as a way of supporting children's voices in the curriculum. These practices include observing children and asking questions about their interests and skills in developing the curriculum. In many situations the content of curriculum is then driven by the children and educators' knowledge is silent or secondary (Krieg, 2011). Possible risks for social justice education can occur if teachers are only privileging children's voices and gender fairness, but respectful relationships are never discussed because children haven't explicitly asked to explore gender equity.

Interestingly, the "Change the Story ..." (Our Watch et al., 2015) document calls for society generally and education specifically to move from an intervention model (e.g. wait and when you see a problem then intervene) to a prevention model where equitable environments are created that encourage the exploration of resources and pedagogy that promotes respect for girls/women and creates opportunities for girls and boys to access and participate in activities, storylines and resources equally. The question is raised as to how early childhood frameworks, policies and educator practices generally can take an intervention approach to gender equity and the promotion of respectful relationships. What would intentional teaching strategies look like for preventative critical gender pedagogies, particularly when teamed with action research methodologies like those used in this research project?

Time to Bring Theory and Practice Together in the Everyday

The beauty of using an action research model in research and learning is that the educators were able to explore new ideas during the workshops and then had at least four weeks to observe and reflect with their co-educators between sessions. This provided opportunities to for them to "see" differently through a gender lens and to shift teaching practices and/or consider establishing different environments and promoting different conversations. These behaviors were evident from the second workshop. One of the educators began to show me an observation she had written about how she had changed the room and the ways in which experiences and spaces were set up after she thought about how materials can be gender marked. The educators in the younger room jumped in to talk about how they had observed how one of the younger children had engaged with the wooden blocks they had set out in the room. She and others said that on the surface they saw the blocks as gender neutral, but then watched as one child began to place her own gender marking on the blocks. She picked up one of the larger blocks and labeled it "daddy"; she then chose a block that was small and identified it as "mummy," and then an even smaller block that she labeled as the "baby." The educator questioned the child and holding the larger block said, "This could be the mummy." The child responded, "No this is daddy." Using their gender lens, the educators discussed how very young children begin to gender mark based on size. We reflected on how picture books often illustrate the adult male/daddy as bigger than the female/mummy. We asked, "Do we pay attention to the illustrations in children's books or how we talk about physical characteristics of people?" and "How does this reinforce or introduce gender norms and attitudes?" – that is, the strong, big, protective man who is the hero or savior and the weak, small woman who is in need of protection or rescuing. The power and multiple effects of gender circulate in and through early childhood education in our intentional and unintentional thoughts, feelings, actions and words. However, these can be destabilized with collective actions authorized within the neoliberal curriculum frameworks.

Thinking Forward: Implications for Educators

This research project also explores alternative spaces for negotiations regarding the definition of the "good teacher." In doing so there is a call to push back against the focus on individualism and (re)create collective communities that can challenge and change social and structural gender norms and behaviors and create more respectful gendered relationships. Practical implications for educators who want to engage with and enact gender pedagogy are the following:

- First, start by reflecting on your own gender stories growing up and think about how your experiences have shaped how you consciously and unconsciously develop and intentionally teach gender pedagogy that supports girls and boys to access diverse materials and experiences that are not limited or reinforced by biology.

- Second, review your educational philosophy and your service's mission statement or vision. Specifically, check to see if gender equity is named in your policy documents, and if not, consider how you might include it. Many educational documents have statements, like "respect diversity." However, diversity can mean many things. How do children, families, co-educators and community members know that you are specifically looking at respect for gender diversity? Further, does respect for diversity mean challenging moments of inequity and disrespect?

- Third, shift from an intervention approach to gender pedagogy where you act when you hear a child being biased. Intentionally, create environments and activities, and importantly plan times to talk about gender fairness. Discussions might occur at circle time or during individual or small group activities.

- Fourth, it is not enough for children to be able to identify bias; they need skills and knowledge to deal with bias. Children need to be resilient and acquire self-help and help-seeking skills. They must be able to recognize and manage their own feelings, learn to self-regulate, listen to others and show empathy.

- Fifth, educators need opportunities to engage with theory to realize how they conceptualize gender development and behaviors and the effect of reflections on the way they see, listen and act in the classroom. Gender pedagogy is not just the acquisition of materials (e.g. story books or puzzles) but the understandings that are drawn on and resisted to create classrooms as sites for advocacy.

- Sixth, creating time to talk with others and share questions, concerns and successes opens space to build a collective community that grows over time as educators, families, children and community members are invited into the dialogue. A community approach means that one voice does not have the ability to silence feminist pedagogy but recognizes adults and children as active citizens who are strategic and political.

Notes

1 Vocational qualification.
2 Vocational qualification.

References

Ärlemalm-Hagsér, E. (2010). Gender choreography and micro-structures – early childhood professionals' understanding of gender roles and gender patterns in outdoor play and learning. *European Early Childhood Education Research Journal*, 18(4), 515–525.

Australian Children's Education and Care Quality Authority (ACECQA). (2017). *Guide to the National Quality Framework*. Retrieved from http://files.acecqa.gov.au/files/Nationa l-Quality-Framework-Resources-Kit/NQF-Resource-03-Guide-to-NQS.pdf

Blaise, M. (2005). *Playing it straight*. Routledge: New York.

Bryant, W., & Cussen, T. (2015). *Homicide in Australia: 2010–11 to 2011–12: National homicide monitoring program report*. Canberra: Australian Institute of Criminology. Retrieved from: http://www.aic.gov.au/media_library/publications/mr/mr23/mr23.pdf

Campbell, S., Alexander, K., & Smith, K. (2017). Are we there yet? Gender equity journeys in early childhood practice. In S. Campbell, K. Alexander, & K. Smith (Eds.) *Feminism(s) in early childhood* (pp. 179–192). Singapore: Springer.

Campbell, S., Smith, K., & Alexander, K. (2017). Spaces for gender equity in Australian early childhood education in/between discourses of human capital and feminism. *Australasian Journal of Early Childhood*, 42(3), 54.

Council of Australian Governments. (2009). *National plan to reduce violence against women and their children 2010–2022*. Canberra: Commonwealth of Australia. Retrieved from: http s://www.dss.gov.au/sites/default/files/documents/08_2014/national_plan1.pdf

Cox, P. (2016). *Violence against women: Additional analysis of the Australian bureau of statistics' personal safety survey, 2012* (ANROWS Horizons: 01.01/2016 Rev. ed.). Sydney: ANROWS. Retrieved from: http://media.aomx.com/anrows.org.au/PSS_2016update.pdf

Davies, B. (2003a). *Frogs and snails and feminist tales*. Cresskill: Hampton Press.

Davies, B. (2003b). *Shards of glass*. Cresskill: Hampton Press.

Department of Education, Employment and Workplace Relations (DEEWR). (2009). *Belonging, being and becoming: The early years learning framework for Australia*. Canberra, Australia: DEEWR. Retrieved from: http://files.acecqa.gov.au/files/National-Quality-Framework-ResourcesKit/belonging_being_and_becoming_the_early_years_learning_framework_for_australia.pdf

Derman-Sparks and the ABC Task Force. (1989). *Anti-bias curriculum: Tools for empowering young children*. Washington, DC: National Association for Education of Young Children.

Early Childhood Australia. (2016) *Start early, respectful relationships for life*. Retrieved from: http://startearly.earlychildhoodaustralia.org.au/category/respectful-relationships

Krieg, S. (2011). The Australian early years learning framework: Learning what? *Contemporary Issues in Early Childhood*, 12(1), 46–55.

MacNaughton, G. (1995). *The power of mum*. Watson, ACT: Australian Early Childhood Association.

MacNaughton, G. (2000). *Rethinking gender in early childhood education*. St. Leonards: Allen & Unwin.

MacNaughton, G. (2005). *Doing Foucault in early childhood*. New York: Routledge.

Munsch, R. (2006) *The paper bag princess*. Gosford: Scholastic.

Office of Preschool and Child Care. (1993). *Equal play, equal work*. Melbourne: Department of Health and Community Services.

Our Watch, Australia's National Research Organisation for Women's Safety (ANROWS) and VicHealth. (2015). *Change the story: A shared framework for the primary prevention of violence against women and their children in Australia*. Melbourne: Our Watch.

Penn, H. (2013). Raw and emerging childcare markets. In E. Lloyd & H. Penn (Eds.), *Childcare markets: Can they deliver an equitable service?* (pp. 173–190). Bristol: Policy Press:

Robinson, K. H. (2013). *Innocence, knowledge and the construction of childhood: The contradictory nature of sexuality and censorship in children's contemporary lives*. London: Routledge.

Robinson, K. H., & Jones Diaz, C. (2006). *Diversity and difference in early childhood education: Issues for theory and practice*. Berkshire, England: Open University Press.

Shutts, K., Kenward, B., Falk, H., Ivegran, A., & Fawcett, C. (2017). Early preschool environments and gender: Effects of gender pedagogy in Sweden. *Journal of Experimental Child Psychology*, 162, 1–17.

Smith, K. (2015). Action research with children. In O. Saracho (Ed.), *Handbook of research methods in early childhood education – volume 1* (pp. 547–576). New York: Sage.

Smith, K., Tesar, M., & Myers, C. (2016). Edu-capitalism and the governing of early childhood education and care in Australia, New Zealand and the United States. *Global Studies of Childhood*, 6(1), 123–135.

Victorian Department of Education and Training. (2016). *Victorian early years learning and development framework*. Retrieved from: http://www.education.vic.gov.au/Documents/childhood/providers/edcare/veyldframework.pdf

Victorian Department of Education and Training (2017a). *Social and emotional learning*. Retrieved from: https://www.education.vic.gov.au/school/teachers/health/mentalhealth/Pages/socialemotion.aspx

Victorian Department of Education and Training. (2017b). *Respectful relationships*. Retrieved from: https://www.education.vic.gov.au/about/programs/Pages/respectfulrelationships.aspx

Resources

Challenging gender stereotypes in the early years: the power of parents
https://www.ourwatch.org.au/Media-Resources
Level Playground
www.levelplayground.org.au
Respectful Relationships Education, Our Watch
https://www.ourwatch.org.au/What-We-Do/Respectful-relationships-education
Social and emotional learning, KidsMatter
https://www.kidsmatter.edu.au/mental-health-matters/social-and-emotional-learning

4

EARLY CHILDHOOD TEACHER CERTIFICATION AS A SITE FOR THE RE-PRODUCTION OF RACIAL AND CULTURAL INJUSTICE

Mariana Souto-Manning, Gail Buffalo and Ayesha Rabadi-Raol

Introduction

At a time in which major financial investments are being made in early childhood education, and equity is narrowly and simplistically defined as access to early education programming (Barnett, 2017; Lovejoy, 2013; US Department of Education, 2015), in this chapter we seek to unveil the ways in which Eurocentric conceptualizations of quality in early childhood education may serve to re-produce racial and cultural inequities (Souto-Manning & Rabadi-Raol, 2018). Centering the experiential knowledges and narratives of three early childhood teachers of color[1] within the context of New York State, we unveil how high-stakes teacher certification tests, such as the edTPA,[2] may effectively serve as tools for ensuring the maintenance of an overwhelmingly white early childhood teaching profession, demographically and conceptually (Milner et al., 2013; Ryan & Dixson, 2006; US Bureau of Labor Statistics, 2018). In doing so, we contend that the use of high-stakes certification tests has implications for the demographic trend of the "whiteification" of the early childhood teaching force (Souto-Manning & Cheruvu, 2016).

As teacher educators from diverse racial, ethnic, linguistic, and cultural backgrounds, our work is grounded in a common commitment to interrupting injustice and fostering justice in and through teaching and teacher education (Souto-Manning & Winn, 2017). Across our diverse identities, we share experience working with early childhood teachers of color and a commitment to supporting their preparation and development as a matter of justice. Our understanding of justice is informed by Dowd and Bensimon's (2015) "three theories of justice: justice as care, justice as fairness, and justice as transformation" (p. 61). In our work, we conceptualize justice as transformation. This understanding of justice, rooted in critical race theory, "foregrounds how racism is institutionally reproduced through structures of education" and prioritizes "racial equity, a term that invokes broader social phenomena beyond schooling and that maintains the focus on racism in education" (Dowd & Bensimon, 2015, p. 14). As such, it informs how we read injustices in early childhood teaching and teacher education (centrally accounting for their racial dimensions) and work to redress them in and through our work (taking institutional racism into account).

Theorizing Justice as Transformation

The theory of justice as transformation draws on "critical race perspectives that challenge the efficacy of liberalism and color blindness to enact change toward a more egalitarian society" (Dowd & Bensimon, 2015, p. 62). It rejects simplistic calls to diversify the profession and demands acknowledging "racialized histories of discrimination and exclusion" (p. 78). Such a conceptualization of "justice as transformation operates on the principles of nondiscrimination and nonoppression … [and] calls on educational practitioners, leaders, and policymakers to act as empowerment agents to dismantle institutional and structural racism" (p. 15).

Politically, "justice as transformation calls for policies and practices that seek to identify and deconstruct structural racism … [and] requires structural changes in the systems … which reproduce inequities" (p. 144), as is the case of high-stakes certification tests for teacher certification. Under the guise of impartiality and objectivism, such tests serve to maintain a status quo of inequities (Solórzano & Yosso, 2002). Thus, here, we engage with justice as transformation and employ critical race theory methodological tools (Solórzano & Yosso, 2002) "to 'counter' deficit storytelling" (p. 23), centering the perspectives of teachers of color seeking to become certified as teachers.

Critical Race Methodology

Drawing and expanding on critical race theory, Solórzano and Yosso (2002) proposed "critical race methodology as a theoretically grounded approach to research" (p. 24). This methodology is rooted in the need to simultaneously eliminate racism and entangled forms of bigotry and foster the empowerment of intersectionally minoritized[3] communities. As underscored by Solórzano and Yosso (2002), we understand that race and racism are intercentric "with other forms of subordination" (p. 25), such as class and gender; however, differing from Marxist and other class- and gender-based perspectives, critical race methodologies center the lives and experiences of people of color. To be sure, we purposefully chose to center the voices of teachers of color and thus intentionally did not interview white teachers.

In this chapter, we specifically engaged with *testimonios* as collective counter-storytelling to the dominant stories of the superiority of Eurocentric ways and systems of knowing (Ladson-Billings, 2000). After all, *testimonios* center "experiential knowledge" transdisciplinarily. That is, they afford analyzing "race and racism by placing them both in historical and contemporary contexts" and offer powerful counter-stories to "the ideology of racism [which] creates, maintains, and justifies the use of a 'master narrative' in storytelling" (Solórzano & Yosso, 2002, pp. 26–27). Instead, *testimonios* afford a counter-story to the racism of "'monovocal' stories" (p. 27) told *about* people of color.

Testimonios*: Collective Counter-Storytelling*

We employ *testimonio* as we seek to challenge negative discourses about the experiences of Latinx communities in the United States marked by marginalization, oppression, and/or resistance (Delgado Bernal et al., 2012; Huber, 2009). *Testimonio* affords modes of analysis that are collective and that center and foreground the experiences of our three Latina participants, to challenge the injustices within the "majoritarian" story of teacher certification, which purports that high-stakes tests are needed to measure quality in teacher education and, relatedly, ensure quality in teaching (Anzaldúa, 1990; Cruz, 2006; Moraga & Anzaldúa, 1983; Solórzano & Yosso, 2002)—a neoliberal quality control of sorts. *Testimonio* responds to and resists "majoritarian stories ... As such, they are stories that carry layers of assumptions that persons in positions of racialized privilege bring with them to discussions of racism, sexism, classism, and other forms of subordination" (Solórzano & Yosso, 2002, p. 28). To disrupt "the apartheid of knowledge" (Huber, 2009, p. 639), we collected oral tellings which were transcribed and analyzed. From these audio recordings and transcriptions, we developed *testimonios* coauthored by Latina early childhood teachers as "a form of resistance" (Smith, 2011, p. 24).

Analysis and Findings

The *testimonios* we constructed are multi-voiced. They center the voices and collective experiences of three Latina teachers. Honoring dialogicism and artistic expression, often marginalized within the context of the academy and deemed unscientific (Solórzano & Yosso, 2002), the *testimonios* we present in this chapter are in the form of dialogue and poetry. This is our purposeful attempt to transgress dominant research genres and paradigms (Burdell & Swadener, 1999; Delgado Bernal et al., 2012).

The *testimonios* presented below were fashioned from phenomenological interviews with early childhood teachers of color (at a location of their choice and lasting 40–180 minutes). In these interviews, we invited them to talk about how they experienced becoming a certified teacher. The participants were all Latina teachers who, due to new certification requirements linked to the expansion of Universal Pre-Kindergarten (UPK) in New York and related policies pertaining to certification requirements, went from being "highly qualified teachers" to uncertified educators. They were either first- or second-generation Latina immigrants from Mexico, Guatemala, or the Dominican Republic. They each identified as women and had prior experience teaching at the time they undertook certification (ranging from five to 34 years). Two of the three identified as Afro-Latinas. At the time the interviews took place, they had all sought and achieved teacher certification in New York State.

At the time they were asked to share their stories of becoming certified, the participants (pseudonyms Barbara, Eliana, and Lucia) had recently completed the New York State certification requirements. Each of us conducted an interview with each one of the participants asking them about their experiences navigating mandated certification requirements. During the interviews, we asked questions such as: *How did you navigate your teacher certification program?; What were some of the most memorable moments?*; and *What were some of the biggest obstacles to becoming certified?* Based on their responses and their identification of the edTPA as an obstacle, we followed up with questions such as: *How would you describe the edTPA?; What do you think is the purpose of the edTPA?*; and *Tell me more about your experience with the edTPA.* Here, we focus on the section(s) of their interviews pertaining to their identification of the edTPA as an obstacle. None of the participants identified the edTPA as a positive aspect of their journey to becoming certified as a teacher.

As each interview was conducted and audio recorded, we wrote researcher memos. We engaged in recording observational notes (jotting down what we were observing) and theoretical notes (thoughts, connections, and initial interpretations) (Schatzman & Strauss, 1973). Through observational notes, we specifically attended to non-verbal behaviors and displays of emotion, seeking to account for the affective dimensions of interviews not typically or fully captured in audio recordings.

After we transcribed each interview, we listened to the audio recordings and consulted our researcher notes to identify emotional hot points (Cahnmann-Taylor et al., 2009). Specifically seeking "[t]o capture the emotional qualities" and to understand our data (interviews and transcripts) more fully, we "responded artfully' crafting … *trans/scripts*: compressed renderings of original transcripts that utilize techniques from poetry and the dramatic arts to highlight emotional 'hot points' and heightened language from the original discourse in our data" (p. 2548). Trans/scripting allowed us to privilege what was important and critical to the three Latina teachers and to purposefully and intentionally honor their prioritizations. Trans/scripting also allowed us to put participants in conversation with one another by combining participants' perspectives to produce a coauthored counter-story, a *testimonio*, a powerful "space for collective representation" (Burdell & Swadener, 1999, p. 23).

The following trans/scripted testimonio captures "hot points" in Barbara's, Eliana's, and Lucia's interviews, as they pertained to their experiences with the tests:

BARBARA: Test taking … was challenging … the style of testing changed too. Every time I turned around there was some changes. I just went like, OK, this is too much. I'm going to leave it alone for a while. And then coming back to it made it more difficult.

ELIANA: Plus tests, you know … I would say it's a privilege thing … if you think about who is able to get into the programs and who is able to afford the programs. And then who can afford the test … That sort of thing.

LUCIA: Yes, you know, I think the cost is a huge factor. And it's not like they [are] paying you more after. You are making the same thing. You have to pass just to keep your job [not to be demoted to an assistant teacher position]. Like the edTPA.

BARBARA: What bothered me the most about the edTPA is that I think that a lot of times things are done unfairly for teachers, because when I completed my master's I had a practicum binder that I had to submit, and the practicum binder is exactly like the edTPA … so it was a bit redundant for me to have to go back.

ELIANA: Um, I don't really know. It's interesting cause I don't know what the purpose of edTPA, I mean, I had to do it. I know it comes from Stanford, but, but besides that I'm just like, you're doing it because you want money.

LUCIA: I get it that New York want this certification for all teachers … but it's not fair how they go about it. Someone who [has] been teaching for [over ten] years like me and someone who is new. There is no differentiation.

ELIANA: I kind of just, was like: yay I'm great; I passed. I don't need to think about it anymore. I think perhaps the only thing I really kind of took away from it was the language.

BARBARA: When I came to the United States I was three-and-a-half years old. I turned four here. And when I arrived I did not speak English.

LUCIA: And if your first language is not English, like mine is not, you are disadvantaged. Because many of the tests is more about reading. And the other is about writing a lot and doing what they want you to do, even though they don't know the kids … How is this about better teachers? It isn't.

BARBARA: I'm not a lawyer so I don't need to sit down and learn about how I'm going to argue this against that, against the next. This, against that yes. Point of view, yes, so that my students are focused and have an understanding that they need to be able to present their facts even as a very young child, what comes first, what comes second, what comes third … but I am against teaching information just for the test purposes. I would much rather [address] questions that relate to … teaching children how to take care of things in the world … [such as] "What do you do with the clothing and no longer fits?" I think that's more important to building a world-class citizen.

In the trans/scripted dialogic *testimonio* above, all three participants offered critiques of the tests required for obtaining certification in New York State. Eliana clearly linked certification tests to financial privilege and later with language (coherently with Lucia's observations—e.g., "if your first language is not English, like mine is not, you are disadvantaged"). That is, they underscored the intercentricity of racism—linking financial privilege to linguistic privilege and racial privilege. Denouncing the financial burden of new certification requirements, Lucia explained that her compensation was not increased as a result of new certification requirements—e.g., "like they [are] paying you more after. You are making the same thing. You have to pass just to keep your job." Thus, they clearly articulated how they were bearing the brunt of new requirements with no additional resources or compensation. Barbara added additional critiques of the tests, explaining that exams like the edTPA are often "redundant" with what she learned in her teacher education program. At other times, test questions were not aligned at all with what she identified as needed for teaching in early childhood; it was "just for test purposes." She also recounted her experience pertaining to ever-changing tests and test formats, which at one point discouraged her from continuing to take exams because it was "too much." Thus, she shows how becoming certified is a protracted and difficult process. Although not visible in the *testimonio* above, each of these women acquired debt in order to complete teacher preparation programs to become certified and thus they were in more precarious financial positions than they had been prior to certification mandates linked to UPK.

Their *testimonio*, whereby they made sense of how they experienced certification mandates, unveils some of the shortcomings associated with new certification requirements, which purport to foster higher quality early childhood education. In particular, they discussed the lack of differentiation for early childhood educators who had been in the profession for a number of years and those who did not engage in teaching prior to becoming certified. This is visible in Lucia's comment: "Someone who been teaching for years like me and someone who is new. There is no differentiation."

They also denounced the insidious nature and (un)intended consequences of new certification requirements when tests pathologize multilingual teachers and privilege "white English," as articulated by Eliana. As Lucia explained: "And if your first language is not English, like mine is not, you are disadvantaged." Their *testimonio* clearly addresses the question of "how language shapes our ideas about race" (Alim, Rickford, & Ball, 2016), re-producing the white English speaking teacher as the ideal prototype of the early childhood teacher. The sort of raciolinguistic privileging identified by Eliana and by Lucia may have dire consequences for diversifying the early childhood teaching profession and for addressing the demographic disproportionality between early childhood teachers (overwhelmingly white) and students (a majority of whom are children of color). Finally, the *testimonio* fashioned from Eliana's and Lucia's collective voices and experiences reaffirm how "the development of Standardized American English … [is] a raciolinguistic project … to discursively produce the American bourgeoisie in opposition to the racialized Other" (Flores, 2016, p. 16).

Based on the voices and experiences of early childhood teachers of color, such a project, when applied to teacher certification—thus determining who becomes a teacher—has serious consequences. It cannot remain unexamined, as it constructs early childhood teachers of color as "the racialized Other" (Flores, 2016, p. 16). Teacher certification processes are thereby clearly "implicated in the reproduction of racial normativity by expecting language-minoritized students [of teaching] to model their linguistic practices after the white speaking subject" (Flores & Rosa, 2015, p. 149).

Additionally, the following trans/scripted poem captures the emotional "hot points" (Cahnmann-Taylor et al., 2009) of their responses acknowledging "the power of human collectivity … revealing oppression through lived experiences, which are rooted in the histories and memories of a larger community" (Huber, 2009, p. 645).

> These tests
> Are all about the money
> They don't affect how I teach
> I am against teaching information just for the test purposes
> I paid a lot of money to go to school and get certified
> It was hard for me to give up those 300 dollars
> I didn't grow up rich
>
> Plus tests, you know
> What can I say?
> I would say it's a privilege thing
> If you think about
> Who is able to get into the programs
> And who is able to afford the programs
> I'm not a lawyer so I don't need to … argue this against that, against the next
>
> Pretty much BSing
> They didn't make me a better teacher
> I … was like: yay, I'm great; I passed
> I don't need to think about it anymore
> On paper you could be a good teacher
> But in practice you might not
> Instead, ask me about building a world-class citizen
>
> It is a lot of writing
> It's not really about teaching
> What are they trying to get at?
> OK, this is too much
>
> Maybe you know how to write?
> The only thing I really kind of took away from it was the language
> Academic language as being that of white English

The poetic *testimonio* above, coauthored by Barbara, Eliana, and Lucia, is comprised of phrases that at once capture emotionality and representativeness— offering perspectives and experiences present within and across interviews and eliciting emotional qualities, thus heightening the language in the original narratives (interviews). That is, the phrases selected represent ideas associated with emotional "hot points" in their narrative tellings (Cahnmann-Taylor et al., 2009).

The poetic *testimonio* above has four stanzas. The first stanza introduces three topics, which are further developed in the following stanzas (2–4), each pertaining to a different lesson rooted in their lived experiences becoming certified teachers. The first stanza denounces how these certification tests: (a) serve as intercentric racist tools; (b) do not lead to improved teaching; and (c) incur a financial burden to those seeking to become teachers (especially those who do not have generational wealth, as indicated elsewhere in the interview transcripts) while simultaneously serving as mechanisms whereby corporations (such as Pearson) make money.

Being described as a "privilege thing," in the poetic *testimonio* above explains how getting into programs and paying for tuition and certification tests further reifies inequities and reinscribes the myth of the superiority of the white teacher—without acknowledging how this is racist and related to other forms of bigotry (e.g., linguicism, classism)—resulting from a history of intergenerational dispossession and racial disproportionality in college admissions.

The three women whose experiences are centered in the *testimonios* presented in this chapter call these tests "BS." They refute the claim that edTPA ensures quality teaching and results in quality teachers. Instead, they position teaching in juxtaposition to performing and/or writing about teaching (e.g., "On paper you could be a good teacher; But in practice you might not"). They denounce that these tests are "not really about teaching," and introduce the idea of writing in white English as indexing teaching quality per certification tests.

Overall, findings indicate that albeit well intentioned, Barbara's, Eliana's, and Lucia's experiences denounce how certification tests may further exacerbate the existing reproduction of racial inequities in early childhood education. Their *testimonios* unveil obstacles they experienced as women of color seeking teacher certification in the state of New York State. They beg us to consider how certification tests in early childhood education may be serving to uphold the overwhelming whiteness present in early childhood teaching and teacher education (Sleeter, 2017a; 2017b)—demographically and conceptually—thereby Otherizing early childhood teachers of color and young children of color. After all, "we teach what we value" (Ladson-Billings, 2017).

Discussion: On Testing (and) Quality

Educational researchers have exposed how the term "quality" is highly contested and how narrow Eurocentric conceptualizations of quality may in effect serve as a guise for the maintenance of the interests of those in power in society, upholding an inequitable status quo (e.g., Leonardo, 2004; Oakes, 1986; Souto-Manning & Rabadi-Raol, 2018). As illustrated by the experiences featured in the trans/scripted testimonios we shared, the notion of quality has been used to support arguments for the imposition of standardization, accountability, accreditation, and certification (Darling-Hammond, 2007; Ravitch, 2016). These measures, although purporting to ensure quality, confound the debate about quality—what that actually means and to whom (Leonardo, 2004; Souto-Manning & Rabadi-Raol, 2018; Zhu et al., 2017). Related to calls for accountability as a remedy to address the purported American educational crisis and improve teaching, the field of teacher education has recently seen a marked rise in the ways accountability has shaped the rhetoric and the purpose of teacher education programs, heightening the attention towards standardized certification as the end goal for teachers (Philip et al., 2019; Zeichner, 2014). The edTPA is thus a situated representation of a pervasive trend.

As visible in the testimonios presented in this chapter, there is a "deceptive rhetoric" that testing will lead to increased quality in teaching and teacher education (Oakes, 1986; Ravitch, 2016), which fails to recognize the power of the experiences teachers of color such as Barbara, Eliana, and Lucia have. Such rhetoric is divorced from historical lessons on how such tools tend to be biased and may in effect uphold inequities, such as those linked to the displacement of Black teachers in the post-*Brown* South (Ladson-Billings, 2004) and SAT racial biases impacting college access and admissions (Fish, 1994; Reeves & Halikias, 2017). Based on Barbara's, Eliana's, and Lucia's lived experiences and with the understanding that standardized testing when combined with high-stakes licensing decisions are likely to result in educational inequity (Froese-Germain, 2001), we purport that testing (even when seeking to ensure quality) may in effect uphold injustice. Thus, we underscore the need for teacher educators to commit to fostering justice in early childhood teacher education by problematizing these discourses and interrupting such practices.

Conclusion

In this chapter we unveiled how despite having significant experience in the teaching profession, teachers of color (such as Barbara, Eliana, and Lucia) are bearing the onus of newly established measures of quality in early childhood teacher certification, such as high-stakes certification tests. In alignment with a long history of racist practices perpetuated in and through standardized tests (e.g., Fish, 1994; Skiba et al., 2002), these tests privilege whiteness, characterized by factors such as generational wealth and white English. Further, they are aligned with the very Eurocentric ways of being and behaving that dominate the early childhood teaching profession (Pérez & Saavedra, 2017; Souto-Manning & Rabadi-Raol, 2018).

Through the analysis of Barbara's, Eliana's, and Lucia's collective experiences and the construction of *testimonios*, we unveiled whose knowledges are deemed worthwhile in and by teacher certification and what interests are served by high-stakes teacher certification assessments, shedding light onto the ways in which paradigmatically, early childhood teacher certification must stop ontologically centering whiteness and move to center teacher education on the lives, voices, values, and experiences of historically minoritized communities (those deemed to be minorities, even when numerically they are the majority—McCarty, 2002).

Situated within the long history of racism as assimilation (Kendi, 2016) enacted in and through high-stakes testing (e.g., Fish, 1994; Hartlep & Anthrop-Gonzalez, 2018), the *testimonios* we shared urge the field of early childhood education to consider how high-stakes certification tests privilege whiteness and re-produce racism in the early childhood profession, invisiblizing and/or attempting to erase the experiences and expertise of individuals and communities of color. Given how early childhood teacher certification has been constructed as a site for the re-production of racial and cultural injustice, we urge the field of early childhood teaching and teacher education to problematize how certification tests, while purportedly espousing concepts such as "rigor" and "quality," may effectively serve as tools for the continued re-production of inequitable status quos in and through early education. As such, we propose that the field of early childhood education has much to learn from the collective experiences of women of color.

Notes

1 We employ the term teacher for certified teacher and educator for uncertified teacher.
2 The educative Teacher Performance Assessment (edTPA), developed by SCALE and administered by Pearson, is a high-stakes assessment tied to New York State certification. It purports to measure teacher quality. As of July 2018, 18 states had established policies identifying edTPA passing scores required for teacher licensure and two states were in the process of establishing such policies (AACTE, 2018).
3 As Souto-Manning and Martell (2019), "[w]e use the term intersectionally minoritized instead of minority because '[a]s a characterization of people, "minority" is stigmatizing and often numerically inaccurate … "Minoritized" more accurately conveys the power relations and processes by which certain groups are socially, economically, and politically marginalized within the larger society' (McCarty, 2002, p. xv). Combining minoritized with intersectional acknowledges 'prejudice stemming from the intersections of racist ideas and other forms of bigotry, such as sexism, classism, ethnocentrism, and homophobia' (Kendi, 2016, p. 5)")[. 37..

References

Alim, H.S., Rickford, J.R., & Ball, A. (Eds.). (2016). *Raciolinguistics: How language shapes our ideas about race*. New York, NY: Oxford University Press.

American Association of Colleges for Teacher Education (AACTE). (2018). edTPA: Participation map. Retrieved from http://edtpa.aacte.org/state-policy

Anzaldúa, G.E. (1990). *Making face, making soul/haciendo caras: Creative and critical perspectives of feminists of color*. San Francisco, CA: Aunt Lute Books.

Barnett, W.S. (2017). *Getting the facts right on pre-k and the president's prek-k proposal*. New Brunswick, NJ: National Institute for Early Education Research.

Burdell, P., & Swadener, B.B. (1999). Critical personal narrative and autoethnography in education: Reflections on a genre. *Educational Researcher*, 28(6), 21–26.

Cahnmann-Taylor, M., Souto-Manning, M., Wooten, J., & Dice, J. (2009). The art & science of educational inquiry: Analysis of performance-based focus groups with novice bilingual teachers. *Teachers College Record*, 111(11), 2535–2559.

Cruz, C. (2006). Toward an epistemology of a brown body. In D. Delgado Bernal, C.A. Elenes, F.E. Godinez, & S. Villenas (Eds.), *Chicana/Latina education in everyday life: Feminista perspectives on pedagogy and epistemology* (pp. 59–75). New York, NY: SUNY Press.

Darling-Hammond, L. (2007). Race, inequality, and educational accountability: The irony of 'No Child Left Behind." *Race Ethnicity and Education*, 10(3), 245–260.

Delgado Bernal, D., Burciaga, R., & Flores Carmona, J. (2012). Chicana/Latina testimonios: Mapping the methodological, pedagogical, and political. *Equity & Excellence in Education*, 45(3), 363–372.

Dowd, A., & Bensimon, E. (2015). *Engaging the "race question": Accountability and equity in U.S. higher education.* New York, NY: Teachers College Press.

Fish, S. (1994). Affirmative action and the SAT. *The Journal of Blacks in Higher Education*, 2, 83.

Flores, N. (2016). A tale of two visions: Hegemonic whiteness and bilingual education. *Educational Policy*, 30, 13–38.

Flores, N., & Rosa, J. (2015). Undoing appropriateness: Raciolinguistic ideologies and language diversity in education. *Harvard Educational Review*, 85(2), 149–171.

Froese-Germain, B. (2001). Standardized testing + high-stakes decisions = educational inequity. *Interchange*, 32(2), 111–130.

Hartlep, N., & Anthrop-Gonzalez, R. (2018). Cultural biases persist in national licensure exam for teachers. Retrieved from http://diverseeducation.com/article/111104/

Huber, L. P. (2009). Disrupting the apartheid of knowledge: Testimonio as methodology in Latina/o critical race research in education. *International Journal of Qualitative Studies in Education*, 22(6), 639–654.

Kendi, I. (2016). *Stamped from the beginning: The definitive history of racist ideas in America.* New York, NY: Nation Books.

Ladson-Billings, G. (2000). Racialized discourses and ethnic epistemologies. In N. Denzin, & Y.S. Lincoln (Eds.), *The SAGE handbook of qualitative research* (2nd ed., pp. 257–277). Thousand Oaks, CA: SAGE.

Ladson-Billings, G. (2004). Landing on the wrong note: The price we paid for Brown. *Educational Researcher*, 33(7), 3–13.

Ladson-Billings, G. (2017). The (r)evolution will not be standardized: Teacher education, hip hop pedagogy, and culturally sustaining pedagogy 2.0. In D. Paris & H.S. Alim (Eds.), *Culturally sustaining pedagogies: Teaching and learning for justice in a changing world* (pp. 141–156). New York, NY: Teachers College Press.

Leonardo, Z. (2004). Critical social theory and transformative knowledge: The functions of criticism in quality education. *Educational Researcher*, 33(6), 11–18.

Lovejoy, A. (with Szekely, A., Wat, A., Rowland, C., Laine, R. & Moore, D.) for the National Governor's Association. (2013). A governor's guide to early literacy: Getting all students reading by third grade. Retrieved from www.nga.org

McCarty, T. (2002). *A place to be Navajo: Rough Rock and the struggle for self-determination in Indigenous schooling.* New York, NY: Routledge.

Milner, H.R., Pearman, F., & McGee, E. (2013). Critical race theory, interest convergence, and teacher education. In M. Lynn and A. Dixson (Eds.), *Handbook of critical race theory in education* (pp. 339–354). New York, NY: Routledge.

Moraga, C., & Anzaldúa, G. (1983). *This bridge called my back: Writings by radical women of color.* Brooklyn, NY: Kitchen Table.

Oakes, J. (1986). Tracking, inequality, and the rhetoric of reform: Why schools don't change. *The Journal of Education*, 168(1), 60–80.

Pérez, M.S., and Saavedra, C. (2017). A call for onto-epistemological diversity in early childhood education and care: Centering global South conceptualizations of childhood/s. *Review of Research in Education*, 41, 1–29.

Philip, T.M., Souto-Manning, M., Anderson, L., Horn, I., Andrews, D.J.C., Stillman, J., & Varghese, M. (2019). Making justice peripheral by constructing practice as "core": How the increasing prominence of core practices challenges teacher education. *Journal of Teacher Education*, 70(3), 251–264.

Ravitch, D. (2016). *The death and life of the great American school system*. New York, NY: Basic Books.

Reeves, R., & Halikias, D. (2017). Race gaps in SAT scores highlight inequality and hinder upward mobility. Retrieved from https://www.brookings.edu/research/race-gaps-in-sat-scores-highlight-inequality-and-hinder-upward-mobility/

Ryan, C.L., & Dixson, A.D.(2006). Rethinking pedagogy to re-center race: Some reflections. *Language Arts*, 84(2), 175–183.

Schatzman, L., & Strauss, A. (1973). *Field research: Strategies for a natural sociology*. Englewood Cliffs, NJ: Prentice-Hall.

Skiba, R., Knesting, K., & Bush, L. (2002). Culturally competent assessment: More than nonbiased tests. *Journal of Child and Family Studies, 11*(1), 61–78.

Sleeter, C. (2017a). Critical race theory and the whiteness of teacher education. *Urban Education*, 52(2), 155–169.

Sleeter, C. (2017b). Wrestling with problematics of whiteness in teacher education. *International Journal of Qualitative Studies in Education*, 29(8), 1065–1068.

Smith, K. (2011). Female voice and feminist text: Testimonio as a form of resistance in Latin America. *Florida Atlantic Comparative Studies Journal*, 12, 21–37.

Solórzano, D., & Yosso, T. (2002). Critical race methodology: Counter-storytelling as an analytical framework for education research. *Qualitative Inquiry*, 8(1), 23–44.

Souto-Manning, M., & Cheruvu, R. (2016). Challenging and appropriating discourses of power: Listening to and learning from early career early childhood teachers of color. *Equity & Excellence in Education*, 49(1), 9–26.

Souto-Manning, M., & Martell, J. (2019). Toward critically transformative possibilities: Considering tensions and undoing inequities in the spatialization of teacher education. *Teachers College Record*, 121(6), 1–42. Retrieved from https://www.tcrecord.org/Content.asp?ContentId=22731

Souto-Manning, M., & Rabadi-Raol, A. (2018). (Re)Centering quality in early childhood education: Toward intersectional justice for minoritized children. *Review of Research in Education*, 42, 203–225.

Souto-Manning, M., & Winn, M. (2017). Where do we go from here?: Foundational understandings as show ways for interrupting injustice and fostering justice in and through educational research. *Review of Research in Education*, 41, ix–xix.

US Bureau of Labor Statistics. (2018). Employed persons by detailed occupation, sex, race, and Hispanic or Latino ethnicity. Retrieved from https://www.bls.gov/cps/cpsaat11.pdf

US Department of Education. (2015). A matter of equity: Preschool in America. Retrieved from https://www2.ed.gov/documents/early-learning/matter-equity-preschool-america.pdf

Zeichner, K. (2014). The struggle for the soul of teaching and teacher education in the USA. *Journal of Education for Teaching*, 40(5), 551–568.

Zhu, X., Goodwin, A.L., & Zhang, H. (Eds.). (2017). *Quality of teacher education and learning: Theory and practice*. Singapore: Springer.

PART II

Social Justice in the Classroom: Democratic and Anti-bias Practices

5

HISTORICAL AND CONTEMPORARY PERSPECTIVES ON DEMOCRATIC EDUCATION IN EARLY CHILDHOOD

Shirley A. Kessler

Introduction

This chapter begins as a personal account of how I came to advocate for an approach to early childhood education that promotes social justice based on education for democratic living. Social justice for me draws upon Roosevelt's "Four Freedoms" (Roosevelt, 1941): Freedom of Speech, Freedom of Worship, Freedom from Want, and Freedom from Fear. I emphasize "Freedom from Want" and focus on economic justice, a belief that all humans should be able to provide for themselves and their families, through their labor, basic needs – including housing, food, health care, and education – as well as opportunities for the establishment of positive relationship with others of all races and creeds and the more-than-human. An economic system that enriches the top 1% of the population and leaves others living from pay check to pay check, unable to afford basic health care, forced to live in dangerous neighborhoods, and to send their children to underfunded schools is unjust. Developing a democratic classroom and teaching students to understand and act on democratic principles can promote the kind of social justice I envision.

The following examination of the historical and contemporary views of democratic education in early childhood arose out of research I was conducting on the history of the early childhood curriculum. As I read the works of Henry Barnard (1811–1900), sometimes called the father of the kindergarten in the United States, I was reminded of the similarity between his views and elements of "revisionist history" and/or "human capital theory." Next, I studied the vast literature about and by Elizabeth Peabody (1804–1894), a tireless advocate of the kindergarten in the later part of the 19th century. I realized the extreme differences between her views and those of Barnard. Peabody's views promote love in the classroom and a classroom community, both of which reminded me of one important component of a "democratic curriculum." I conclude that their ideas represent different views as to the social purposes of education, including different visions of the "good life" (Kessler, 2018) and a just society, as well as what should be taught in the early childhood classroom. These issues which are still debated today can serve as background information and perhaps provide a rational for developing a democratic early childhood curriculum, one of several aspects of social justice education (Hytten & Bettez, 2011).

Theoretical Background

Revisionist History

In the late 1970s I studied the history of educational thought with well-known historian Clarence Karier. What I learned was both surprising and perplexing. Karier claimed that "the central purpose of public education was not designed to equalize wealth and opportunity ... but ... designed to help fit people into the social system" (Karier, 1975, p. xx). Statements such as this one, and others, caused me much dismay. I asked myself, "Is this what I, as an educator, was teaching?" I learned later that Karier was at the forefront of what has been called "a modest revolution" in the historiography of education that challenged traditional accounts of education where schools were depicted as providing equal opportunity for all as well as engines of social progress. Karier and other like-minded historians, called "revisionists," further claimed that schools were instruments of social and economic power for elite groups by inculcating the values and attitudes in workers necessary to maintain a particular economic system based on laissez-faire capitalism and/or neoliberalism. The social purpose of the common school, he stated, "was to impart new, common values to prevent political, social or economic revolution" (p. 11). In conducting research on the thinking of early school psychologists and sociologists, and the work of John Dewey, Karier pointed out that he had left out of his research a focus on so-called "child-centered" traditions and movements that he claimed deserved a different book. And so, I began to study the history of early childhood education and early childhood curriculum(s) with the proclamations of revisionist historians in mind. Did Karier's views as to the reproductive nature of educational theory and practice apply to early childhood?

Friedrich Froebel (1782–1852)

I read carefully the works of Friedrich Froebel, the founder of the kindergarten in Keilau, Germany in 1837. Did Froebel believe that the purpose of the kindergarten was to help children fit into the existing social system? I don't believe so. As you may know, he believed the purpose of education was, as he put it, "the realization of a faithful, pure, inviolate, and hence holy life" (Froebel, 1887, p. 4). He continued, "Education should lead and guide man to clearness concerning himself and in himself, to peace with nature, and to unity with God ..." (p. 5).

Early in his career, Froebel had visions of an education different from that admired by State officials in Prussia. He pointed out in 1828 that if he had educated children for futures as shoemakers, servants or merchants, he would have won support from the State. But, if so, he wrote, "I should have become a State-machine; I should have been busy cutting out and shaping other machines. But I wanted to educate men to be free, to think, to take action for themselves" (Froebel, 1828, p. 41). Aren't these goals of a democratic education?

Further, Froebel maintained that in founding the school at Keilhau he had hoped to provide a basis for creating a "united and transformed" society (Lilley, 1967) that would include the political and moral freedom of nations (Marenholtz-Bulow, 2007, p. 38). This was Froebel's "utopian vision" (Kessler, 2018). Thus, rather than seeing the kindergarten as a means for socializing the young to internalize the values of dominant forces in society, Froebel believed the kindergarten had the potential for changing society for the better. Creating free thinking individuals in order to promote a society based on more democratic ideals was a threat to Prussia, that had just survived the revolution of 1848, putting down an uprising of liberals and workers who wanted to depose the authoritarian rule of Frederick IV and establish a unified Germany based on democratic ideas. In 1850 the kindergarten was forced to close – a prohibition which lasted until 1860.

Henry Barnard (1811–1900)

What happened to Froebel's vision when the kindergarten was introduced in the United States in 1856? I next studied the work of Henry Barnard who described the kindergarten to American educators in the *American Journal of Education*, which he edited and supported financially. He wrote,

> One of the most interesting and instructive contributions to the London Educational exhibition in 1854 was made by Mr. Hoffman, of Hamburg, in specimens of the cheap and simple apparatus devised by Frederick Froebel to be used in his system of Infant Garden training and instruction – which has been introduced into the principal cities of Europe.
>
> *(Barnard, 1856, p. 449)*

The kindergarten could not have had a more highly esteemed and politically well-placed advocate than Henry Barnard. Appointed the nation's first Commissioner of Education, he submitted a report to the Senate in 1868 and the House of Representatives in 1870, calling for the kindergarten to be included in the primary school (Barnard, 1890). At this formative period, he wrote, there ought to be some formal arrangement to promote "language, manners, observation, and all that constitutes the early development of the human being …" (Barnard, 1890, p. 370). I wondered to what extent his vision of the purposes of the kindergarten was compatible with those of Froebel's.

Barnard was born into a family of privilege. He attended a private school before graduating from Yale, after which he traveled extensively in Europe. While he saw the evils of capitalism, he did not believe in systemic change, but sought to address the growing dissatisfaction of workers through education. Like others of his social class, Barnard is said to have feared the uneducated masses, afraid they would rise up as they had in Germany in 1848. In his unpublished notes, he wrote,

> We may think … we can with safety drive it [the working class] to grind at the mill for our pleasure and convenience – but we must take care how we sport with its awakened feelings lest the spirit of vengeance and of strength return upon it … and destroy the social structure, though itself perish.
>
> *(Curti, 1971, p. 146)*

Such sentiments shed light on Bernard's support for the establishment of a kindergarten in the Workingman's School, founded in 1878 by Dr. Felix Adler, president of the New York Society for Ethical Culture. A kindergarten was added to the school in 1881, the purpose of which was to prepare children for their future as common laborers. Adler wrote, "The founders hoped it would avert 'future unhappiness and misery by educating skillful, intelligent, and independent working men'" (Ross, 1976, p. 21). Barnard described the kindergarten as a model of the kind of instruction that should be given to children of "the people." Such as program, he stated, would "enable them when grown up to be men and women, to help themselves, and at the same time to give the dignity of intellectuality to labor, and to the workingmen as a class" (Adler & Barnard, 1890, p. 687).

Adler, who was influential in promoting the kindergarten in California and elsewhere, recognized the fact that there was a "pauper" class emerging among the populace who were not capable of lifting themselves up to enjoy better conditions, and, thus, could be dangerous. He explained that the workers had come to believe in their equality with others, which the American political institutions had inspired in them. However, he stated, civic leaders must take time now, before conditions became as bad as they had been in Germany, to foster what he claimed were "sounder" views of "equality" and individual "rights." All had equal rights, such as liberty, personal protection, and the right to the pursuit of happiness, Adler wrote, but equal rights did not mean that there was equality of "natural fitness" and "endowment." He maintained that individuals must recognize this distinction and accept that society was based on a hierarchy, and those in positions of authority deserved their status because they were more fit to lead. As he put it,

> Let us impress upon the minds of the children that the business of life will always be carried on in the hierarchy of services and that there is no shame in doing a lesser service in this hierarchy; that all honor accrues to us only in doing the

function well to which we are committed, and taking and finding dignity in its performance.

(Adler & Barnard, 1890, p. 691)

In their view, kindergarten education was to aid children to fit in to the current political and economic hierarchy and, thus, contribute to the economic growth of the new nation. I wonder, are early childhood programs today agents of the State, "stamping out" children who have uniform characteristics in the service of the ideals of elite members of society? Neoliberal policies that have led to school privatization and the standardization of curriculum planning and education evaluation, such as the testing programs initiated by the Organization for Economic Co-operation and Development (OECD), would lead one to think this is the case (OECD, 2018a; OECD, 2018b; OECD, 2018c). (See Chapter 12 in this volume.)

Human Capital Theory

The belief that the primary purpose of education is to teach students job skills, so they will become productive members of society and promote economic prosperity in a global economy, corresponds to what has been termed "human capital theory." The emphasis is on schools "selecting students and preparing them for different segments of the labor market. Standardized tests, ability grouping ... and the separation of high school students into differing educational programs ... are considered important components in linking schools to the economy" (Spring, 2011, pp. 8–9). Originally, public support for universal free education promoted the goals of teaching Protestantism, citizenship, and skills needed to promote a capitalist economy (Kaestle, 1983). Human capital goals have now to a great extent replaced other important purposes of education, especially citizenship education (Lightfoot-Rueda & Peach, 2015; Spring 2011, p. 236). I doubt that we early childhood educators believe that the primary social purpose of education is to help children acquire the skills and attitudes to obtain worthy employment as adults in order to strengthen the U.S. economy at home and abroad, and yet the emphasis on teaching skills to preschoolers and testing to learn if those skills have been achieved corresponds to that purpose.[1]

Elizabeth Peabody (1804–1894)

Bernard's views about the purposes of education differ greatly from those of Elizabeth Peabody, another prominent figure in the kindergarten movement in the United States. Elizabeth Peabody was a lifelong educator and worked tirelessly to promote the kindergarten, beginning in 1860 when she opened the first English speaking kindergarten in Boston until her death in 1894. Both Barnard and Peabody were very religious. He was a strong Protestant who believed the Bible should be a required text in all classrooms and used to teach reading; she was a follower of many precepts of William Channing and Unitarianism. At that time, Unitarianism emphasized service to mankind. Channing preached that individuals were responsible for each other's happiness and promoting such happiness was the essential duty of all mankind (Baylor, 1965, p. 52).

Peabody believed that the purpose of education was not to teach just knowledge, but should focus on developing the moral character of children (Peabody, 1890a, p. 617). Echoing Channing, moral development meant educating children to act to make others happy, not to simply enjoy themselves (Peabody, 1890b, p. 570). Unlike Barnard, Peabody held that moral education could not be achieved by direct teaching, but by leading children to understand concepts of good/bad and right/wrong through play with other children, where they would learn to "do unto others as they would have others do unto them" (Peabody, 1887, p. 76).

An important component in moral education was "education of the heart." In *heart education* children's hearts would be educated in social situations when they learned to be kind, just, magnanimous, and deny themselves for the sake of others (Peabody, 1887). Peabody believed a kindergarten that was based on moral education and education of the heart had the potential for the redemption of humanity. Furthermore, Peabody believed the kindergarten teacher had to be truly religious and "committed to cultivating a heaven on earth" (Ross, 1976, p. 9). This was Peabody's utopian vision. Love was a vital element in moral education. In the kindergarten, children's love of self and love of others interacted until a healthy balance was achieved; then they would experience "spiritual goodness: wherein the Holy Ghost could dwell" (Mann & Peabody, 1870, p. 3). Peabody's statements about moral development reminded me of writings about the importance of building a loving community (see Chapter 10 in this volume) in the classroom, an important component of educating for democratic living and social justice education (Hytten & Bettez, 2011).

Like the beliefs of Froebel, Peabody saw creative play as an art form and an expression of God's creativeness in man (Peabody, 1890c). Even "make-believe play" seen in all children was thought to be an artistic endeavor. Furthermore, during such activities children became aware of the power that was within, power that flowed to him from the Creator (Peabody, 1890c).

Merle Curti (1971) examined the social ideas of American educators, wherein he identified three categories into which certain individuals could be placed. Educators could support the status quo, advocate for the education system to be modified, or call for a radical change to the system. Curti claimed that Barnard was a member of the first group, one who wanted to conserve the current system of education. Unlike Barnard, Peabody wanted to modify the current system of education or possibly call for radical change. Her views on the nature of work are revolutionary. Unlike Bernard who envisioned limited opportunities for workers, Peabody saw work as problematic. She recognized that most labor was unattractive because it was not artistic. She maintained that the only way to make the laborer equal to the professional in terms of social status was to make industrial labor artistic (Peabody, 1890c), an interesting thought for today. Can we conclude that Peabody's vision of the future included work that contained a creative element? Furthermore, Peabody saw the kindergarten as a "commonwealth or republic of children," "...as opposed to the traditional school which was like an absolute monarchy" (Peabody & Mann, 1863, p. 14).

Thus, in Peabody's writings I found views incompatible with the ideas of revisionist historians and human capital theorists Her ideas are more compatible with ideas about how to educate citizens to participate in a democracy. Her view of kindergarten as a "republic" as opposed to a "dictatorship" supports this view. Furthermore, Peabody valued creativity in the kindergarten classroom, where she claimed it was the first step in art education for children. She maintained that during creative activities, children experienced and strengthened their inherent power to express themselves and control their immediate environment. The late Maxine Greene (Greene, 1986) likewise argued for the importance of the arts in the curriculum in promoting alternative visions of current realities and possibilities for envisioning a future that would promote a fairer and just means of associated living. I maintain that in a kindergarten curriculum that promotes children's creative play as well as love for others holds the promise of strengthening children's sense of self and perhaps assist them in developing alternative ideas about the present and perhaps future opportunities. I believe heart education and art education are vital components of a democratic early childhood curriculum.

Contemporary Perspectives on Democratic Education

The contrasting views of Barnard and Peabody as to how to educate children for democratic living provide a context for the examination of this same issue today. There are many views as to what a democracy looks like and ways to realize its possibilities. Hytten (2017) maintained along with many others (Apple & Beane, 2007; Dewey, 1916; Goodman, 1992; Wolk, 1998; Wood, 1998) that "Democracy is more than a political system or process, it is also a way of life that requires certain habits and dispositions of citizens, including the need to balance individual rights with commitments and responsibilities toward others (p. 1). She argued further that democracy was an "ethical ideal that must be deliberately fostered and nourished [and is] ... ever a work in progress ..." (p. 1). Likewise, Beane (2005) argued that democracy was finally a belief "about how people can live together in ways that are equitable, just, enriching, and fulfilling" (Hytten, 2017, p. 5). The Institute for Democratic Education in America (n. d.) characterizes democratic education as "participatory," "empowering," and "democratic," that includes student choice in the curriculum, student-led reform movements, and shared decision-making.

Steven Wolk (1998) described several characteristics of a democratic classroom: children are respected and multiple voices are honored and strengthened, learning is meaningful as in project work, the classroom is a community, and there is a healthy balance between freedom and control. Beane and Apple (2007) argued that schools should foster cooperation rather than competition and teach children how to work together on projects that address current problems in the community (Hytten, 2017,

p. 16). George Wood (1998) described a democratic curriculum as including "critical literacy" that gives children the ability to evaluate what is heard and what is read; using children's own histories in historical inquiry; empowering students to make decisions about their learning, including choices about what to study; and teaching the values of equality, liberty, and community. Beane (2005) also maintained that in a democratic classroom, students must learn to be compassionate and could do so by caring for others (Hytten, 2017).

As was mentioned in the introduction to this volume, Ann Pelo offers further suggestions that put concerns for social justice education, along with ecological teaching, at the forefront of curriculum planning in early childhood. One important characteristic of such programs is that they prioritize "anti-bias, culturally sensitive teaching and learning" (Pelo, 2008, p. ix). In addition, early childhood programs should stress coaching children in understanding multiple perspectives as well as children collaborating with each other.

Social Skills

What would democracy in an early childhood classroom look like? Dan Gartrell offers suggestions for teaching young children what he calls, "democratic life skills" (Gartrell, 2012). These skills include children finding acceptance as a member of the group; learning to express strong emotions in non-hurting ways; solving problems creatively, independently, and in cooperation with others; accepting unique human qualities in others; and thinking intelligently and ethically (p. 111). These skills are best taught in a developmentally appropriate classroom (National Association for the Education of Young Children (NAEYC), 2009). Gartrell's book focuses on promoting children's so-called "social-emotional" development; unfortunately, Gartrell does not included recommendations for curriculum content in the early childhood classrooms, although the checklist he provides of specific "prosocial" skills in the appendix is helpful.

Likewise, NAEYC (2009) includes in its guidelines for developmentally appropriate practices a section called, "Creating a Caring Community of Learners." A few recommendations include valuing each member of the community, providing contexts for children to interact in small groups where they have opportunities to cooperate to solve problems, and expecting everyone to respect others and behave in ways that enhance learning and the well-being of all. Like Gartrell's checklist, this statement does not suggest curriculum content that would enhance the development of democratic behaviors in the classroom.

Curriculum Content

When I began to research programs that provide examples of the content of the curriculum in early childhood classrooms that would promote democratic education and citizenship, I was surprised. There is a substantial literature on this subject. For example,

Georgina Ardalan, a Title One preschool teacher in Washington, DC, provides an example of what the curriculum in a democratic classroom might be (Ardalan, 2017). Her action research project began by asking, "How can I expand my three-year-olds' understanding of citizenship beyond the classroom?" She asked children "What is a Citizen?" Children wondered if a bunny could be a citizen, or plants. Their working hypothesis was a citizen is a person, big or small, an animal, or a plant that lives in Washington, DC. An expert, a "Mr. Allen," was called in to discuss the question of citizenship with the children. After his visit, the children seized upon his remark that an important part in being a good citizen was being kind to people. The children decided to make other people happy by creating cards to distribute to strangers as they walked to field trip sites in DC. During six fieldtrips, the children created and handed out about 300 cards, adding an email address for those who wanted to respond to their messages. Ardalan concluded that educators do not have to wait until children are in high school or are 18 years old and eligible to vote to teach them to take civic action. She concluded, children are citizens in the "here and now" and play an important part in the well-being of their school and community.

Project Zero, based at the Harvard Graduate School of Education, likewise addressed the question of citizenship in early childhood classrooms. The project collaborated with "Ready to Learn Providence," a community-based school readiness initiative, and asked educators to think of children as citizens in the here and now (Mardell & Carpenter, 2012). One teacher-researcher told the children in her class that a group of teachers were planning a visit to Providence and wondered about places to play in the city. Children proposed a project whereby they would inform visiting teachers of where they liked to play in Providence. They wrote a booklet called, "Places to Play in Providence" that was displayed in the city library and elsewhere. It had wide influence, demonstrating to the local community the importance of early childhood programs and a view of children as "protagonists" in their educational endeavors, not simply as individuals with specific needs to be fulfilled. In addition, the booklet was read by educators in places such as Louisiana, Ohio, Oregon, Japan, and Hong Kong. This initiative demonstrated the benefits of encouraging children to participate in civic life and the significance of embracing the rights of children as citizens.

Another aspect of Project Zero, called "Children as Citizens," produces a yearly booklet by young children. The 2017 edition contained stories from children about what they thought about Washington, DC (Project Zero, 2017). Teachers helped children research the city and share their ideas with their classmates and children in other programs. Children called the 2017 booklet, "What Children Like Most is in This Book," referring to what children liked most about Washington, DC.

Conclusion

When planning a curriculum for democratic living, we must ask ourselves: "What vision of the future guides curriculum planning in early childhood classrooms?"

(Kessler, 2018). Do we want to promote a future where children are treated as human capital in service of a vision that promotes a particular economic system, or do we envision a future where children learn to live in a community where regard for others and the "common good" prevail? Bill Ayers urges us to ask: "What does it mean to be human today? What kinds of people do we want to become? How shall we live? (Ayers, 2016, pp. 86–87). Ayers further encourages us to ask "What if" questions to unleash our imaginations to envision a better future for ourselves and our children. Based on this prompt, I ask us to consider the following: What if schools were liberating factors organized around the vision of community held by children, parents, and teachers? What would the curriculum look like if it fostered intellectual freedom first articulated by Froebel? What if schools in the US were funded equally, and adequate resources provided to educational efforts in wealthy and poor neighborhoods? What if there were no basic standards articulated by the state that drive curriculum planning today? Answers to these questions, as well as debates regarding the social purposes of education, must guide curriculum planning in early childhood education, including answers to the important question: What knowledge is of most worth?

Note

1 Recently, historians have criticized the revisionist perspective as being limited. For example, Reese and Rury (2008) maintained that revisionist's themes of injustice and exploitation have remained an important aspect of historical accounts, but such accounts also link education to growth and opportunity. These authors claim that education is now seen "as a process of change, entailing struggle and the hope of progress" (p. 6).

References

Adler, F., & Barnard, H. (1890). Free kindergarten and working man's school: Work education for the workingman. In H. Barnard (Ed.), *Kindergarten and child-culture papers* (pp. 687–704). Hartford: Office of Bernard's American Journal of Education.

Apple, M.W., & Beane, J.A. (2007). *Democratic schools: Lessons in powerful education*, (2nd ed.). Portsmouth, NH: Heinemann.

Ardalan, G. (2017). Spreading happiness: A preschool classroom in Washington, D.C. investigates citizenship and makes a statement – "Be happy!" *Young Children*, 72(2) 78–80.

Ayers, B. (2016). *Demand the impossible: A radical manifesto*. Chicago: Haymarket Books.

Barnard, H. (1856). *Froebel's system of infant-gardens. The American Journal of Education* (pp. 449–451). Hartford: F. C. Brownell.

Barnard, H. (1890). *Plan of publication: Kindergarten and child-culture papers*. Hartford: Office of Barnard's American Journal of Education.

Baylor, M. (1965). *Elizabeth Palmer Peabody: Kindergarten pioneer*. Philadelphia, PA: University of Pennsylvania Press.

Beane, J.A. (2005). *A reason to teach: Creating classrooms of dignity and hope*. Portsmouth, NH: Heinemann.

Beane, J.A., & Apple, M.W. (2007). The case for democratic schools. In M.W. Apple, & J. Beane (Eds.), *Democratic schools: Lessons in powerful education* (2nd ed.) (pp. 1–29). Portsmouth, NH: Heinemann.

Curti, M. (1971). *The social ideas of American educators*. Totowa, NJ: Littlefield, Adams & Co.

Dewey, J. (1916). *Democracy and education*. Toronto: Collier-Macmillan Canada, Ltd.

Froebel, F. (1828). Letter to Karl Christoph Friedrich Krause. In I. M. Lilley (Ed.) (1967). *Friedrich Froebel: A selection from his writings*. New York: Cambridge University Press.

Froebel, F. (1887). *The education of man*. Translated from the German and annotated by W. N. Hailmann. New York: D. Appleton & Co.

Gartrell, D. (2012). *Education for a civil society: How guidance teaches young children democratic life skills*. Washington, DC: National Association for the Education of Young children.

Goodman, J. with assistance from Kuzmic, J. & Xiaoyang, W. (1992). *Elementary schooling for critical democracy*. New York: State University of New York Press.

Greene, M. (1986). In search of a critical pedagogy. *Harvard Educational Review*, 56, 427–441.

Hytten, K. (2017). Democracy and education in the United States. *Oxford Research Encyclopedia of Education*. doi:10.11093acrefore/9780190264093.013.2.

Hytten, K., & Bettez, S.C. (2011). Understanding education for social justice. *Educational Foundations*, Winter-Spring, 7–24.

Institute for Democratic Education in America (n.d.). What is democratic education? Retrieved http://democraticeducation.org/indes.php/features/what-is-democratic-education/

Karier, Clarence (Ed.) (1975). *Shaping the American educational state*. New York: The Free Press.

Kaestle, C.F. (1983). *Pillars of the republic: Common schools and American society 1780–1860*. New York: Hill & Wang.

Kessler, S.A. (2018). Reconceptualizing the early childhood curriculum: An unaddressed topic. In M. Bloch, B. B. Swadener, & G. Cannella (Eds.), *Reconceptualizing early childhood care & education: A reader: Critical questions, new imaginaries & social action* (2nd Ed.) (pp. 35–45). New York: Peter Lang.

Lightfoot-Rueda, T., & Peach, R. L. (Eds.). (2015). *Questioning the discourses of human capital theory in early childhood education: Reconceptualizing theory, policy and practice*. New York: Palgrave.

Lilley, I.M. (1967). *Friedrich Froebel: A selection from his writings*. New York: Cambridge University Press.

Mardell, B., & Carpenter, B. (2012). Places to play in Providence: Valuing preschool children as citizens. *Young Children*, 67(5), 78–80.

Marenholtz-Bulow, B. (2007). *How kindergarten came to America*. New York: The Free Press.

Mann, M., & Peabody, E.P. (1870). *Moral culture of infancy and kindergarten guide with music for the plays* (3rd Ed). New York: J.W. Schemerhorn & Co.

National Association for the Education of Young Children (NAEYC). (2009). *Developmentally appropriate practice in early childhood programs serving children from birth through age 8: A position statement of the national association for the education of young children*. Washington, D.C.: author.

Peabody, E.P. (1887). *Education in the home, the kindergarten and the primary school*. London: Swan Sonnenschein, Lowrey & Co.

Peabody, E.P. (1890a). Necessity of kindergarten culture in our systems of public instruction. In H. Barnard (Ed.), Kinder *garten and child culture papers* (pp. 617–642). Hartford: Office of Barnard's American Journal of Education.

Peabody, E.P. (1890b). Froebel's principles and methods in the nursery: A lecture to young Kindergartners. In H. Barnard (Ed.), *Kindergarten and child culture papers* (pp. 561–574). Hartford: Office of Barnard's American Journal of Education.

Peabody, E.P. (1890c). Plea for Froebel's kindergarten as the first grade of primary art education in school. In H. Barnard (Ed.), *Kindergarten and child culture papers* (pp. 673–678). Hartford: Office of Barnard's American Journal of Education.

Peabody, E.P., & Mann, M. (1863). *Moral culture of infancy and kindergarten guide.* Boston: T. O.H.P. Burnham.

Pelo, A. (2008). *Embracing social justice in early childhood education.* Milwaukee, WI: Rethinking Schools.

Project Zero (2017) Children as citizens. Retrieved from pz.harvard.edu/resources/children-are-citizens-book-2017

OECD (2018a). What is PISA? Retrieved from http://www.oecd.org/pisa/aboutpisa/

OECD (2018b). The International Early Learning and Child Well-being Study – The Study. Retrieved from www.oecd.org

OECD (2018c). Definition and Selection of Competencies (DeSeCo). Retrieved from http://www.org/education/skills-beyschool/definitionandselectionofcomop etenciesdeseco

Reese, W.J., & Rury, J. (Eds.). (2008). *Rethinking the history of American education.* New York: Palgrave Macmillan.

Roosevelt, F.D.R. (1941). *The Four Freedoms: The 1941 State of the Union.* January 6. Retrieved from wwwamericanrhetoric.com/speeches/fdrthefourfreedoms.htm

Ross, E.D. (1976). *The kindergarten crusade: The establishment of preschool education in the United States.* Athens, OH: Ohio University Press.

Spring, J. (2011). *The American school: A global context from the Puritans to the Obama era.* New York: McGraw-Hill.

Wolk, S. (1998). *A democratic classroom.* Portsmouth, NH: Heinemann.

Wood, G.H. (1998). Democracy and curriculum. In L. Beyer and M. W. Apple (Eds.), *The curriculum: Problems, politics and possibilities* (2nd ed) (pp. 177–198). New York: State University of New York Press.

6

"SHE DOESN'T *WANT* TO BE A BEAUTIFUL PRINCESS!"

Language, Power, and Teaching for Democracy in the Early Childhood Classroom

Dana Frantz Bentley and Betty Chan

Teaching for Democracy and Social Justice: Classroom Foundations

The difficulty in defining teaching for democracy and social justice is in our practice of not-knowing. It is quite a conundrum because to teach is to know … isn't it? And yet we find in our pedagogy teaching for democracy and social justice work is a matter of questions, not answers (Ayers, Kumashiro, Meiners, Quinn, & Stovall, 2016). It is a matter of wondering, of not-knowing. Daily we wonder:

> What does social justice mean in the life of a young child?
> What does it mean to teach toward democracy?

These questions, and the myriad answers they bring, guide and shape our social justice work as teachers. I can offer no finite definitions of teaching toward democracy and social justice; they are our foundation because they are limitless, too lively to be contained by one definition (Souto-Manning 2013). But in our classroom, they include:

- Children and teachers are members of a community.
- No one "holds" the knowledge. We co-construct our learning.
- We are all citizens with the ability and responsibility to impact the world.
- We question the *status quo*.
- We live in questions.
- Empathy, critical questions, advocacy, and engagement are essential.
- We listen to each other and to the world around us.
- We wonder, and we change.

Classroom Talk: What Is a Princess?

It is a tired Monday afternoon in February, the cold weeks and months of school stretching before us in the PreK classroom. The children huddle together on the carpet, in that weary-yet-wiggly post-nap time, our circle melting in on itself as they lean, and poke, and sometimes listen. Today is Priya's "Word Wizard" day, and she takes the stage with some authority, sitting tall on her stool, slightly above the group, awaiting full attention. I cannot say that I have been looking forward to this Word Wizard day. Priya has chosen the word "princess" to sound out, illustrate, and define for the class, and I am less than enthusiastic. We are working hard to disrupt traditional gender dynamics in the classroom, but our girls in particular cling to these ideas of "princesses," "beauties," and "boyfriends." It feels to me like a failure in my teaching, that we have reached February and I have not managed to make these ideas dissipate. But princess is Priya's word, and princesses we shall have. I sit back, three children melting in my lap, and listen to her.

> "My word is princess," Priya explains. "Princesses are beautiful people with jewels. They are not just normal people. They are beautiful people who live in a kingdom. Other people live in homes," she explains, pointing to a blond-haired, blue-eyed illustration of a princess in a long gown and crown.
> "I agree," Carla says, as Priya calls on her, "but I also think that some princesses live in castles that have jewels with lights that light up at Christmas."
> "Yes, I agree." Priya acquiesces.

My spirits sink deeper as she shares these ideas. Have I taught them nothing at all? The circle as a whole lacks energy. There is a quiet, almost defeated acceptance in the air combined with the agitated need to move onto the next thing. These are princesses. They are beautiful. Fine. Can we go outside now? In a last-ditch attempt to shift the conversation, I raise my hand and Priya calls on me.

> "Are princesses all the same?" I ask, hoping for a miracle.
> "No," says Priya, "some can be Indian princesses, and some can be other languages."

Suddenly, the air in the room shifts. Some of the children sit up a bit taller. Hands begin to shoot up in the air, fingers wiggling, awaiting Priya's acknowledgement. Something is happening.

> "Adliz!" Priya calls.

This is it. Adliz is the social powerhouse in our classroom. Her comment will determine the path of the conversation, for better or for worse …

Classroom Practice: Teaching Toward Democracy

We open this chapter with the story of Priya the Word Wizard because it is a beginning, both of a story, and a beginning of the delicate dance of structure and resistance that characterizes our pedagogy. In the space of this classroom narrative, we witness children following a highly organized system whose very structure is designed to invite resistance, questioning, and criticality – a system of democracy.

"What does it mean to teach toward democracy?" (Mardell & LeeKeenan, 2016)

This question written in large font hangs in the center of our PreK classroom, reminding us as teachers to ask ourselves this question with persistence and consistence. What does it mean to teach toward democracy? As a teacher in today's world, the issue is essential, to know that above all things we are teaching toward democracy.

But what does that mean? In a room filled with four- and five-year-olds, how is democracy grown and practiced? There are many misconceptions around this kind of teaching – the "progressive," "emergent," or "child-centered" philosophy that we espouse as teachers, the most common being that the curriculum is "totally unstructured." I use the last term because it was used with me just a few days ago to describe my classroom. It is also highly inaccurate. Resistance and criticality are grown through careful structure, structure that invites criticality and questions authority. This is the story of education that we tell our children from their very first days in school. School is for questions. School is for resistance (Souto-Manning , 2013).

This chapter tells a story of the structure of teaching for social justice and democracy, the structure of freedom that is developed and is ever-developing in our PreK classroom. Emergent, social justice work with young children is always a balancing act of facilitation, structure, freedom, and faith that provides the space for democracy and leadership from the children (Rinaldi, 2001b; New & Mallory, 1994). Precision and planning create the foundation of our classroom community's space of freedom, expression, and respect.

The classroom narratives that shape this chapter follow a story of teaching for democracy and social justice, making visible the power of the children's thinking, the structure, and the unstructuring that occur in our work together. Within the context of culture circles (Souto-Manning, 2010), the children develop a practice of critical discussion, of leadership, of listening, and of meaning-making in collaboration with the community.

Classroom Talk: Princess, Overthrown

I wait with bated breath for Adliz's response, and the direction the princess journey it will either deny or confirm. Are we off to the realm of damsels in distress? Might there be a better way?

"I agree," Adliz says boldly, then pausing for effect. "This is my idea. Mulan is a princess. She doesn't have a crown or a castle. She doesn't want to be a beautiful princess!"

There is silence for a moment. Is it possible that a princess would not *want* to be beautiful?

"Yeah! I think princesses don't always live in a castle!" adds Aisha, speaking out of turn in her excitement.

"I disagree. This is my idea. They are not real princesses!" Priya protests, re-asserting her construct of the word. But the moment of the blue-eyed damsels has passed, and the deconstruction rages on.

"Some princesses are Chinese!" asserted the usually quiet Maia in a surprisingly loud voice.

"And some are like Moanna!"

"What is a real princess?" murmured Hema wonderingly.

"My idea is that it's just a kind of special person," Priya explained, in revision.

"There are actual real princesses in the world," adds Ryan gruffly, not sure about entering this discussion of princesses but needing to make his point.

"Everyone is special," insists Meagan.

And this is the tipping point. Our tired conversation erupts into debate about the construct of princess, who can be a princess, what princesses look like, and what powers they might have. There is a feeling of beginning here, a feeling of where we might go. I ease into the waterfall of "I agree!" and "I disagree!" that pours into our circle space. I do not know exactly where we are going, but we are certainly in motion.

Classroom Practice: Ritual and Structure

There is a particular practice, a ritual and structure, that guides and shapes the work of words in our classroom. At this point we are joined by my co-teacher, Betty Chan, who brought Word Wizard to our classroom. Below, she explains the work of the Word Wizard.

Word Wizard: Structures

Word Wizard is a dedicated practice in the classroom in which children take on distinct roles. It begins with the role of Word Wizard itself; individual children take on the responsibility and pride in all that the name implies. When a child is the Word Wizard for the day, it becomes their responsibility to come up with a word of their choosing to guide the exploration. The teacher poses the question, "What is a word you know about? What is a word you wonder about?" These open-ended questions lead to the most authentic study of words. Once the word is chosen, the child then draws their representation of the word, uses inventive spelling to curate the word, and comes up with her or his definition of the word. When curating this definition, the children come up with descriptions of their chosen word, personal feelings about the word, and even questions to explore during the conversation. Once this preparation is complete, the rest of the children gather as a group and we have a conversation about the chosen word, led by the child.

(Betty Chan)

Who carries the power of words? What is the power of words in the life of a child? As teachers of young children, we think a great deal about the power of words, "using your words," listening to children's words, and finding our own as we collectively make meaning about the world. Who is speaking? Who is raising her hand? Who is silent? As participants in the larger society, we are highly aware of the power of words, often a power that is denied to children in school settings, where "goodness" or "success" is often defined by their ability to sit quietly and listen (Foucault, 1975/1995). The practice of Word Wizard is a reframing of the role of the power of words as it pertains to who holds the knowledge of the word itself. As illustrated in the children's conversation, as well as Betty's explanation, our classroom practice of Word Wizard places the power of definition in the minds and hands of the children themselves. This is a reframing of the practice of Freirian culture circles, with a direct focus on the powers of language (Souto-Manning, 2010).

"Reading is not walking on words. It is grasping the soul of them" (Freire, 1985, p. 19). These are lofty intentions to live with, certainly, but what do them mean? How might we inspire this perspective in children? How might we rethink the concept of "reading" words with children who do not traditionally "read" yet? Through practices such as Word Wizard, we deliberately invite a "grasping at the soul" of words, a question of passion, of personal investment, and of leadership. The structure of this work invites children to resist the rote acceptance of the *status quo* at the very moment they begin in the formal space of schooling.

Classroom Talk: Princess, Unleashed

The princess discussion was rich with the scent of possibility, and as teachers we moved forward in hot pursuit of non-conformity and the overthrow of gendered constructs. Despite over 16 years of experience, I still laugh regularly over my clearly anticipated paths, and the powerful divergences brought about by the children, if we have the courage to follow them.

Following our princess discussion, we introduced the text, *The Water Princess* (Verde, 2016), which chronicles the life of Princess Gie Gie, who must walk many miles each day to gather water for her family in Burkina Faso. We shared this book in order to explore and imagine new possibilities of "real" princesses, envisioning perhaps a study of diverse princesses in the world. This was not the path the children chose. They listened, rapt, to the book, and the end was followed by that awe of the "good story" silence. They waited. And then their words crashed into the space.

> Andrew said, "But that's not a real book. Like, it's real, but it was a long, long time ago. Not now."
>
> Quest responded, "I disagree! Look on the board! Dana writed down my words on the board (pointing to our dry erase board). This is a real, true book. That's cause I readed it first with her, and sawed the real pictures in the back. It's a real story. Look!"

We looked together at the photos, and read a bit of the biographical information in the back of the book.

> Cyrus added, "So, it's because it's Africa and they don't have water there. Look at the houses! They don't have pipes."
>
> Michael said, "I agree with that. And it's a long time ago. People have water now, but maybe not a long time ago."
>
> Quest added, "I have a different idea! Look at those pictures. Dana, show them! That's in the back of the book. Those are real pictures, not a long time ago. It's now!"
>
> Cyrus said, "Ok, so, I know! We can mail them some water. We can save a little each day, and then mail it on the airplane. There's these shuttles with writing on them. I've seen them!"
>
> Adliz said, "Yeah! We will mail some and then they don't have to walk so far!"

Betty and I scrambled with the unexpected re-routing of the conversation. Water. Not princesses. Water. Mailing water to Africa. Yet again, we found ourselves at the beginning of an unexpected journey, led by words and the worlds that words have the power to invoke.

Classroom Practice: Authority and Its Relinquishing

There is a particular, somewhat uncomfortable, feeling that accompanies the unfolding of a child-led curriculum. The structure, the teaching toward democracy, enables just that: democracy. For us, in our classroom, this inherently means that we do not know exactly where we are going. As teachers, we must be willing to accept this unknown-ness; we cannot ask the children to lead, and then be unwilling to be led by them. But with this rethinking of authority comes a quite disconcerting feeling of free fall. This way of teaching flies in the face of the traditional construct of the "good teacher" (Freire, 2005; Freire, 2000; Greene, 1973), who is always in control of the paths of learning. As we turn the story of the curriculum over to the children, the role of authority in the classroom is

rewritten, and one might expect chaos. Yet, amidst a relinquishing of authority –
the uncertainty of the unknown, and the nausea of free fall – the structure
remains. It carries us – a structure of democracy. And even in the terror of the
fall, there is the tingle of possibility.

Word Wizard and Leadership Intentions

> Upon the completion of the word study, the class gathers to have a conversation led
> by the Word Wizard. Although initially some children still look to the adult for gui-
> dance, we teachers continually turn the leadership back over to the children. After the
> child introduces her or his chosen word, the teacher reads their definition and the
> conversation begins with an invitation to wonder together, led by the Word Wizard.
> We offer the language "I agree," "I disagree," and "this is my idea" as ways to respond
> to their classmates' ideas. Although there is always a sense of dissonance when there is
> disagreement, we make it clear from the beginning that people will have different
> ideas. Through this discord, the children are challenged to think critically about their
> ideas in conjunction with those of their classmates. Through this synthesis, the children
> build not only a wider repertoire of knowledge, but more importantly, the skills
> necessary to engage in critical conversations throughout their lives.
>
> *(Betty Chan)*

The Princess Unleashed narrative represents a curricular story unfolding,
grown out of this delicate balance of teacher facilitation, child leadership, and
democracy. Formal, or "official" spaces signal to children what is valued in
the classroom (Lindfors, 2008); so how do we create spaces that invite resistance and the questioning of the status quo? This process "always involves critical
perception, interpretation, and *rewriting* of what is read" (Freire and Macedo,
1987, pp. 35–36), and in this rewriting, we invite resistance. We invite the
children to crack open the status quo of expectation or social construct, welcoming in dissonance, questions, and possibilities, all within the power of words:

I agree
I disagree
This is my idea.

And the wondering begins again: Can we mail water to Africa?

Classroom Talk: Water Theories:

In the Water Project, the story of Princess Gie Gie was a touchstone in our many
conversations as a classroom community. The children were drawn back to her, a
fairy tale, a real princess, a person who they knew as we struggled to imagine:
How can we help? The idea of mailing water to Africa persisted in the classroom,
and we followed it, questioning, offering new resources, and wondering with the

children. We knew they needed to arrive at a different possibility, but they had to do so in their own way. We read, showed clips from the Georgie Badiel Foundation (on whom the story is based), always resisting the urge to simply say, "A well. We could help dig a well!"

We worked on a series of water explorations at our sensory table, attempting to clean the water of rocks, small stones, sand, and dirt. With each iteration of this process, the children edited, suggesting new tools and examining the "drafts" of the water. Late one morning, weeks into our work with water, we sat around another "water draft," once again wondering together.

> "How are we gonna get the water to them?!" Quest asked in pure, five-year-old frustration. "This was simply taking too long."
>
> "Mail it," offered the ever-pragmatic Simone.
>
> "We have to make more because there's more than two people at Africa," declared Rachel, gesturing authoritatively at the two "clean" jars of water in the center of our rug.

Yes! I thought, and leapt in with a question, "I'm thinking about what Rachel said. They are drinking water every day. Is this enough water for us to send?" The children sat, silent, staring at their work. It was a lot of work to get that water clean. It still didn't look like much water.

> "I wish they lived here," sighed Quest.

Then suddenly,

> "Wait! This is my idea! We could do the same thing that Gie did!" cried Adam. "She dug a holey thingy – a very deep hole – and then water came out! We can do that!"
>
> "I agree!" added Alexis, "They would be happy then because they didn't have water and now they do."
>
> "But how can we get there to dig the hole?" the ever-logical Steven added, returning us to the possibility or impossibility of a field trip to Africa.

Classroom Practice: Environments of Questions

So much hinges on a question. Children's work pivots on the willingness to ask that question, the freedom to ask the question, the ability to live in a question. As we teach toward democracy, and engage in social justice work with children, we are teaching amidst and about questions. We teach to wonder, and about wondering. Our "Water Theories" narrative illustrates children living and working within questions and provocations. These provocations are the different experiences we curate within the classroom, inviting children to explore and to wonder: how can water be cleaned? How does water move? Why do some people have water while others do not? Their (and our) thinking deepens and becomes more complex as we experiment, read new texts, and speak to different sources, all of which inform our journey.

A classroom structure of questions invites two powerful elements in our teaching toward democracy and social justice. The first is the questioning of the *status quo*. The children are invited to question the meanings of words themselves, to unmoor language and the structure of authority in the classroom, opening to new possibilities. In the words of Freire (2000):

> When a word is deprived of its dimension of action, reflection automatically suffers as well; and the word is changed … into verbalism … It becomes an empty word, one which cannot denounce the world, for denunciation is impossible without a commitment to transform, and there is no transformation without action.
>
> *(p. 87)*

These structured yet unstructured classroom spaces are malleable frameworks for transformation; the nature of these spaces represents our commitment to transform with, and to be transformed by the children (Freire, 2000; Souto-Manning 2010). The practice of culture circles also develops the ability to live amidst questions rather than answers. As illustrated by these conversations, and the length of the study, our community is willing to take time to wonder. Children live with many ideas, with dissenting voices expressed (generally) with respect as we work on through our thinking.

The desire to give the simple answer, to lead the children to a solution, is always strong, always pushing us as well. This is the good teacher at our shoulder, insisting that we "know" and "teach" (Green, 1973). But then the work would be ours, not theirs. Then the destination would reify the structure we ask children to reject – the teacher with knowledge, the children waiting to be filled. And so, we question. We question with the physical nature of the classroom, through experiments and explorations. We question with books, offering diverse perspectives and ideas. We question with resources, wondering what new voices we can bring to our thinking. We create a structure of learning built and sustained by questions.

Classroom Talk: Water Stories, Water Connections

The emergence of Adam's idea of a "holey thingy" initiated more discussion of wells and our knowledge of these tools. While the children are very much the leaders of this process, as teachers we wonder, research, and seek resources. We began corresponding with the Gie Gie's foundation, learning about what we might do and the contact that the children might have with the organization. We read portions of the book *One Well: The Story of Water on Earth* (Strauss, 2007), and began to discuss. "What do you notice? What do you think?" we asked the children.

It is April now, and the children are seasoned in the shape of culture circles. They leap confidently into the conversation, impatiently waiting for any "teacher talk" to finish so that they can begin their work of questioning and leading. Hand-raising becomes somewhat optional during these cascades of impassioned discussion, although we have to be hauled back from the brink by teacher reminders when the cacophony becomes incomprehensible.

MICHAEL: "It's a thing – you pump it and goes into the bucket and you take it back."
FRED: "I saw this before in a book. The well was so deep you need a bucket and you need a rope to pull, pull, pull."
PRIYA: "If Africa is so hot, why don't they have water?"
SIMONE: "Because if water was so hot, it dries."
JAMIL: "It's so sandy and hot so the water evaporates."

And our story continues. As I write this, we have spent the morning skyping with Russell Stevens, of the Cape Town Aquarium, where we learned more about water insecurity and "day zero." The children asked the good questions, wondering:

How do you flush your toilet?
How can you have an aquarium? Did the fish take all the water?

Russell's Cape Town story wove into our stories of Gie Gie, making intimate connections on global issues.

ADAM: "Well, they need one of those holey thingys. The well. But how do they dig it? Gie Gie knows how!"
ADLIZ: "Yes, and she's real! We can ask her how to do it. I think. Can we Dana?"

We are onto new theories, hopefully moving the ways we might help in digging wells in a land far away. Apparently, we will need to call Gie Gie to get more information. I hope she won't mind. I hope we can make it happen.

Classroom Practice: Imperfect Advocacies

Before you protest, I want to make very clear that I see the issues of the story we are presenting to you. It is very clear that a classroom of predominantly affluent children, looking at a culture far away, and wanting to help, is filled with issues of power, privilege, and the "othering" of a different people, a different experience. You are right. You win.

And yet, we keep on. We continue the work, imperfect as it is, because it is the work of teaching toward democracy. As we learn with the children, we strive to circumvent the othering, drawing closer through the power of stories, connections, real people like Gie Gie and Russell. We are clear about our limitations, asking questions such as: Will this be enough water for all of the people? Will this solve the problem for everyone? We turn the lens to ourselves, noticing our own water usage, changing the ways we live. We are not perfect. If you are looking for critiques, you will find them. But still, we are better because of this experience. The feeling of the classroom is focused, purposeful, questioning. They know about water. Their understandings of the world have shifted; some people don't have water. We know real stories, real faces; the world that we know has changed.

Through this process, we invite a different conception of child: we frame the children as capable advocates (Rinaldi, 2001a; Cowhey, 2006). Through the democratic process of the classroom, the children have been presented with a genuine problem for which they feel the responsibility to develop a solution. This work is balanced by much free play, snack, and story reading, but the work is there as well, the heartbeat of the classroom that leads the children to new understandings of themselves as citizens who have the power and responsibility to understand and to make change in the world. Imperfect as it is, it is a deeply satisfying imperfection. And I would rather try, replete with mistakes and imperfections, than hide for fear of our mistakes.

Classroom Practice: Inconclusive Conclusions

Ours is a story of dissent, questioning, critical engagement, and social action (although I do not yet know exactly what that action will be). The challenge of writing about the classroom is that our stories happen in real time. They are the circuitous, non-fiction adventures of a room full of young children and two teachers, who are in the process of discovering where they will go. It is messy. And it is very real. So, I do not have an ending to offer you today, a conclusion to tie up our tale securely and neatly. We are still in the telling. I can only leave you where we are now in our wonderings, our theorizations, and our rewritings of the words and worlds around us.

Classroom Talk: Water Princesses in our Room

It is lunchtime, and the classroom is in a constant state of movement. That is something to be aware of in the PreK classroom. As soon as a meal is being consumed, literally everyone needs to get up for something, usually at the same time. We keep at least two mops nearby.

Over the past year, we have discontinued using disposable cups for water and milk, and now ask the children to wash their cups and utensils in the classroom sink. Yes, yes, it is a mess. And we rewash everything. But it's worth the trouble. One challenge of the children-washing-dishes plan is … well, children washing dishes. The water is always running as overzealous washers enjoy the suds and feel of the water pouring over their hands. We roll with it. It's part of the process.

Today, I sat at the table with one of our more truculent eaters, trying to convince her to take just one more bite of her sandwich, totally unaware of the sound of the water running. Suddenly, Dominique's strident voice rang out across the classroom:

"Hey – turn off the water! You're wasting it! You don't need that much!"

Her voice was joined by others.

"Yeah, Gie Gie needs that water!"
"And Russell too!"

The water was expediently turned off. What strikes me about this moment is that it was entirely led by the children. These water stories, stories of Gie Gie and Russell, are alive in their classroom, informing children's own awareness and relationship to water. And, what more could we hope for? That our children might ask a question that we could never have anticipated, reshaped our curricular journey, and arrived at a moment where these new stories are alive and shaping their independent thinking. This is the stuff of democracy, born of a structured questioning of words and worlds.

Faced with the question of, "Why did it stop raining in Cape Town?" we are currently beginning to explore the concept of climate change with our children. Please wish us luck.

Implications of the Research: Practical Applications

While this chapter tells a particular story of one classroom, the practices are accessible to any early childhood classroom. Below I share a few elements that are central to our social justice work with children.

Culture Circles

Culture circles are the central space in which children develop their work of critical conversations (Souto-Manning, 2010). Children learn the practice of leading and listening, integrating thinking and respect for the ideas of others. They are framed as leaders and collaborators in these open exchanges of ideas.

Teachers as Learners

In order to develop social justice work that feels safe for children, teachers must frame themselves as learners and wonderers as well. Teachers must be willing to learn from children, to admit their mistakes, and to make visible the changes in their own thinking. In this way, we become a genuine community, and we model these practices for young children.

Questioning the Status Quo

When children enter formal schooling settings, they are not socially positioned to question the structures or power dynamics that surround them (Foucault, 1975/1995). Within our work, we must teach children that school is a place for questioning, for wondering about "the rules" or the "one story" that they know. We must sanction the school space as a place where they might question the world.

Children as Advocates

In US culture, children are not framed as powerful or able to make change. Our classrooms are a space in which to change that, to support children in their ability to engage in critical conversations, and to lead real advocacy. Children have the ability to be change makers, and we have the opportunity to begin that journey with them.

Structured Resistance

Teaching toward democracy and social justice is not a free-for-all. As illustrated in this chapter, conversations, project planning, and goal setting are all facilitated by structures that support children in developing their social justice work. Take time to teach children the structure of dissent and resistance, through rich and respectful conversation, through sharing common language such as "I agree" and "I disagree," and through collaboration in the planning and goal-setting inherent in this work.

References

Ayers, W., Kumashiro, K., Meiners, E., Quinn, T., & Stovall, D. (2016). *Teaching toward democracy: Educators as agents of change* (2nd ed.). New York: Routledge.

Cowhey, M. (2006). *Black ants and Buddhists: Thinking critically and teaching differently in the primary grades.* Portsmouth, NH: Stenhouse.

Freire, P. (1985). Reading the world and reading the word: An interview with Paulo Freire. *Language Arts* 62(1), 15–21.

Freire, P. (2000) *Pedagogy of the oppressed* (30th anniversary ed.). New York: Continuum.

Freire, P. (2005). *Teachers as cultural workers: Letters to those who dare to teach.* New York: Routledge.

Freire, P., & Macedo, D. (1987). *Literacy: Reading the word and the world.* Westport, CT: Bergin & Garvey.

Foucault, M. (1975/1995). *Discipline and punish: The birth of the prison* (A. Sheridan, Trans.). New York: Vintage Books.

Greene, M. (1973). *Teacher as stranger: educational philosophy for the modern age.* Belmont, CA: Wadsworth.

Lindfors, J.W. (2008). *Children's language: Connecting, reading, writing, and talk.* New York: Teachers College Press.

Mardell, B. & LeeKeenan, D. (2016) "If Trump wins, my family will have to go back to El Salvador…": Talking to young children about the election (and other challenging topics). Presentation at the Lesley University Innovations Series, Cambridge, MA.

New, R. S., & Mallory, B. L. (1994). Introduction: The ethics of inclusion. In B. Mallory and R. New (Eds.), *Diversity and developmentally appropriate practices: Challenges for early childhood curriculum* (pp. 1–13). New York: Teachers College Press.

Rinaldi, C. (2001a). Documentation and assessment: What is the relationship? In *Making learning visible: Children as individual and group learners*. Reggio Emilia, Italy: Reggio Children.

Rinaldi, C. (2001b). Infant-toddler centers and preschools as places of culture. In *Making learning visible: Children as individual and group learners*. Reggio Emilia, Italy: Reggio Children.

Souto-Manning, M. (2010). *Freire, teaching, and learning: Culture circles across contexts*. New York: Peter Lang.

Souto-Manning, M. (2013). *Multicultural teaching in the early childhood classroom: Approaches, strategies, and tools, preschool-2nd grade*. New York: Teachers College Press.

Strauss, R. (2007). *One well: The story of water on earth*. Toronto, Canada: Kids Can Press.

Verde, S., & Badiel, G. (2016). *The water princess*. New York: G.P. Putnam's Sons Books for Young Readers.

7

ACTIVISM IN THEIR OWN RIGHT

Children's Participation in Social Justice Movements

Lacey Peters

Defining Social Justice

When I think about social justice, the words that come to mind are freedom, human rights, happiness, equity and fairness, appreciation, diversity, acceptance, understanding, compassion, empathy, care, and community. Social justice means eradicating injustices, making the invisible visible, creating inclusive and caring spaces, valuing people's diverse backgrounds and abilities, fostering acceptance, and appreciating the richness of our pluralistic society. Nieto (2006) defines social justice as a "political project" because it is about power. When there is social justice, there is shared decision making and mutually beneficial outcomes. Nieto sees social justice as being a "democratic project" that requires active participation among all people.

Participation can take many forms; people can engage in social justice actively or through peripheral participation. Children's socialization is influenced by their participation in their cultures and communities, and their participation is fluid and dynamic and (re)shapes the ways in which adults view and act in the world. Malaguzzi (1994) stated that "children are very sensitive and can see and sense very quickly the spirit of what is going on among adults in their world" (p. 3). Although participation is vital to elevating justice, many social groups are excluded from dialogues or decision-making, including children and younger people. More often than not, adults exclude children from important social justice activities because of fears and anxieties they have about exposing children to complex social issues too early. Childhood is considered to be a period of innocence and adults attempt to shield younger people from the darker sides of the human experience, due largely to the belief that they are inexperienced, less capable, and inferior because of their young age (MacNaughton, Hughes, & Smith, 2009).

A key element to social justice is listening to all people, and understanding their thoughts and opinions on matters that affect their daily life experiences. Children are known to express themselves in "100 different languages" (Malaguzzi, 1998), yet it is not very often their views and perspectives are sought or taken into consideration. Corsaro (2015) argues that children and childhood are constrained by existing social structures and societal expectations (e.g. preconceptions of children and childhoods). Many adults assume they know what it is like to be a child today because they were all once children themselves. Mandell (1988) refers to this as the "adult ideological bias" and believes that it must be diminished in order for children's views to be taken seriously. While children's perspectives can be different from adult perspectives, children's perspectives are not inferior (MacNaughton, Hughes, & Smith, 2009). In order to challenge the dominant perspectives of children as innocent or inferior beings, adults and children should build shared understandings about their life experiences. Once shared understandings are established, adults and younger people can work together with greater empathy and broader perspective to influence change. Further, by privileging the voices of children, we can give deeper meaning their concerns about their social worlds and the ways in which they try to make things better.

Collective action is another key element of social justice. As a means to fight for social justice, people turn to advocacy and activism to elevate peace, equity, acceptance, and inclusion. Advocacy is defined as the act or process of supporting a cause or proposal; whereas activism is a doctrine or practice that emphasizes direct vigorous action especially in support of or opposition to one side of a controversial issue (Merriam-Webster Dictionary, 2019b; 2019a). The results of the 2016 election in the US have (re)ignited activism, and more and more people show an increased interest or responsibility in confronting socio-political injustices. Yet as different forms of advocacy take shape, questions emerge about the inclusion of marginalized groups, including young people. It is not unusual to hear adults wonder if children understand complex social issues such as racism, xenophobia, sexism, or other forms of prejudice. Adults also ask, "Should children be brought to marches? Can they protest?" or "What can they really do?" The agency and activism of children/youth are thus diminished and the views and voices of younger people are rarely taken seriously.

Social Justice and Young Children

Social justice in early childhood is typically associated with topics related to equity, diversity, acceptance, and inclusion. Early childhood educators are encouraged to facilitate learning experiences related to family, community, belonging, culture, caring for the earth, or ecological teaching. Pelo (2008) describes social justice in early childhood education as being a multi-faceted approach that encompasses anti-bias, culturally sensitive teaching, addresses issues of fairness and unfairness, and privileges cultural funds of knowledge. Early childhood is a time when children are constructing their sense of self, and a number of factors have influence over their concept of self-esteem or self-worth. Anti-Bias Education (Derman-Sparks & Edwards, 2010) is often used to address social justice education in early childhood. Its aims are to help adults and children alike embrace their diverse backgrounds and social identities. There are four goals of anti-bias education and these involve building self-awareness and positive social identities, appreciating and being comfortable with diversity, recognizing unfairness, and taking action against prejudice and/or discriminatory actions.

Whereas certain topics were once taboo, adults who work with young children are increasingly being encouraged to discuss issues related to race/racism, gender identity and expression, family structures, class differences, and other topics around personal and social identities. Children show us their capacities to grapple with complex issues in numerous ways. Literature on the sociology of children and childhood uses the term "agency" to talk about the potential for children to have autonomy, power, and influence over the construction of their own life experiences. In various contexts, there is a growing recognition of children as "public actors" or "social actors." The phrase, social actors, is used to talk about children as contributing members of society who have the power to influence processes and structures around them (James, Jenks, & Prout, 1998). Sociologists also refer to children as "social agents." According to Mayall (2002) as cited in Mason and Hood (2011, p. 490), social agents are understood as actors whose contributions to interactions make "a difference to a relationship or decision, to the workings of a set of social assumptions or constraints" (p. 490).

History of Children's Participation and Activism in the United States

There is a long and often overlooked history of children's participation in the United States. Children played an integral role in the Civil Rights Movement in the 1960s. Younger people attended meetings, marches, and demonstrations, engaged in violence, and were sometimes imprisoned. Ruby Bridges was six years old when she attended the first desegregated school in the United States in 1960. Images of her entering the school building and video footage of that morning conveyed the harsh reality of hatred and bigotry. In an interview, Ruby mentioned that her parents told her that she was going to a new school and that she needed to behave. She pointed out that she was unaware of her role in history, as it is difficult for adults to explain to a young child the significance and implications of such a life experience (Bridges, 2013). The "Children's Crusade" in Birmingham, Alabama in 1963 was a pivotal moment in the Civil Rights movement in the United States. It was during this time that adults witnessed the power of youth participation and activism in influencing change. Yet, as Angela Davis recounts, the role children played is often forgotten and, in this moment, their influence was forgotten in the sense of "breaking the silence regarding racism" (Davis, 2016, p. 37). During the "Freedom Summer" of 1964, 40 freedom schools were established, serving close to 2,500 students, including parents and grandparents. The freedom schools created opportunities for black people to learn through a progressive curriculum that sought to help young individuals learn that they could become public and political actors.

Children in other marginalized groups have also had a strong influence on the course of history. Indigenous children challenged colonizing and assimilative forces in schools. Throughout time, children and youth have been involved in activism around child labor, social class issues, pay equity, education reform, better school conditions, stronger communities, gun control, among other issues.

We continue to see younger people engaged in social action today. At 15 years old, Malala Yousaufzi became a revolutionary in promoting girls' education after getting shot in the head for going to school, although it is important to note that she and her family had spent her lifetime trying to elevate gender equity in education to Pakistan. Marlee Dias was 11 years old when she launched "#1000blackgirlbooks," with the goal of collecting 1,000 books about black girls. She began this crusade after growing frustrated by the lack of diverse representation in children's literature. Indigenous youth are credited for starting the opposition movement to halt the construction of the Dakota Pipeline across the Standing Rock Sioux Reservation. In 2018, the youth of Parkland, Florida launched "March for our Lives," a student-led demonstration, that brought people to the streets to advocate for gun control. At one of the largest demonstrations for March for our Lives in Washington DC, 11-year-old Naomie Waddler gave an impassioned speech about the disproportionate number of black girls who are killed from gun violence.

Each of these examples demonstrates the power of younger people's advocacy and influence. Many people in the United States are inspired by the actions of youth today and look to them for hope. They believe that they will be instrumental in shaping the future into a better place. While children/youth are in fact carrying out important work, their efforts aren't wholly recognized as being effective because they are not yet 18 years old – the age of majority in the US. Further, older children and youth are primarily recognized for doing important equity and advocacy work.

Children's Activism in the Current Socio-Political Climate

My own interest in children's participation in social justice movements grew after the 2016 presidential election. A number of large marches and demonstrations were organized in New York City, and throughout the country, in response to Donald Trump taking office, and in opposition to racism, xenophobia, homophobia, and other forms of prejudice and oppression. As I marched through the streets of Manhattan, I could not help but notice the children and youth in attendance. Many of them were holding signs or standing along-side adults to convey their anger and discontent or desire for change. Some of the signs I read included messages like "Not My Future" or "Keep Us Safe in School" and "If Kids Are Old Enough to be Shot They Are Old Enough to Have an Opinion on Being Shot." At the March for Our Lives, I saw two children selling water and snacks to people in the street. Each dollar they raised would be donated to an organization that aims to end gun violence.

As I observed children at marches, I wondered about how are children making sense of their participation in these moments and movements. Did adults ask these younger people if they wanted to attend, or did they just bring them along without consultation? Are they there as informed citizens? Have they been used as props or in a more tokenistic way? To what extent are adults having conversations with children about current events and their responses to them? I was also curious to know what it was like for them to experience social action or to be a part of these demonstrations. How did the children create their signs? Was this a collaborative effort and did more knowledgeable others (Vygotsky, 1978) build shared understandings around the messages each person wanted to share?

Around the same time, I was also a part of an organizing committee that planned a Children's March in Brooklyn, New York. People of all ages attended the first meeting, and I was encouraged to see that younger people were a part of the decision-making process at the onset. As we continued to organize the march, however, I noticed that children stopped attending the meetings and that their views and opinions were left out of conversations about different aspects of that day. Adults also overrode some of the youth's perspectives because they did not like their ideas (e.g. a design for a logo) or were unsure about how or whether to include their ideas in the demonstra-tion and march. This uncertainty created tension between adults' perceptions of what they wanted the march to be about and what younger people thought was important. With this experience, I saw first-hand the ways in which well-intentioned adults move children and youth to the periphery and diminish their participatory roles in social action.

More recently, I have been involved with an organization called Little Chairs Big Differences; a primary intention of this organization is to build conversations around identity and intersectionality with young children and adults within the early childhood community. The organization is comprised of individuals who hold a deep commitment to shifting people's mindsets about the potential and possibilities of young children to build critical con-sciousness and to take action. Little Chairs holds an annual meeting to provide educators and care providers with ideas and actions they can take to foster inclusion and acceptance. There are also events whereby children are invited to attend and unpack issues related to race and racism, as well as gender identity and expression.

Children's Participation in Social Justice

There are different models of children's participation used to help adults understand the ways in which children can be included in decision making. For instance, Roger Hart (1992) conceptualized the ladder of participation, building on this work of Shier (2009; 2001) who uses the metaphor "pathway" to describe a trajectory of children's participation. Shier conceptualized pathways to participation to help adults see how children's involvement in social action ranges from tokenism to children sharing power and responsibility in decision making. Lundy (2007) looks carefully at the United Nations Convention on the Rights of the Child (UNCRC; Office of the United Nations High Commissioner for Human Rights, 1989), specifically examining Article 12 and children's right to express themselves. In Lundy's view, children must be provided with space, voice, audience, and influence in order for their views to be adequately heard.

Numerous "openings" (Shier, 2001) for advocacy present themselves in children's daily lives, and adults can use these pivotal moments to co-construct opportunities with children and youth to support their participation and engagement in social action. More and more frequently adults are learning about younger people's abilities to understand complex social issues and how children and youth make meaning of certain situations. This in turn leads to obligatory or embedded practices around involving children and youth. Together, people of all ages can develop plans or solutions to eradicate or diminish unfairness, injustice, or negativity. Adults and children must generate and sustain shared understandings of cultural routines, rules, and mores. Then "guided participation" (Rogoff, 2003) can occur when adults and children are both active participants in the construction of knowledge, structure activities together, and mutually benefit from any interactions. Adults are responsible for guiding an overall experience, and children engage in the management of their own learning and processing. For instance, when children are being and becoming part of a family or community, they familiarize themselves with the nuances of cultural routines and practices.

Challenges persist in children's participation and involvement in promoting social good; many adults still maintain the idea that children are too young, inexperienced, or incapable to talk about or engage with complex social issues. These ideas are particularly true for children who are younger than age eight. Additionally, there are many marginalized social groups that find themselves unable to engage in social action. Systems of oppression and societal barriers reduce the "cultural capital" (Bourdieu, 1986) of people of Color, people living in low income communities, and people who speak languages other than English. Cultural capital is a concept used to describe the ways culture and class are used to reinforce social stratification. Adults may also perceive children's interests in social action to be situated at the micro-level and restrict their participation because of the bias there. Adults also are nervous about relinquishing power to children and youth in fear that young people will misuse their rights. Despite the challenges, there are many things adults can do to elevate children's participation in social action.

Strategies for Promoting Social Justice with Children and Youth

Help Children Understand Their Influence

Research demonstrates the number of ways children learn about their social worlds, process complex social issues, form biases or judgments at early ages, and engage in social action. We also know that children face discrimination and prejudice because of their age, race or cultural background, gender, dis/ability, and other social identities. The development of empathy and understanding is a cornerstone of early childhood teaching and learning. Adults bring a lot of attention to helping children develop self-regulation and self-awareness. These learnings can evolve into shared understandings, relationship building, and cooperative and collaborative play and learning. Scholars have shown that infants and toddlers actively construct knowledge about others and the ideas of fairness and responsiveness in play activities (Hamlin, Wynn, & Bloom, 2007). Additionally, research demonstrates that children two years of age have already constructed ideas around morality and social justice (Brownell & Kopp, 2007).

Literature is a powerful way to help children build awareness around the diversity of our social worlds. Literature also brings attention to and explains social justice issues, in addition to showing children how they can take action. Children's books provide "windows and mirrors" (Bishop, 1990) and can reflect one's own life experiences or can broaden worldviews by showing that there are other ways of living and being. In recent years organizations such as "We Need Diverse Books" have advocated for diverse representation in children's books and are making significant gains in creating characters and stories that reflect the beauty of our pluralistic society.

Teachers have a unique opportunity to bring critical pedagogies into early childhood and can use children's literature or can teach lessons that combat the monocultural curricular models premised in White, middle-class norms (Long, Souto-Manning, & Vasquez, 2016). By using children's literature as a teaching tool, adults generate dialogue about the messages or issues that are embedded within a story's plot. Zeece (2009) emphasizes the role open-minded adults and children's literature play in fostering kindness and caring behaviors in children. By coupling intentional teaching with books that are inclusive of diverse back-grounds, and abilities that convey messages of fairness, kindness, and social justice, children engage in critical dialogue around social action and activism.

Create "Openings and Opportunities" for Children to Participate in Social Action

Schools are sites for social action and change, and there is a growing body of literature around teachers' engagement with social justice in early childhood. Further, educational leaders have the responsibility to prioritize social justice work in schools and care settings. In reference to how adults can support children in social justice work, Boutte (2008) explains the shortcomings of teachers' professional learning in fully addressing issues of equity and diversity. She writes, "Few of us have developed tools to address difficult issues such as discrimination and oppression, and we likely naïvely believe that if we respect the individual child, all will be well" (p. 165). Hyland (2010) asserts that the failure to counter the White and Eurocentric frames of reference in schools is inherently unjust, and urges early childhood educators to engage in "equity pedagogies" and culturally relevant teaching. Anti-bias education (Derman-Sparks & Edwards, 2010) is an approach that can be used to help translate complex topics into ideas that children can more easily understand. Yet, as Bentley (2012) points out, "These are not easy practices; it is far easier to say that we believe in multiculturalism, diversity, and social justice than it is to actually find and implement the meaning in the lives of our young students" (p. 195). I believe early childhood educators have a moral imperative to address social justice and anti-bias education.

Manifestations of injustice occur in classrooms in a myriad of ways, whether as a result of implicit bias impacting how a child is seen or heard, pressure to conform to standardized approaches to teaching, or peers excluding one another based on perceived difference(s). It is important to note, however, that children are entrenched in systems that are inherently racist or discriminatory. When contemplating how to create openings and opportunities to counter discriminatory practices, adults must first think about how to disrupt dominant approaches to curriculum and teaching and we must constantly challenge deficit views of children and families in schools and society.

Therefore, in looking at children's advocacy and activism, it is essential to understand what teachers are doing to embed social justice curriculum into the daily life experiences of the youngest learners. Pelo (2008) shares a collection of narrative accounts of teachers and children's experiences in early childhood settings to illustrate the power of social justice and ecological teaching. Teachers share examples of how they advocated for equity alongside children, using young people's ideas as a catalyst for change. In one chapter, Katie Kissinger (2008) writes that she and children in her Head Start class wrote to Lakeshore Learning Materials Company (a large educational toy manufacturer) and explained to them that they had made a mistake when they created a figure sitting in a wheelchair. A child noticed that the feet were not resting on the footrest, and that in reality this would lead to discomfort or tiredness. Cole and Verwayne (2018) discuss anti-racist pedagogies in early childhood. The authors unpack the possibilities and challenges that Ms. Verwayne, a kindergarten teacher, the parents in her classroom, along with the children, experienced when she decided to bring racial identity into the curriculum. McLennan (2018) describes the power of integrated learning and used math-based lessons that occurred during a school-wide food drive to showcase ways teachers could maximize their instructional time to encompass the many facets of prosocial learning. This experience enabled children to meet content-based objectives and at the same time connect to their broader community.

Build and Maintain Critical Dialogue with Children

Young children care a lot about fairness, equity, and justice. In my own research on children's perspectives about going to kindergarten, I learned about the ways in which it is hard for them to make sense of teachers' approaches to classroom management. In one example, a child was confused about why their friend always had their name on "yellow" when the teacher would laugh at their jokes. Often teachers will use "stoplights" in their classrooms as a tool for classroom management. The stoplight is a way to reflect a continuum of good and bad behavior, with green being good and red being bad. Yellow indicates that a child is not demonstrating good behavior, but not serious enough to fall on the red. In the case of the child interviewed, what seemed to be a positive interaction was met with a negative consequence. Adults often withhold information from children as a way to maintain control of children's behaviors. Behavior charts like the one alluded to by the child are also indicative of the ways children are shamed in classroons and these management tools take away their agency. In contrast, there are programs that encourage younger people to "fill buckets," to encourage them to be good citizens or to be caring people. This approach stems from a book entitled *Have You Filled Your Bucket Today?* (McCloud & Messing, 2006) a story that encourages children to engage in acts of kindness and appreciation in order to "fill a bucket" or to be a caring individual. Additionally, curricular frameworks have been created to help children learn how to be "upstanders" and to speak up or act when they witness or experience teasing, bullying, or other forms of oppression. Additionally, engaging in culturally responsive and sustaining pedagogies enriches children's prosocial behavior(s). Within responsive classrooms, adults use inclusive practices and embrace "funds of knowledge" (Moll, Amanti, Neff, & Gonzalez, 1992) to build meaningful relationships with children and families. Rather than imposing adult expectations on prosocial behavior, teachers and children are co-constructing ideas about fairness and respect.

Schools also have the potential to help children understand that they are citizens in their own right and that their views and perspectives should be given "due weight." Due weight is a phrase used in the United Nations Convention on the Rights of the Child and is used to explain how factors such as a child's age or individual abilities should influence the extent to which their voices should be heard.

In the current climate of public school in the United States, it can be difficult for teachers to balance all aspects of the curriculum and there can be a constant push and pull between addressing more academically-oriented content and social-emotional related work. However, it is absolutely necessary for teachers to seek out the "wiggle room" (Nieto, 2019) to find a balance.

Mutually Structuring Children's Participation in Social Action

Adults and children can unite in collective action. Parents and other family members must be included in the conversations around social justice. In doing so, teachers and children can help build the shared understandings needed to carry forward social justice work. Silva (2016) emphasizes the use of children's lived experiences to engage children in critical multicultural curriculum. She worked with one art teacher over the course of a school year to foster consciousness building, critical thinking, reflection, and ultimately collective action with first grade students. This teacher, Ms. Monet, aimed to connect children's lived experiences, and the lived experiences of various artists, to broader social issues. Silva (2016) points out that Ms. Monet was concerned that children are told about social issues, but are rarely given explanations about why these problems exist. In a similar vein, Duncan-Andrade (2009) discusses the notion of "hope deferred" and uses it to explain how teachers often construct idealistic notions of hope and change without acknowledging the deeply rooted issues within underserved and under-resourced communities. He then discusses "audacious hope" as a way to transform educational models so that they bend toward culturally sustaining pedagogies.

In many cases, families are extending conversations with children to broaden their understandings about living in their social worlds. A number of organizations and online forums have been established to help adults talk to children about different social justice issues. "Raising Race Conscious Children" is a blog space where people share ideas on how to build conversation with children about racism and racial justice.

Strategies for Children's Social Action

In her 2010 TED Talk entitled, What Adults Can Learn from Kids, Adora Stivak urges people to rethink the meaning of "childish" and argues that it should no longer be associated with "irresponsible behavior and irrational thinking." She then asks, "Who's to say that certain types of irrational thinking aren't exactly what the world needs?" (Stivak, 2010). Children carry a wealth of ideas about their social worlds, and adults must honor these as being important and valid. Let's help children carry these ideas into action. At the most basic level, children and youth can engage in social justice by being kind, and getting to know their neighbors, friends, and family members in deep ways. Adults and children can participate in service projects together. Adults should continue to bring children to marches and demonstrations, and, as they prepare for them, remember to build dialogue around the purpose of attending and develop plans for future action(s).

Pictures of children help adults see social injustices in a different way and these portrayals can evoke strong emotions. More recently, we have seen pictures of refugee and immigrant children in the mainstream media. This imagery is used to depict the dehumanization of certain cultural groups and the human rights violations of people the world over. Pictures by children tell another story. Photo-voice is an approach to qualitative research that can be used to elevate children's voices and perspectives. Through photo-voice children can use a particular lens to shed insight on the important facets of their lives. Photography and art can also be used to help children express their hopes and desires for the future.

In September 2016, a letter that a six-year-old boy wrote to Barack Obama went viral on the internet as he asked the president to give permission for a Syrian boy to live with him and his family. Letter writing campaigns are an effective way by which children can share their opinions and hopes for a different world with broader audiences. Children can also use their drawing and writing skills to create posters to share within their schools or communities. One recent afternoon, I was walking by a park and public-school playground in New York City. Posted on the fence surrounding the play areas were posters children created to remind adults to throw garbage away and to keep their space clean. The public display of children's posters reminds adults that younger people have a voice and that they are an integral part of the community. Adults can work with children to draft their letters or to create their signs and help them strategize ways to get their views across – whether it be finding out where to send letters or emails, or giving them a chance to post their signs and posters.

There is no doubt children play important and influential roles in society and engage in social action in their everyday lives. Younger people's participation in advocacy and activism has the transformative power to dispel the ageist perspectives that are prohibitive. It is important for adults to seek out the openings and opportunities to elevate children's position(s) in society. This chapter discussed some ways to promote children's participation including building awareness on children's participatory rights, opening dialogue with children (and adults), and taking action. There are a variety of other strategies for promoting children's advocacy and activism. The question that remains is what other approaches can be employed to advance children's participatory roles in social justice movements?

References

Bentley, D. F. (2012). "Rights are the words for being fair": Multicultural practice in the early childhood classroom. *Early Childhood Education Journal*, 40(4), 195–202.

Bishop, R. S. (1990). "Mirrors, windows, and sliding glass doors." *Perspectives*, 6(3), ix–xi.

Bourdieu, Pierre (1986). *The forms of capital*. In J. G. Richardson (Ed.), *Handbook of theory and research for the sociology of education*. New York: Greenwood Press.

Boutte, G. S. (2008). Beyond the illusion of diversity: How early childhood teachers can promote social justice. *The Social Studies*, 99(4), 165–173.

Bridges, R. (2013, November 19). Ruby Bridges goes to school. Retrieved from https://www.pbs.org/wnet/african-americans-many-rivers-to-cross/video/ruby-bridges-goes-to-school/.

Brownell, C. A., & Kopp, C. B. (2007). Transitions in toddler socioemotional development. In C. A. Brownell and C. B. Kopp (Eds.), *Socioemotional development in the toddler years: Transitions and transformations* (pp. 1–40). New York: Guildford Publications

Cole, K., & Verwayne, D. (2018). Becoming upended: Teaching and learning about race and racism with young children and their families. *YC Young Children*, 73(2), 34–43.

Corsaro, W. A. (2015). *The sociology of childhood*. Thousand Oaks, CA: Sage Publications.

Davis, A. Y. (2016). *Freedom is a constant struggle: Ferguson, Palestine, and the foundations of a movement*. Chicago: Haymarket Books.

Derman-Sparks, L., & Edwards, J. O. (2010). *Anti-bias education for young children and ourselves 2012*. Washington, DC: NAEYC.

Duncan-Andrade, J. (2009). Note to educators: Hope required when growing roses in concrete. *Harvard Educational Review*, 79(2), 181–194.

Hamlin, J. K., Wynn, K., & Bloom, P. (2007). Social evaluation by preverbal infants. *Nature*, 450(7169), 557.

Hart, R. A. (1992). *Children's participation: From tokenism to citizenship* (inness92/6).

Hyland, N. E. (2010). Social justice in early childhood classrooms. *Young Children*, 65(1), 82–90.

James, A., Jenks, C., & Prout, A. (1998). *Theorizing childhood*. New York: Routledge.

Kissinger, K. (2008). Holding Nyla: Lessons from an inclusion classroom. In A. Pelo (Ed.), *Rethinking early childhood education* (pp. 147–150). Milwaukee: Rethinking Schools.

Long, S., Souto-Manning, M., & Vasquez, V. (Eds.). (2016). *Courageous leadership in early childhood education: Taking a stand for social justice*. New York: Teachers College Press.

Lundy, L. (2007). "Voice" is not enough: Conceptualising Article 12 of the United Nations Convention on the Rights of the Child. *British Educational Research Journal*, 33(6), 927–942.

MacNaughton, G., Hughes, P., & Smith, K. (Eds.). (2009). *Young children as active citizens: Principles, policies and pedagogies*. Newcastle upon Tyne: Cambridge Scholars Publishing.

Malaguzzi, L. (1994). Your image of the child: Where teaching begins. *Child Care Information Exchange*, 52–52.

Malaguzzi, L. (1998). Part I: History. *The hundred languages of children: The Reggio Emilia approach—advanced reflections*, 49, Greenwich, CT: Abelex Publishing Corporation.

Mandell, N. (1988). The least-adult role in studying children. *Journal of Contemporary Ethnography*, 16(4), 433–467.

Mason, J., & Hood, S. (2011). Exploring issues of children as actors in social research. *Children and Youth Services Review*, 33(4), 490–495.

Mayall, B. (2002). *Towards a sociology for childhood: thinking from children's lives*. Buckingham, UK: Open University Press.

McCloud, C., & Messing, D. (2006). *Have you filled a bucket today. A guide to daily happiness for kids*. Brighton, MI: Bucket Fillosophy.

McLennan, D. P. (2018). Counting kindness: A food drive inspires rich mathematical thinking. *YC Young Children*, 73(1), 63–68.

Merriam-Webster.com. (2019a). Activism. Retrieved February 17, 2019 from https://www.merriam-webster.com/dictionary/activism

Merriam-Webster.com. (2019b). Advocacy. Retrieved February 17, 2019 from https://www.merriam-webster.com/dictionary/advocacy

Moll, L. C., Amanti, C., Neff, D., & Gonzalez, N. (1992). Funds of knowledge for teaching: Using a qualitative approach to connect homes and classrooms. *Theory into Practice*, 31(2), 132–141.

Nieto, S. (2006). Teaching as political work: Learning from courageous and caring teachers. The Longfellow Lecture at the Child Development Institute, Sarah Lawrence College.

Nieto, S., & López, A. (2019). *Teaching, a life's work: A mother–daughter dialogue*. New York: Teachers College Press.

Office of the United Nations High Commissioner for Human Rights. (1989). *Convention on the rights of the child*. New York, NY: United Nations.

Pelo, A. (2008). *Rethinking early childhood education*. Milwaukee: Rethinking Schools.

Rogoff, B. (2003). *The cultural nature of human development.* Oxford: Oxford University Press.

Shier, H. (2001). Pathways to participation: Openings, opportunities and obligations. *Children & Society*, 15(2), 107–117.

Shier, H. (2009). *20 pathways to participation revisited.* In B. Percy-Smith and N. Thomas (Eds.), *A handbook of children and young people's participation* (pp. 215–229). London: Routledge.

Silva, J. M. (2016). Reading, writing, and revolution: Facilitating social activism in first grade. *The Social Studies*, 107(5), 171–178.

Stivak, A. (2010, February). What adults can learn from kids [Video file]. TED talk. Retrieved from https://www.ted.com/talks/adora_svitak?language=en.

Vygotsky, L. (1978). Interaction between learning and development. *Readings on the Development of Children*, 23(3), 34–41.

Zeece, P. D. (2009). Using current literature selections to nurture the development of kindness in young children. *Early Childhood Education Journal*, 36(5), 447–452.

8

THE CULTURAL POLITICS OF CHILDHOOD EDUCATION FOR DEMOCRACY IN REGGIO EMILIA'S *SERVIZI DELL'INFANZIA*

Rebecca S. New

Over 25 years ago, in an article about social studies, Carol Seefeldt described the joy, excitement and "euphoria of freedom" following democratic revolutions in central and eastern Europe. She bemoaned the brevity of those celebrations, given the "difficult, violent and life-threatening task of building new social and economic systems" (Seefeldt, 1993, p. 9); and urged teachers – even those of very young children – to promote children's active participation in the democratic life of the classroom. She emphasized the need for shared decision-making, collaboration and reflection as essential to promoting children's critical thinking and empathy, vital dispositions of curious, "knowledgeable and connected" children with "regard for each other as human beings" (Ibid). That these words were written for teachers of young children, rather than for economists or political scientists, is noteworthy. There was no reference to early childhood educators in Reggio Emilia, Italy, whose ideals and *praxis* resonate with many of those outlined by Seefeldt.

When first introduced to US early childhood educators in the late 1980s, little attention was directed to Reggio Emilia's political history as a source of pedagogical practices (New, 1990).[1] Reggio Emilia's example was appropriated by US early childhood educators (this author included) to assist in our own professional controversies, including potential risks of pre-academic instruction, the benefits of child-initiated versus teacher directed instruction, and the limits of NAEYC's guidelines for developmentally appropriate practice (DAP) (Bredekamp, 1987). Within a decade, Reggio Emilia had inspired a surge of publications on "the Reggio Emilia approach" (Edwards, Gandini & Forman, 1993, 1998; New, 1997) and hosted delegations to Italy for those who wanted to see for themselves. Illustrative of its influence in the US were references to Reggio Emilia as exemplars of quality environments and challenging pedagogy in revised DAP guidelines (Bredekamp & Copple, 1997). By the turn of the century "doing Reggio" was shorthand for US educators attempting to incorporate educational practices from this Italian city into their own childcare and early education programs for young children.

Today, tens of thousands of early childhood and teacher educators actively explore various features of the Reggio Emilia approach; and the existence-proof fact of Reggio Emilia serves as a touchstone for those who believe that young children *and their* teachers are capable of much more than is typically allowed or encouraged. And yet, in spite of growing concerns about increasingly standardized curriculum and assessment mandates in increasingly non-standardized classrooms amid heightened awareness of educational inequities and social injustices in US society at large, few outside Western Europe (c.f., Dahlberg & Moss, 2005) have closely examined Reggio Emilia's example of an ethical education for democracy.

This chapter draws on several sources in describing Reggio Emilia's interpretation of an early education for democracy, beginning with decades of study of Italian child care and early education in collaboration with Reggio Emilian and other Italian colleagues.[2] The scholarship of psychological anthropologists and contemporary cultural models theory also inform this discussion, aided by a review of English and Italian literatures in which the people of Reggio Emilia speak for themselves. Primary aims of this chapter are to describe the historic roots and political underpinnings of pedagogical characteristics most often associated with the Reggio Emilia approach and to highlights ways in which those political values are reflected in their *servizi dell'infanzia,* [3] (municipally funded early childhood services) including the guiding principles of transparency, debate and community engagement. The "unpacking" of Reggio Emilia's commitment to children, families and teachers will also illuminate their evolving interpretation of an education for democracy. The chapter concludes with a cautious consideration of lessons from this Italian community that might inform efforts on behalf of more democratic and equitable early childhoods in the United States.

Cross-Cultural Perspectives on Early Childhood

Reggio Emilia's early childhood services are among many developed in 20th century Italy and in other settings around the world. In each nation and sub-cultural setting, decisions are made about the most efficacious settings and strategies appropriate for the early care and education of young children. Psychological anthropology offers a valuable lens with which to view cultural diversity and decades of inquiry into how children are socialized to become competent members of their respective cultural settings. A brief review of this work includes theoretical advances in understanding the role of cultural contexts in human development that will assist in this effort to better understanding Reggio Emilia's municipal early childhood services.

Over the last century, anthropologists and socio-cultural scholars have generated a wealth of empirical data on the cultural nature of child development (Rogoff, 2003), including robust cultural differences in such parenting behaviors as sleeping arrangements, discipline practices, and whether or not to talk or play with babies (LeVine & New, 2008). This work has identified the central role of parental belief systems *aka* ethno-theories (Harkness & Super, 1996), including views on children's early learning (New, 1999), as explanations for diverse parenting practices. A conceptualization of children's proximal environments as "developmental niches" (Super & Harkness, 1986) highlights the interface between culture and child development. This cumulative body of work challenges universal theories of cognition, attachment and socio-emotional development, among other prevailing beliefs about children's development on which many early childhood educators rely (New, 2003).

Recent work by psychological anthropologists includes studies of cultural differences in early childhood education. Multi-vocal video ethnographies illuminate changing cultural and ideological underpinnings of preschool in China, Japan and the US (Tobin, Hsueh & Karasawa, 2009); and Western European parent and teacher perspectives on diversity in early childhood settings (Tobin, Arzubiaga & Mantovani, 2007). My research with Italian colleagues notes sub-cultural differences in beliefs about what should be learned at home and at school (New, Mallory & Mantovani, 2000). This scholarship joins other critiques of standardized interpretations of quality (Dahlberg, Moss & Pence, 1999) and problematizes the very possibility of an "anti-bias" early childhood curriculum (Vandenbroeck, 2007). This corpus of work on culture-as-developmental context (Goodnow, Miller & Kessel, 1995) also resonates with an integrated theory of cultural models.

Cultural Models Theory

Similar to cultural-historic-activity theory in tracing contemporary practices to historic events, cultural models theory also highlights a society's future goals, conceptualized as moral goods or a "moral direction" (LeVine et al., 1994). Contemporary cultural models theorists have expanded notions of a moral direction (in the sense of a desirable pathway for a developing child or society) to include more explicit goals or "moral imperatives" (Li, 2012). The power of moral imperatives is in guiding decision-making and insuring socialization strategies are consistent with the promotion of culturally valued virtues. This conceptual framework is especially useful when comparing diverse societies' approaches to the care and education of young children.

For example, many US ECE practices, such as teaching very young children to put on their own coats—and discourses of "you can do it by yourself"—can be traced to US history in which independence was both a goal and a necessity, as was self-sufficiency, leading to rewards of personal achievement. Many aspects of contemporary American society are consistent with this model, including disdain for those in need of public assistance and a view of children's early education as an investment for future economic returns and global stature.

With this theoretical lens in mind, what is it about Reggio Emilia that has captured the imaginations of so many educators, including those in nondemocratic societies around the world, and what are the cultural and historic sources of these accomplishments?

Reggio Emilia's Cultural Model of Early Childhood

It's important to note that Reggio Emilia is one of several Italian cities with high quality municipal early childhood services (New, 1993), playing leadership roles in the passage of two laws, the first (in 1968) ensuring the rights of all Italian children ages 3–5 to *scuola materna;* the second (1971) mandating provision of infant-toddler care (*asili nido*). Then and now, municipal services are one of several early education options (state, private, cooperative) for young children in Italy. References in this chapter, whether to Reggio Emilian educators, classrooms or "the Reggio Emilia approach," are specific to the municipal services. Some characteristics of Reggio Emilia's municipal *servizi dell'infanzia* are present in other municipal services, but many features of Reggio Emilia's services reflect decades of effort, experimentation and innovation, including: the environment as a "third teacher," the importance of children's multiple symbolic languages as creative and cognitive resources, documentation as a major tool in teacher inquiry, *progettazione* as a cultural project, and home-school-community relationships as foundational to the origins and sustainability of the municipal early childhood services. These pedagogical practices, described in detail in numerous publications (c.f., the three edited volumes on *The Hundred Languages of Children* by Edwards, Gandini & Forman, 1993; 1998; 2012), are also forms of *praxis* central to the city's cultural model of early childhood education. A brief look at the historic context helps explain the personal and cultural sources reflected in Reggio Emilia's contemporary interpretation of an early childhood education for democracy.

A History of Resistance and Social Activism

In the early 20th century, many Italians were persuaded by the young Mussolini to join the Italian Socialist Party. Reggio Emilia's Socialist mayor opened the area's first school for young children, with the aim of promoting socialist ideals of education as a tool for freedom (Rinaldi, 2006). As Reggio Emilia citizens continued pushing back against the doctrines of the Catholic Church, by 1922 Italy had the world's first fascist regime. The new fascist governor of the Reggio Emilia province quickly closed the socialist school and, just as quickly, a new movement known as *La Resistenza* (the Resistance) was formed to oppose Fascism and encourage collective action. Loris Malaguzzi grew up during this period and Reggio Emilia's citizens were key protagonists of this movement.

Reggio Emilia's traditions of resistance were honed in the decades leading up to and throughout World War II. Motivated by opposition to what Mussolini represented, others were inspired by the writings of Antonio Gramsci on workers' rights and participatory governance. The concept of *gestione sociale* (social management) resonated with resistance activists as the newly formed Italian Communist Party gained ground in Reggio Emilia. By the late 1930s Reggio Emilia resistance workers were sabotaging German aircraft and bombing bridges used by German transports. The region's long history of cooperatives in which farmers worked closely together on common goals contributed to a confidence and trust instrumental to the solidarity of the resistance movement. In the intense period between Italy's signing of the armistice in 1943 and Hitler's surrender in the spring of 1945, other cooperative relationships were established as resistance workers were joined by partisans, both men and women. By war's end, women in Reggio Emilia had established the first of Italy's *Gruppi di defesa della donna* (Groups in Defense of Women). Later renamed the *Unione delle Donne Italiane* (Union of Italian Women), Reggio Emilia was the hub of the Italian women's movement. Women from diverse political and socio-economic backgrounds were instrumental in extending the agenda of *La Resistenza* into the post-war period and gaining support, first in Reggio Emilia, then nationally, for public early childhood services.

Jerome Bruner has written extensively on the role of narratives in capturing the meanings of culture (Bruner, 1996) and Reggio Emilia has many stories about the city's culture of resistance and activism. The story of *Villa Cella* was a favorite of Loris Malaguzzi's, who often recounted his amazement, in the days following liberation, upon hearing about "inconceivable" acts of peasant women and men building a school for their children on the outskirts of Reggio Emilia in an area previously the target of massive bombings and reprisal executions by German soldiers. Malaguzzi's description of women cleaning bricks from the ruble of bombed out buildings was followed by other narratives of children passing bricks along to a row of men who, brick by brick, built up the walls of their new school, using funds obtained by finding and selling a German military tank and a few horses (Barazzoni, 1985). Their hopes for their own and subsequent genera-tions of children who would attend this school are expressed in the school's name—*XXV Aprile* (April 25), Italy's Liberation Day.

Over the next two decades, Italians dedicated human and material resources to the rebuilding of a nation in a state of shock and physical ruin, and the bringing together of opposing factions left over from the war. In Reggio Emilia, memories of *La Resistenza* and the growing women's movement contributed to much-needed optimism that they *could* rebuild and, in critical ways, re-imagine Italian society, and fueled a growing press for more public early childhood schools inspired by the grass-roots efforts that led to the *Scuole XXV Aprile*. By 1963, Reggio Emilia had opened its first municipally funded public schools for young children even as signs of unrest surfaced at the national level due to wage stag-nation, a lack of social services and an influx of Southern Italy migrants seeking employment in northern Italy. As noted previously, State Law 1044 (1968) declared the rights of all children ages 3–5 to high quality *scuole materna* [4] (nursery school), a policy achievement attributed to unrelenting demonstrations by Italian women, many from Reggio Emilia. While early childhood advocates celebrated, the political turmoil surrounding labor contracts reached a tipping point[5] as trade unions struggled unsuccessfully for workers compensation and the right to elect delegates. By the summer of 1969, as 100,000 metalworkers marched in Milan, a socialist leader predicted an *autunno caldo* (hot autumn). By September, the "social earthquake" had begun and quickly spread throughout Italy.

Italian news archives, many with photographs (Guizzardi, 2015), depict this period as one of intense political anxiety characterized by waves of protests by growing numbers of Italians. Workers in large factories were joined by hotel concierges, custodians and women working as seamstresses, telephone operators and nurses. Women's demands for pay equity, maternity leave and public services including child care added to the growing chorus of discontent. Students mobilized for extending the right to education to all social classes, joining workers' demonstrations. The growing solidarity around these collective public demands attracted bankers and members of the middle class to the movement. The number, size and frequency of strikes paralyzed Italy.

Results of this "wave of madness" were unprecedented in Italy and Western Europe. Final agreements, signed into law in 1970, sanctioned workers' collective and individual rights, a reduction of the work week to 40 hours, salary increases for all, 10 hours of paid union meetings and union representation. A new law guaranteed high school graduates access to state universities. Italian women benefitted from workers' rights legislation and laws establishing rights to divorce and abortion as well as the abolishment of laws criminalizing female adultery. Building on the 1968 law establishing children's rights to *scuola maternal*, the groundwork was laid for a 1971 law for *asili nido* for working mothers. Italian historians describe the *autunno caldo* as a time of solidarity and courage—an "epochal push to change society."[6]

This history, including the values, discourses and ambitions of *La Resistenza* and the Women's Movement, is very much alive in Reggio Emilia. The democratic principles of "freedom," "quality" and "social" justice, core values of the Resistance Movement, today serve as moral imperatives. The Women's Movement added complexity to these aims by elaborating on the multiple means and meanings of *l'emancipazion* (liberty, freedom, emancipation). In response to their close encounters with fascism, Reggio Emilian educators, and especially Loris Malaguzzi, expanded these principles to include the importance of diversity—of *people and opinions*—to a democratic society. Reggio Emilia and other progressive Italian communities have sustained this early commitment to dialogue and debate as alternatives to violence and oppression (Davidson & Wright, 1998). The theory of cultural models would consider these values as the "guiding lights" in the city's determination to change the culture of childhood.

The Socio-cultural and Political Roots of Reggio Emilia's *Praxis*

A closer look at prominent features of the "Reggio Emilia Approach" reveals ties to the city's radical history and political principles that inform their work with young children, their families and the larger community. This cultural ethos is also evident in community discourses and educators' descriptions of their work (New, 2007).

Environment as a "Third Teacher"

Much has been written about Reggio Emilia's *asili nido* and *scuole* environments, filled with natural light and plants, spaces for adults to visit and linger, open access kitchens, and large and small *ateliers* where children explore a variety of creative and recycled materials. Surprises such as a life-size skeleton in the hall, a peacock in the courtyard or climbing ropes and ladders insure that these learning environments are far from standardized. In this sense these environments represent intentional developmental niches in which human and material resources are chosen to inspire *and provoke*. They also reveal the political roots and values underlying their existence. While some *scuole* are in former homes, such as *La Villetta,* others are named for artists (*Nido Picasso*) and literary figures (*Gianni Rodari*) and prominent social critics—*Scuole Paolo Freire* and *Scuole Tondelli*. Still others are named for victims of past wars—*Nido G. Cervi,* the mother of seven brothers killed by German soldiers, the first of many local heroes of the Italian Resistance. And some, like *Scuola Anna Frank,* are named for child war victims. *Scuole Iqbal Masih* is named for a Pakistani child assassinated at age 13 while riding his bike, for having spoken out against abusive child labor. These names are not just to honor the dead or impress foreign visitors, although they invite questions and further discussion. More important to a pedagogy for democracy is that the narratives of those being recognized, their valor and contributions to society, are shared with children and families. Children's views of events surrounding those being recognized are often included in "identity" brochures. In the *Iqbal Masih* brochure, drawings of children on bicycles are accompanied by children's declarations that children should be safe and not have to work.

Documentation

Carefully curated photographs are on ample display in these environments, of children working intently on a painting, playing with friends or engaged in serious debate. More than bulletin-board decorations, documentation images are organized and displayed in places most likely to attract the attention of adults and children, sparking questions and discussions of children's early learning. Teachers share their observations, whether audio-recordings or a series of photographs, with each other and with the children, providing opportunities to re-visit and reflect on their experiences. Documentation notebooks and panel displays are often accompanied by text dictated by children or teachers' notes of children's questions and hypotheses. In this way documentation supports teachers' planning and helps families understand the origins of activities based on children's questions, whether it's why a shadow has moved or how to attract more birds to their playground. Documentation of adults engaged in deep conversations during parent meetings are accompanied by notes of what was discussed, for the benefit of those who were not in attendance. This documentation also serves as an invitation to join the next conversation, as their perspective is also needed.

In addition to these pedagogical incentives, Reggio Emilia uses documentation to intentionally invite parent questions, sometimes generating conflict, each premises for sustained conversations. For example, a debate among three-year-old children about gender identity as a function of boys' or girls' clothing led one teacher to propose *una prova* (test) in which one boy and girl would exchange clothing. According to images captured by the other teacher, this was a frightening prospect for some children as they watched two peers agree to exchange items of clothing. This single-event documentation was posted immediately in the front door, making visible children's responses to this experience, leading to intense discussions among parents and teachers about children's identity development. Other examples of intentional provocations were teachers' audio-recordings of children's conversations when playing with peers in different areas of the classroom, about the Gulf War. They were shared with parents after many had claimed that their children "had no idea" about the war waging nearby. After hearing children talk about sinking boats and bombs, parents agreed to teachers' proposals to invite children to draw what they were afraid of, giving the adults disturbing but much-needed insights into what very young children grapple with, often on their own. In this light, documentation serves as a major tool for learning about children, sharing diverse perspectives and developing adult relationships in the process.

Progettazione

Many Italian early childhood educators eschew a pre-determined curriculum, yet Reggio Emilia's interpretation of curriculum in the form of *progettazione* is one of the most distinctive features of their work with young children, and one of the most challenging for US educators to understand. The open-ended nature of *progettazione* is but one of the ways in which it is distinct from other examples of project-based curriculum. The origins of pedagogical explorations are often teachers' observations of children's interests, but could also be parent concerns, community events or children's disagreements as potential topics worthy of exploration. These projects often lead children into the community in search of information or resources, as was the case when a small group of five-year-olds spent weeks devising a means of measuring a broken table so that it could be replaced by a local carpenter. Some projects, including those initiated by children, lead to the exploration of concepts generally considered far beyond their abilities, such as when a group of four-year-olds spent months trying to draw a dinosaur to scale. And some *progettazione* serve as professional development opportunities for teachers, as when a whole *scuole* of 75 three-, four- and five-year-olds explored the origins of early literacy—a project launched when three-year-olds began creating "messages" of colorful ribbon and leaves to put into envelopes for their friends. Discourses associated with Reggio Emilia's history of resistance may emerge in these contexts, as illustrated in one four-year-old boy's "letter of protest" to his teachers. Documentation throughout these *progettazione* provides families and teachers with valuable information about children's experiences and capabilities. Some *progettazione* also represent compelling occasions for families, teachers and community members to join in exploring such topics as the rights of children, families—including grandparents!—and their teachers. More recent projects have grown from children's confusions about diverse religious beliefs and cultural traditions—in each case risking controversy and compelling the participation of diverse families and community members.

Multiple Symbolic Languages

Lorix Malaguzzi was adamant that children's expressions of ideas, insights and imagination should not be limited to talk and text, followed by hiring an *atelierista* (someone trained in the arts) in each setting to work closely with children and their teachers. Numerous examples of children's explorations with diverse materials are displayed throughout the *nidi* and *scuole* environments, in some cases from previous years, reminding children that their school has a history. Multiple means of representation are also a major resource in children's project work. For example, children's complaints about crowds at the beach inspired a project involving trips to the market and the central piazza, where children observed people of all ages coming and going. Back in the *atelier,* some created figures out of clay while others drew people, one at a time, to be cut out and gathered together to create their own crowds. Another example grew from an argument about a "girls only" tree when four-year-old boys returned from playing outside, leading to a project in which the boys were invited to use clay to express what it means to be a "macho boy"—in this case, an array of snakes was the collective response.

Throughout these and other *progettazione,* documentation of children's efforts and their uses of multiple representational media contributes to "making learning visible" for the children, their teachers and their families (Giudici, Rinaldi & Krechevsky, 2001). The values of conflict and debate are also evident when children explore their multiple symbolic languages. In a long-ago project associated with a local drought, children were invited to represent the roots of a tree that had gone too long without ample water. Some were provided with pencils, others with fine-tipped felt pens, still others with hollow blocks of clay. They went back and forth among their various renditions, debating whether or not a shriveled root might manage to keep a tree from falling. Their teacher joined them, not to quell the discord but to take notes on their various hypotheses for further exploration.

Home-School-Community Relationships

The final but most significant feature of the *Reggio Emilia Approach* is also the least visible to casual observers of this Italian city's *servizi dell'infanzia*—the relationships among and between parents, teachers and community members. Relationships between children, families and teachers are nurtured in part due to the Italian practice of keeping groups of children together throughout the time they are in a particular setting, e.g. three years in a *nido* and another three in a *scuole dell'infanzia*. In Reggio Emilia, structural features such as *gestione sociale*—the social management proposed by Antonio Gramsci—offers parents and community members the opportunity—and the responsibility—to collaborate in such decisions as continuing the use of linens on children's tables, hiring auxiliary staff and determining criteria on which to admit new cohorts of children to the municipal services. True to Gramsci's prediction, *gestione sociale* offers transparency in the workings of *servizi dell'infanzia* and promotes relationships and skills in conflict negotiations that contribute to the sort of solidarity seen when hundreds of parents and community members appear at city council meetings when budgets for early childhood services are determined. A final example that resonates with Reggio Emilia's values of conflict and dialogue as fundamental to a democracy began one afternoon when three boys were told to sit quietly and wait for their parents, as other children settled down for a nap. When one father arrived to pick up his son, he observed the teacher scolding the boys, who were playing noisily with each other. That evening, at a class parent meeting, the father made an impassioned speech to the effect that he did not send his son to school "to learn to sit down and be quiet!" He reminded the other adults—"remember what happened when Italians did just that?" That disruption launched a year-long public debate involving hundreds of *Reggiani* citizens on the purposes of an early childhood education.

New challenges in home-school-community relations have emerged in this formerly wealthy homogeneous community due to an influx of immigrants and refugees from more than 100 countries with diverse cultural, religious and (as many as 200) linguistic traditions. Described as a process of transformation (Edwards, Gandini & Gorman, 2012), Reggio Emilia educators have responded to this diversity in a variety of ways, such as increasing spaces in the municipal *nidi* and *scuole* for children, forming culturally and linguistically diverse parent advisory councils and exploring ways to capitalize on (and promote) children's multilingual diversity as among their symbolic languages. A persistent challenge is how to modify traditional parent participation practices, as many new and immigrant parents are unaccustomed to the level of engagement associated with Italian interpretations of *partecipazione* (New & Mallory, 2005). Documentation of children's play and collaborative project work has proved especially valuable as means of sharing the "life of the school" with families. Also popular with new (and old) families are *"serata nella cucina"* (nights in the kitchen) events in which grandmothers prepare traditional recipes to share with school cooks and other families.

Beyond Early Childhood: Democratic Values in the Community

As Reggio Emilia educators seek ways to communicate and collaborate with new families, what hasn't changed is their commitment to their rights and freedoms to belong, engage, collaborate and participate are respected (New & Kantor, 2013).

For half a century, those democratic values have served as *moral imperatives* that drive and sustain their municipal *servizi dell'infanzia*. These values are also evident in community responses on behalf of migrants, as detailed in a World Health Organization (WHO) report on health care provisions for immigrants and refugees in Western Europe. The WHO report attributed the dramatic increase in the numbers of families seeking residence in the city to a regional policy "aimed at facilitating the social integration of migrant groups" with dedicated health services, including multilingual literature and interpreters. Management criteria emphasized "equity through sensitivity to and acceptance of diversity," and "increasing quality … through more personalized services that take the individuality of each person into account." The report highlighted Reggio Emilia's commitment to developing "equitable participatory processes" in health care and local governance (Chiarenza & Chiesa, 2018, pp. 88–89). Although Italian policy regarding migrants' residency status is far from resolved, discourses of rights, quality and participation were dispersed throughout the report.

It's More Than an Approach: It's a Commitment to Democratic Activism

Within an increasingly fragile global context, the example of Reggio Emilia warrants a much closer look at what is possible when a community determines to co-construct a new culture of childhood in which its democratic ideals are represented, debated and openly evolving. Granted, the accomplishments and failures of the US do not have a common source of inspiration such as Reggio Emilia's history of fascism and *La Resistenza*—nor does that explain why the moral compasses of our respective cultural models are so far apart. Yet numerous scholars have noted the potentials of conflict and trauma to inspire social and cultural change (Turiel, 1999). Given the growing recognition of social injustices and inequitable education in the US, it's hard to ignore Reggio Emilia's example of citizens working collaboratively and persistently on behalf of a more democratic and just society, beginning in early childhood. That Reggio Emilia continues doing this work in an increasingly diverse community makes it all the more compelling and relevant.

In acknowledging our differences, how might we use what we've learned from Reggio Emilia's story? At the least, we should

- Remember that talk matters (Fennimore, 1999) and pay more attention to professional discourses, avoid deficit labels and replace references to children's *needs* by highlighting their emerging skills and understandings;
- Be strategic in seeking attention from educational and community leaders with documented examples of what young children are capable of learning, in the classroom and the community;

- Dare to bring the notion of children's rights into policy and community discussions, e.g., about heritage language maintenance in addition to English learning outcomes;
- Create and seek occasions for diverse and mixed groups of parents, educators, community members to share the virtues they hope children might acquire during childhood;
- Extend our reach beyond the profession, developing new relationships with others with whom we disagree—and use the disagreements as the first step in learning how to listen, before we discuss, debate, negotiate a common ground dedicated to a collective and insistent voice in *defense of childhood* in our community, school district, state, nation.

These efforts will not result in dramatic changes in US educational inequities nor will they lead to more democratic classrooms. But they may lead to new insights about how to engage others in examining the dialectical tensions of our freedoms and responsibilities to children (Greene, 1988), first steps in identifying partners and possibilities for meaningful change in our particular communities. In asking ourselves to take risks beyond those of our everyday experiences and expertise, we can remember the peasant women scrapping old mortar from bricks, determined not to give up, to build a new school for their children, where they would learn what it means to live in a democracy. And someday, should a US school for young children be named *Otto Marzo* (March 8) like the one in Reggio Emilia, in honor of the New York garment workers strike that inspired the first women's union in the United States, we'll recall Malaguzzi's feelings, after first proclaiming "it's impossible!" only to hear someone respond *"nothing is impossible."*

Notes

1 The original manuscript submitted to *Young Children* began by describing the city's political affiliation and history of social activism. Following editorial concerns that early childhood educators might not read the article if it seemed "too political," the paragraph was removed.
2 Two major grants from the Spencer Foundation (1996 and 1999) were instrumental to this discussion. My role as *rapporteur* of OECD's (2001) review of Italian early care and education also informed my understanding of common and diverse features of Italian *servizi dell'infanzia.*
3 This term refers to municipally-funded early childhood services, including *scuole dell'infanzia* for children 3–5 years and *asili nido* for infants and toddlers.
4 Italy's earliest services for children ages 3–5 years were known as *scuole materna.* Reggio Emilia was among the first to reject this gendered label and to hire male teachers in spite of state prohibitions.
5 I was living in Florence in the spring of 1968 and witnessed many events associated with the resistance movement.
6 https://www.corriere.it/foto-gallery/cronache/14_ottobre_03/1969-l-anno-cui-italia -scoppio-l-autunno-caldo-34d087ec-4aec-11e4-9829-df2f785edc20.shtml

References

Barazzoni, R. (1985). *Mattone su Mattone: Storia della Scuola per Bambini "XXV Aprile" di Villa Cella. [Brick by brick: The history of the "XXV Aprile" People's Nursery school of Villa Cella.]* Reggio Emilia: Centro Stampa Municipio di Reggio Emilia.

Bredekamp, S. (1987). *Developmentally appropriate practice in early childhood programs serving children from birth through age eight.* Washington, DC: National Association for the Education of Young Children.

Bredekamp, S. & Copple, C. (Eds.) (1997). *Developmentally appropriate practice for early childhood programs serving children from birth through age eight* (Rev. ed.). Washington, DC: NAEYC.

Bruner, J. (1996). *The culture of education.* Cambridge, MA: Harvard University Press.

Chiarenza, A. & Chiesa, V. (2018). The provision of migrant- friendly health care in Reggio Emilia, Italy. In *COMPENDIUM of health system responses to large-scale migration in the WHO European Region.* Copenhagen, Denmark: WHO Regional Office for Europe.

Dahlberg, G. & Moss, P. (2005) *Ethics and politics in early childhood education and care.* London: Routledge.

Dahlberg, G., Moss, P. & Pence, A. (1999). *Beyond quality in early childhood education and care: Postmodern perspectives.* New York: Routledge.

Davidson, A. & Wright, S. (Eds.) (1998) *"Never give in": The Italian resistance and politics.* New York: Peter Lang.

Edwards, C., Gandini, L. & Forman, G. (Eds). (1993). *The hundred languages of children: The Reggio Emilia approach to early childhood education.* Norwood, NJ: Ablex.

Edwards, C., Gandini, L. & Forman, G. (Eds). (1998). *The hundred languages of children: The Reggio Emilia approach to early childhood education: Advanced reflections* (2nd ed.). Norwood, NJ: Ablex.

Edwards, C., Gandini, L. & Forman, G. (Eds). (2012). *The hundred languages of children: The Reggio Emilia experience in transformation.* Denver, CO: Praeger.

Fennimore, B. S. (1999). *Talk matters: Refocusing the language of public schooling.* New York: Teachers College Press.

Giudici, C., Rinaldi, C. & Krechevsky, M. (Eds.) (2001). *Making learning visible: Children as individual and group learners.* Reggio Emilia, Italy: Project Zero and Reggio Children.

Goodnow, J. J., Miller, P J. & Kessel, E. (Eds.). (1995). *Cultural practices as contexts for development. New directions for child development (67).* San Francisco, CA: Jossey-Bass.

Gramsci, A. (1971/2018). *Selections from the prison notebooks of Antonio Gramsci.* Edited and translated by Q. Hoare & G. N. Smith. New York: International Publishers.

Greene, M. (1988). *The dialectic of freedom.* New York: Teachers College Press.

Guizzardi, G. (2015). *Photographic Museum of Humanity.* Retrieved from https://phmuseum.com/giacomoguizzardi/story/red-emilia-the-hotbed-of-italian-communism-0b7ea7dd56

Harkness, S. & Super, C. (Eds.) (1996). *Parents' cultural belief systems: Their origins, expressions and consequences.* New York: Guilford Press.

LeVine, R. & New, R. (Eds.) (2008). *Anthropology and child development: Selected readings.* Malden, MA: Blackwell Publishers.

LeVine, R. A., Dixon, S., LeVine, S., Richman, A., Leiderman, H., Keefer, C. & Brazelton, T. B. (1994). *Child care and culture: Lessons from Africa.* New York: Blackwell.

Li, J. (2012). *Cultural foundations of learning: East and west.* Cambridge, UK: Cambridge University Press.

New, R. (1990). Excellent early education: A city in Italy has it. *Young Children,* 45(6), 4–10.

New, R. (1993). Italy. In M. Cochran (Ed.), *International handbook on child care policies and programs* (pp. 291–311). Westport, CT: Greenwood Press.

New, R. (1997). Reggio Emilia's commitment to children and community: A reconceptualization of quality and DAP. *Canadian Children*, 1(7–11).

New, R. (1999). What should children learn? Making choices and taking chances. *Early childhood research and practice*, 1(2), 1–25. Retrieved from www.eric.org/ecrp

New, R. (2003). Culture, child development research, and early childhood education: Rethinking the relationship. In D. Wertleib, F. Jacobs & R. Lerner (Eds.), *Handbook of applied developmental science, Vol. 3* (pp. 223–252). Thousand Oaks, CA: Sage.

New, R. (2007). Reggio Emilia as cultural activity theory in practice. *Theory into Practice*, 46(1), 5–13.

New, R. & Kantor, R. (2013). Reggio Emilia in the 21st century: Enduring commitments, new challenges. In J. Roopnarine and J. Johnson (Eds.), *Approaches to early childhood education* (6th ed.) (pp. 331–354). Boston: Pearson.

New, R. & Mallory, B. (2005). Children as Catalysts for Adult Relations: New Perspectives from Italian Early Childhood Education. In O. N. Saracho & B. Spodek (Eds.), *Contemporary perspectives on families, communities and schools in early childhood education*. Greenwich, CT: Information Age Publishers.

New, R., Mallory, B. & Mantovani, S. (2000). Cultural images of children, parents, and teachers: Italian home-school relations. *Early Education and Development*, 11(5), 97–616.

OECD (2001). *Starting strong: Early childhood education and care*. Paris: OECD Publishing. doi:10.1787/9789264192829-en

Rinaldi, C. (2006). *In dialogue with Reggio Emilia*. London: Routledge.

Rogoff, B. (2003). *The cultural nature of human development*. Oxford: Oxford University Press.

Seefeldt, C. (1993). Social studies: Learning for freedom. *Young Children*, 48(3), 4–9.

Super, C. & Harkness, S. (1986). The developmental niche: A conceptualization at the interface of child and culture. *International Journal of Behavioral Development*, 9, 545–569.

Tobin, J., Arzubiaga, A. & Mantovani, S. (2007). Entering into dialogue with immigrant parents. *Early Childhood Matters*, 108, 34–38.

Tobin, J., Hsueh, Y. & Karasawa, M. (2009), *Preschools in three cultures revisited*. Chicago: University of Chicago Press,

Turiel, E. (1999). Conflict, social development, and cultural change. In E. Turiel (Ed.), *Development and cultural change: Reciprocal processes* (No. 83, pp. 77–92). San Francisco, CA: Jossey-Bass Publishers.

VandenbroeckM. (2007). Beyond anti-bias education: Changing conceptions of diversity and equity in European early childhood education. *European Early Childhood Education Research Journal*, 1(15), 21–25.

Way Forward: Stories of Hope and Possibility

9

OUT AND ABOUT

Practicing Hope Through Research

Jeanne Marie Iorio and Clifton S. Tanabe

Acknowledgement of Country

This chapter was written while being with the traditional lands of the Wada-wurrung people of the Kulin nation. We pay our respects to elders past and present and acknowledge that this land continues to be an important place of knowledge creation as it has been for many thousands of years.

Introduction

Social justice for us is rooted in commitment, community, and action. Based on these beliefs, our work is framed by an effort to contribute to democracy while ensuring access and voice for all. Democracy is about making public current issues, ideas, and questions for discussion to empower the public to act. As an academic and administrator in higher education, we have witnessed many conversations but less action, related to articulated commitments to democracy and social justice. For us, the work of social justice requires both conversation and action. The framework we drew upon for pursuing conversation and action is the "practice of hope." The research we share in this chapter is an example of the practice of hope as it supports children, families, educators, and ourselves to act as agents of change and to make visible issues of social justice for debate, dialogue, and action.

We each bring different perspectives to the writing of this chapter. Clifton, positioned as an Asian male who grew up in Hawai'i and is now living and working in a bicultural, binational, and bilingual region with a predominantly Hispanic population, approaches administration with humility and a commitment to learning. Jeanne, positioned as a white settler woman, an American living in Australia, and having lived in Wadawurrung Country for less than five years, understands her learning and experiences as continually evolving as she learns with and "coming alongside" Aboriginal worldviews (Martin, 2016).

Pedagogical Documentation: A Story of Gifting

Sunscreen hits the air; feet moving toward the toilet; large-brimmed hats topping heads; water-bottles fill backpacks – chaos ensues in the first- and second-grade classroom. These movements mark the beginning of the day, a day every fortnight when feet travel down the hill towards the ocean, to Fishermans Beach.

Feet moving quickly at the start, slapping against the pavement, hurrying across the highway, and then the rhythm is set for the remaining 15-minute walk. Ocean watching us as we move closer to Fishos, the nickname we call this beach. We have been learning with/from this place and acknowledge that it has always been a part of Wadawurrung Country. Prior to colonization, Fishos would have been a site of sustenance – a place to find fish, shellfish, and berries. As a result of colonization, Fishos may also have been a site of death as disease, lack of access to traditional food sources, and war killed many of the Wadawurrung people. As a way to respectfully "refigure" (Nxumalo, 2016) Wadawurrung presences, we carefully use Wadawurrung words that have been shared with us to describe land, sea, and sky country, for example, *warri* for the sea and *korrak* for the shore.

Fish fill the shallow and calm waters of Fishos. Yellow Bluff, a tall cliff, stands at the right side of the beach. Layers of rocks, cracks, and tree roots share with us the power and the potential of the cliffs to be both safe and unsafe. Yellow Bluff is the sources of much conversation: "What is Yellow Bluff telling us today? Have parts of Yellow Bluff fallen to the sand? Are there small stones rolling down to the sand? Can we see more of the tree roots? How does Yellow Bluff tell us where to play?"

Backpacks release from our backs and join the sand. Sand invites us to sit for a rest, a snack, a sip of water. Sand holds our feet as we wander and find the spot that calls us into connection at Fishos. Water running from the rainwater drain calls for investigation. *Wordel* (crabs) scurry through the sand, provoking us to follow, watch, and listen. Clay located at the base of Yellow Bluff encourages hands to squish, curl, and pat. *Warri* (sea) covers the sand as feet try and predict where to stand to barely be touched or, in some cases, feet fully covered and testing the temperature. These movements populate the three hours we spend each time at Fishos. We see these movements, these places as gifts – gifts Fishos offers us. Today is a day we "gift back" to Fishos.

Out and About

The pedagogical documentation presented here shares "Out and About" – an early childhood research project which takes place in a coastal town in Victoria, Australia and an urban area in Melbourne. Out and About considers the

devastating current human-induced state of the environment (Solomon et al., 2009) illustrating a poor relationship between humans and the earth. The Out and About project supports building a more positive relationship between humans and the planet in order to reshape the future of the local and global environments. This chapter shares the research, rooted in environmental justice, conducted at this coastal site. Every fortnight over 100 six- and seven-year-old children walk with their teachers to Fishermans Beach intending to think *with* the place as a means of building a relationship between humans and the earth.

Out and About as a Practice of Hope

Out and About is an example of the "practice of hope" – a pedagogy we suggest in order for academics to work towards social change (Iorio & Tanabe, 2015, 2016, 2019). Built on theories of hope and the intent of being "wide-awake" (Greene, 1995) and acting, the practice of hope includes the way in which we see academics (and ourselves as academics) attempting to work in universities towards social justice. We take inspiration from philosopher Maxine Greene (1997) who reminds us "to think of things as if they could be otherwise" (p. 1), pointing out that imagination can offer new ways to see the world and our existence as academics. Greene (1997) describes "dark times" in relationship to society and schools through the image of being "shadowed:"

> I view our times as shadowed by violations and erosions taking place around us: the harm being done to children; the eating away of social support systems; the "savage inequalities" in our schools; the spread of violence; the intergroup hatreds; the power of media; the undermining of arts in the lives of the young.
>
> *(p. 1)*

Greene makes the connection between the realities of the world – violence and inequity – and what is happening in education. She also notes that dark times are the impetus for the urgency for light (Greene, 1997, p. 1). Greene advocates teachers' work as "actions of light" in dark times; light is achievable by disrupting what constitutes our everyday, and imagining what else could be. "Imagination, after all, allows people to think of things as if they could be otherwise; it is the capacity that allows a looking through windows of the actual towards alternative realities" (p. 2).

In these dark times we need a light – a light as Greene (1997) suggests – empowering us to "imagine" what "could be otherwise" and create "alternative realities" where academics lead research that is focused on the common good. We respond to Greene's call and practice hope.

Practicing Hope

The practice of hope is how we as academics can work towards change and is founded in Freire's (1994; 1998) conception of hope as a part of being human. This foundational understanding of hope positions how we envisage the world (Andrews, 2010). It builds on Freire's (1972) ontology of hope and the way in which education can pursue hope and work toward human completeness (Freire, 1998). In this chapter, we focus on ourselves as academics in teacher education engaging in the practice of hope through research, specifically, by engaging in the Out and About project. Throughout this project, we attempt to be "wide-awake" engaging with Greene's (1995) concept of "wide-awakeness" – an "awareness of what it is to be in the world" (p. 35). Wide-awakeness situates how we position ourselves as academics and supports our choices in research projects that consider real world issues and respond in ways that further change.

We also take inspiration from early childhood academics across the field illustrating wide-awakeness as they pursue in research focused on the public good. For example, Quintero (2018) engages in qualitative research using multifaceted storying as pre-service teachers and young children collaborate on building curriculum and conducting research. Through storying, the lives of migrant children and families are made visible, and, thus, contribute to the ways in which pre-service teachers learn to listen and view children and families as capable, competent, and contributing members to the school and community. Pente, Massing, and Kirova (2018) offer another illustration of wide-awakeness as they utilize arts-based methods, participatory action, and ethnographic interviews, focus groups, and observations to "explore sense of place and the role of artistic practice in investigations of biculturalism by immigrant preschool teachers and their immigrant students and families" (p. 111). This research offers ways to think about "knowing" and "being" culturally across a preschool setting. Further, Hamm and Boucher (2018) make meaning by "being present" as a means to respectfully center Aboriginal perspectives in early childhood education. Through narrative, their research shares the stories of teaching in post-colonial Australia and engaging with the complexity of place.

Returning to Out and About

This account brings us back to the story shared through pedagogical documentation at the start of this chapter and how this story communicates the practice of hope for us as academics in teacher education. Framed by "common world" pedagogies (Common Worlds Research Collective, 2014; Taylor & Guigini, 2012; Taylor & Pacini-Ketchabaw, 2015), Out and About research seeks to understand how teachers support children in their learning within their relationships in their common world's human and "more-than-human" relations. "More-than-human" includes the multispecies communities (for example, plants and animals) and the local place where children live. For these children and educators Out and About is geo-historically specific, as it engages with Australia's colonial past, present, and futures and its entanglements with "other beings, non-living entities, technologies, elements, discourses, forces, and landforms" (Common World Research Collective 2014). Common world pedagogies (Taylor & Pacini-Ketchabaw, 2015) reposition learning to respond to the common world legacies and to rethink common futures.

A critical component to this work is "place" and attending to the entanglements and the complexity these entanglements generate. Place in this research is viewed as not "culturally or politically neutral" (Mignolo, 2003 in Tuck, McKenzie, & McCoy, 2014, p. 1), rather place is a "territory that is Indigenous and which has been and continues to be subject to the forces of colonization" (Tuck, McKenzie, & McCoy, 2014, p. 1). Seeing place from this perspective provokes us to pay attention to political, historical, and ethical entanglements, and to practice political, intellectual, and ethical pedagogies.

Approach to the Research

This project draws on multisensory methods (walking, listening, smelling, talking, touching) (Pink, 2008) focusing on the relations between place, people, and the more-than-human. Central to this method is the understanding of the "contact zone" (Haraway, 2008) that recognizes that places are inclusive of more-than-human and human entanglements. This includes "place-making" (Pink, 2008, p. 179) where all participants – children, teachers, researchers – participate and regard place as a pedagogical contact zone (Hamm & Boucher, 2018). Data is collected through a pedagogical documentation process completed by the teachers, including field note and researchers' understandings and reflections throughout the research process. Analysis of the data is ongoing and uses Latour's (2005) notions of "tracing" and "assembling" and paying attention to events within the data. This is inclusive of tracing relations and associations happening as the more-than-human, place, and humans act and interact.

In particular, Out and About uses pedagogical documentation as a way to make visible the place and the relationships with more-than-human. Pedagogical documentation as practiced in the municipal infant-toddler centers and preschools in Reggio Emilia, Italy, makes children's ideas and theories visible to the children, educators, and community, contributing to curriculum development (Dahlberg, Moss, & Pence, 2007; Edwards, Gandini, & Forman, 1998; Parnell, 2011; Rinaldi, 2006). While the pedagogical documentation process used in this research draws inspiration from pedagogical documentation rooted in the early childhood centers in Reggio Emilia, the teachers in this research project evolve a version of pedagogical documentation that is relevant to their context. As a living document that is always evolving with new photos, comments, and questions, pedagogical documentation makes public children and teachers' thinking, listening, learning, and thus informs teaching methods. Meaning making is made through dialogues between children and teachers as they revisit and ponder photos, videos, notes, and creations.

Continuing the Story

We now continue the story of "gifting back" to Fishos, started at the beginning of the chapter. In the following part of the pedagogical documentation, we share an excerpt with the understanding that many discussions, provocations, creations, and visits to Fishos have taken place. These events have indicated to the teachers and researchers that children now recognize how the "place gifts" to the children and the children's actions are "gifts back." For example, children offer that one way of thinking *with* Fishos is to not take the rocks. We ask, "Does the description of the child's action indicate a relationship between place and the child? Is it a shared or common world?" A provocation is then given to the children: "If Fishos has given us so much then what are we going to give back?"

Pedagogical Documentation: Gifting

We gather on the carpet and begin to think with the provocation: "If Fishos has given us so much, then what are we going to give back?" Noticing first what Fishos has given us, and then what are actions of gifting might be, children comment:

> My gift to Fishos is love.
> My gift to Fishos Beach is not climbing the cliffs, not wrecking the sand dunes and planting a seed.
> I'm giving Fishos signs.
> My gift to Fishos beach is putting back nature.

We teachers and researcher gather again to look seriously at the ideas of children made visible through their drawings. Similar ideas come together to create gifting categories: "Education," "Love," "Actions," "Connecting," and "Respect." Each category is written at the top of a sign-up sheet.

Using these categories, we also consider how the children work as a group and how they might think to use the place as provocation for their "gifts" to the place. These words – these descriptions – offer a way to consider how children are defining their relationship with this place; it is more of a kinship relationship. Fishermans Beach is not a place the children and educators possess, rather *it is part of their kin*.

The gifting categories are given to the children; bodies move to the sign-up sheet – some children move straight to the one each they connects with; others move slowly, considering which category to choose. "Education," "Love," "Actions," and "Respect" fill up. Only one child signs the paper, "Connecting." With the intent for group work to take place, we teachers move "Connecting" to "Action" – ensuring each child is part of a group. In the end, all have joined a group – a recognizing what a place can give and, because there is now a shared relationship, there is a gifting back.

To continue the gifting process, we wish to understand how children theorize, or think about a gift. Children explore the following questions in small groups in dialogue with each other and with their teachers.

- Will our gift change the place?
- What is a gift?
- Who gives a gift?
- Are there different types of gift?
- Do you need to be able to see a gift?
- How do you make a gift meaningful and special?
- What does meaningful mean?
- How do you know it's meaningful?

Discussion and questions continue to be considered as small groups of children begin to plan and build their gifts – always returning to the ideas of love, respect, education, and actions. Gifts include rubbish collection at Fishos, seed collection from the plants at Fishos to revegetate the dunes, returning shells taken from Fishos, and sharing information with the public in order to provoke others to engage as custodians of Fishos. These activities include creating and sharing pamphlets, making large signs out of natural materials, and creating a puppet show, poems, and songs. Together these ideas, actions, and creations form gifts for Fishos.

Bodies move towards the dunes, following the local land manager. He leads children to the seeds. Hands pick and separate, finding the seeds of life with the purpose of giving more life to this place. Seeds are moved to new plots of sand/soil the garden will grow at school. This garden is a gift to Fishos.

Wanting others to think with Fishos, a plan is developed to make public the "thinking with the place." Seaweed is collected from the shore; hands move and form letters, ensuring the message is clear for all to read – "Please Don't Litter." This moment eventually stretches into months as the sign remains throughout the summer and is the provocation for dialogue across the community, evident in the local shire notice board on Facebook, with a photo of the sign, comments, and over 200 likes.

Walking feet enter the cafe on the beach; pamphlets on how to engage and care for the place are left for the public on the counter. The public gathered for coffee, a quick bit, and conversations invite the children to share ideas of thinking with Fishos. As the children walk away, conversations continue.

Hands with bags, walking feet move across the sand, collecting rubbish, recording the amounts and kinds. Becoming informed on what is left at Fishos and understanding how colleting rubbish impacts this place.

Bringing back shells is the action of many of the children that have spent days at Fishos, recognizing how their behaviors need to move from thinking, "What can we get from a place?" to respecting the more-than-human that inhabit this place.

Songs, poems, and puppet shows fill the air as the relationship with Fishos is shared with the place – written and practiced prior to this day, with recognition of Fishos as audience – giving back to Fishos, thinking with the more-than-human and living with and in this reciprocal relationship.

Discussion

The practice of hope drives how we act as academics. In this sense, we view the academic as an activist, as effectuated hope. The research enacted through the Out and About project makes visible the researcher as well as the teachers and children as advocates for social change. This research, while focused on teaching pedagogies, is also action – action that comes through a deep relationship with a place by the children, teachers, and researcher. It is about learning with and in relation to the place and the more-than-human. What is most profound is the movement of the children and teachers as they change from possessing Fishos to becoming with and making kin with Fishos (Fraser & Taylor, 2016; Haraway, 2016). Gifting back to Fishos is recognition of Fishos' agency and provokes the children and teachers to change how they act in order to create a common future. Lastly, the process of noticing, connecting with, respecting place through the Out and About

project manifests as a recognition of the nexus of public and hope. The action of gifting, in and of itself, becomes an expression of hope in the public sphere.

Practical Applications and Implications

Both the practice of hope and the Out and About research project offer ways to think and rethink practice across education. The practice of hope offers specific ways to engage as academics, but these ideas are also applicable to educators at all levels.

Becoming Wide-Awake and Acting

Being wide-awake and questioning, rethinking, and resisting are all practices early childhood teachers can implement. These practices include understanding the local policies impacting early childhood and advocating for children and

families to ensure children and families are viewed as capable, competent, and contributing members in the school and community. The Out and About project presents a strong example of connecting issues of social justice to research and bringing together teachers, children and researchers to work toward the common good. These ideas can be an inspiration for teachers, teacher educators, community organizations, or any group attempting to create collective action towards social change.

Committing to Going "Out and About"

During the Out and About project, teachers and children built relationships with the local places and this relationship explains the way they began to talk and act on the current devastating state of the environment. This process began by visiting the same place in the community for over two years and spending extended periods of time in the place. Children and teachers in the research shared in this work, visited Fishos every other week, regardless of weather, during their first- and second-grade school experience. Committing first to visiting the place in this intense manner was critical to how the relationships grew between the humans and this place. This commitment to visiting is one way to begin this work in a variety of contexts.

Walking To and With the Place

Children and teachers walked to Fishos in the Out and About project, creating a ritual of going to the place and leaving the place. Then, in the place,

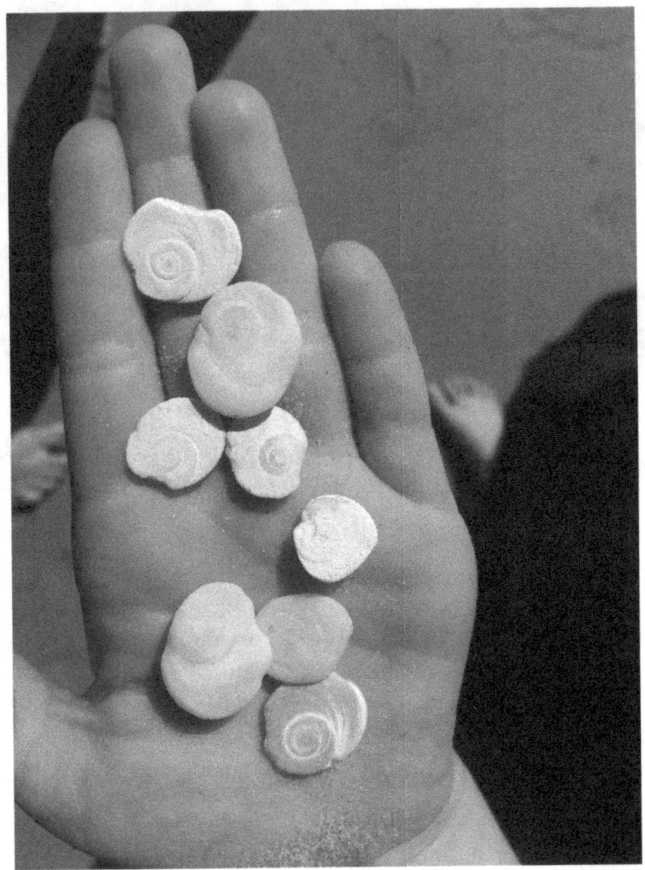

they walked and moved with what called them into connection – the water, Yellow Bluff, and the more-than-human. In other contexts, the movement or ritual to the place is important and should reflect the community. Once in this place, thinking, listening, and walking with the place should be practiced. The emphasis is on being in relationship with the place and the more-than-human, rather than seeing oneself as separate and simply "learning about" the place and the more-than-human.

Understanding the Histories of a Place

Since the Out and About project took place in Australia, we recognize that all teaching and learning must include respectfully coming alongside Aboriginal worldviews of a place (Martin, 2016).

One of the ways we can attend respectfully to Aboriginal perspectives of place is to attune to the places around us in ways that do not always begin with a settler-colonial gaze. Disrupting the settler-colonial gaze requires us (settler colonials) to see places differently, in ways that attend to the ethics and politics of living on stolen land.

(Hamm & Boucher, 2018, p. 61)

In the Out and About project, we begin with the understanding that the children, families, and educators live their lives on Wadawurrung country. The act of knowing whose land it is begins a process of seeing the place differently. In any context, beginning in this way recognizes the entanglements of a place, and practices ethical teaching and learning.

References

Andrews, P. (2010). Hope and the many discourses of education. *Cambridge Journal of Education*, 4(4), 323–326.

Common Worlds Research Collective. (2014). Homepage. Retrieved from http://comm onworlds.net.

Dahlberg, G., Moss, P., & Pence, A. (2007). *Beyond quality in early childhood education and care: A postmodern perspective*. London and New York: Routledge/Falmer.

Edwards, C., Gandini, L., & Forman, G. (Eds.). (1998). *The hundred languages of children: The Reggio Emilia approach: Advanced reflections*. Westport, CT: Ablex.

Fraser, H., & Taylor, N. (2016). *Neoliberalization, universities and the public intellectual*. New York: Palgrave.

Freire, P. (1972). *Pedagogy of the oppressed*. New York: Penguin.

Freire, P. (1994). *Pedagogy of hope*. New York: Continuum.

Freire, P. (1998). *Pedagogy of freedom*. Lanham, MD: Rowman and Littlefield.

Greene, M. (1995). *Releasing the imagination: Essays on education, the arts, and social change*. San Francisco: Jossey-Bass.

Greene, M. (1997). Teaching as possibility: A light in dark times. *The Journal of Pedagogy, Pluralism & Practice*, 1(1), 1–11.

Hamm, C., & Boucher, K. (2018). Engaging with place: Foregrounding Aboriginal perspective in early childhood education. In N. Yelland and D. Bentley (Eds.), *Found in translation: Connecting reconceptualist early childhood ideas with practice*. New York: Routledge.

Haraway, D.J. (2008). *When species meet*. Minneapolis: University of Minnesota Press.

Haraway, D. (2016). *Staying with the trouble: Making kin in the chthulucene*. Durham: Duke University Press.

Iorio, J.M., & Tanabe, C.S. (2015). A modest proposal e-imagined: Disrupting and rethinking educational decision-making. *Teachers College Record*. Retrieved from http://www.tcrecord.org (ID Number: 1882).

Iorio, J.M., & Tanabe, C.S. (2016). Challenging the neoliberal truth of student as consumer: Rethinking student as public intellectual. Paper presented at 24th Early Childhood Reconceptualist Education Conference (RECE), Taupo, New Zealand.

Iorio, J.M. & Tanabe, C.S. (2019). *Higher education and the practice of hope*. New York: Springer.

Latour, B. (2005). *Reassembling the social: An introduction to Actor-Network-Theory*. New York: Oxford University Press.

Martin, K. (2016). *Voices & visions: Aboriginal early childhood education in Australia*. New South Wales: Pademelon Press.

Nxumalo, F. (2016) Towards "refiguring presences" as an anti-colonial orientation to research in early childhood studies. *International Journal of Qualitative Studies in Education*, 29(5), 640–654. doi:10.1080/09518398.2016.1139212

Parnell, W. (2011). Revealing the experience of children and teachers even in their absence: Documenting in the early childhood studio. *Journal of Early Childhood Research*, 9(3), 291–309. doi:10.1177/1476718X10397903

Pente, P., Massing, C., & Kirova, A. (2018). Collaborative landscapes within Deleuze/Guattarian affect and assemblage: Aesthetic notions of place explored by preschool immigrant teachers, parents and children. In J.M. Iorio & W. Parnell (Eds.), *Meaning making in early childhood research: Pedagogies and the personal* (pp. 111–126). New York: Routledge.

Pink, S. (2008). An urban tour: The sensory sociality of ethnographic place-making . *Ethnography, 9*, 175–196. doi:10.1177/1466138108089467.

Quintero, E. (2018). Multifaceted storying among children and preservice teachers as bricoleurs: Ways to gather and care. In J.M. Iorio & W. Parnell (Eds.), *Meaning making in early childhood research: Pedagogies and the personal*. New York: Routledge.

Rinaldi, C. (2006). *In dialogue with Reggio Emilia: Listening, researching and learning*. Abingdon, UK: Routledge.

Solomon, S., Plattner, G.-K., Knutti, R., & Friedlingstein, P. (2009). Irreversible climate change due to carbon dioxide emissions. *Proceedings of the National Academy of Sciences, 106*, 1704–1709. doi:10.1073/pnas.0812721106.

Taylor, A., & Guigini, M. (2012). Common worlds: Reconceptualising inclusion in early childhood communities. *Contemporary Issues in Early Childhood*, 13(2), 108–119.

Taylor, A., & Pacini-Ketchabaw, V. (2015). Learning with children, ants, and worms in the anthropocene: Towards a common world pedagogy of multispecies vulnerability. *Pedagogy, Culture & Society*, 23(4), 507–529.

Tuck, E., McKenzie, M., & McCoy, M. (2014). Land education: Indigenous, post-colonial, and decolonizing perspectives on place and environmental education research. *Environmental Education Research, 20*(1), 1–23. doi:10.1080/13504622.2013.877708.

10

"WHAT'S LOVE GOT TO DO?"

Enacting The Beloved Community Through Early Childhood Education

Mara Sapon-Shevin

Introduction

"Now make sure you're sitting on your bottom on your own carpet square and that you're keeping your hands and feet to yourselves."

"Okay children, over to the story rug. Make sure you're snuggled up nice and close to your friends and that you are all comfortable with each other before we get started."

"I know you're upset that Jonah didn't have much lunch today, but you need to mind your own business."

"You noticed that some kids in our class don't seem to have enough to eat - let's talk as a class about what we could do about that."

"If Nadya's crying, you need to leave her alone to figure out what she needs to do to take care of herself."

"Maybe you could move over closer to Nadya and see if together you can figure out how to help her feel better."

The first proscription above may sound familiar, but the second directive, not only allowing but encouraging physical closeness and touch, is harder to imagine. The second paired quotes ask us to think about how ideas of independence/interdependence and mutual responsibility are conveyed to children. And the third set of quotes speaks to the value we place on helping students to acquire sensitivity to and skills in supporting those in need of help or support.

These contrastive quotes are intended to illuminate that the ways we structure education and the messages we give children - even very young children - about physical closeness, interdependence and support, will have a profound effect on their understandings of themselves and their relationships to others. As early childhood educators we have the opportunity and the privilege to shape early beliefs about how the world is organized and how we can interact with one another, both when things are going well, and when there are challenges and difficulties.

This chapter envisions what early childhood education might look like if building a loving community were the primary focus of our work. How we could operationalize a commitment to social justice in early childhood settings so that students are supported in learning how to interact with one another in loving and caring ways. And, more specifically, what if we recognized and honored that children live *through* their bodies, and believed children's bodies were not merely sites to be regulated, but provided opportunities to envision and enact possibilities of caring, connection and loving touch

I explore what it would mean to put "love" at the center of a social justice curriculum in early childhood education and some of the obstacles to that vision. I share some examples of teachers who have found ways to put love and loving touch at the center of their educational programs, eliminating false dichotomies between social-emotional development and academic achievement. I argue that creating a society that embodies inclusion and social justice requires the development of children as whole human beings who can create a beloved community in which they can connect, support, touch and be touched within a loving context.

Why Is This So Hard? Current Realities

Why is it so hard for discussions about early childhood education to center on love (Aslanian, 2018)? And what gets in the way of loving touch in schools? In an article entitled "Practitioners' Construction of Love in Early Childhood Education and Care," Cousins (2017) speaks to the importance and challenges of defining love in early childhood settings. She says that there is limited (and sometimes contested) discourse about what love is, and

> As long as love in early childhood education remains unspoken, it remains undefined, different in some ways to love in familiar contexts, with some unwelcome connotations, not the same in every situation, natural in some cases more than others, and tough at times.
>
> *(p. 16)*

Cousins (2017) links the lack of discourse about love to a variety of factors. One of the obstacles to talking about love is the domination of neo-liberal discourses on standards in which professionals are expected to perform in particular ways; to be a "professional" is to behave in ways that are predictable and measurable, and which are directly linked to outcomes. Campbell-Barr and Varga (2015), who ask "Where has all the love gone?" in developing early childhood professionals, also link the reticence to use the word love to notions that being a professional means *not* mothering young children, separating the teacher's role from that of a parent or caregiver.

Most significantly, however, I feel that the biggest challenge to naming, discussing and enacting love in early childhood settings is that love is often linked to "touch," thus tapping into what Tobin (1997) and others (Johnson, 1997) have defined as the "moral panic" about child abuse and pedophilia. This becomes particularly salient, of course, when discourses of love are associated with the ways in which teachers (and I would argue children themselves) touch children or interact with them physically.

Schools are often structured so that bodies are unwelcome, viewed as superfluous at best, and dangerous at worst in the learning process (Piper & Smith, 2003; Piper & Smith, 2002a, 2002b, 2002c; Piper & Smith, 1996). Tobin (1997) decries the mind-body split which risks having children (and caregivers) forget the capacity for feeling.

Many schools have eliminated the most embodied parts of the school day, particularly free play and recess. In my local elementary school, recess was eliminated for the entire year in 4th grade because of the pressure of statewide assessments. The children were told, "We don't have time to play." Sadly, this ban on play has also extended to eliminating other activities during the school day that are seen as unrelated to achievement and high stakes testing success, including music, art and physical education. The focus on high-stakes academic achievement has trickled down into early childhood settings with a decrease in playtime and an increase in direct instruction and testing. One of the kindergarten teachers I work with was required to disassemble her block corner, housekeeping corner and art corner and directed to stop singing with her students in order to have more time for children to engage in direct instruction and complete worksheets on reading and mathematics.

A recent thread on Facebook was initiated by a mother who was upset that her child's school had just implemented a "no touch" policy - no touching between children of any kind - even though the school uses the Responsive Classrooms Models[1] where they are allowed to give each other a high-five or a handshake as part of greeting one another in the morning. But touch any other time during the day is now forbidden. Another parent responded,

> I am so sad to hear this. We need to teach students to interact with one another in an appropriate, positive manner. We also need to teach them it is ok to set personal space boundaries and give them the voice to say, "please stop" if someone is crossing those boundaries.

But children are the *essence* of embodiment. They are "in" their bodies and they learn through their bodies. Leavitt and Power (1997) state,

> The body is not only the source of unending and ever-changing feelings and emotions but is also the criterion by which we evaluate our experiences in the world, experiences that may either threaten the self or open the way to fulfillment.
>
> *(p. 43)*

When children are not permitted to be embodied or to learn in embodied ways, they learn not to connect with their own bodies. In many schools, children are not even allowed to urinate when they need to, their bodies so tightly controlled by others. Leavitt and Power (1997) explain that, "A child who fails to learn appropriate body management incorporates this stigma into his or her self-identity" (p. 43).

Concerns about touching have two major foci: one concerns how teachers touch children and the other how children touch one another. If children are not allowed to be in their own bodies, they are certainly not supposed to interact with other children's bodies either. A colleague's five-year-old came home from kindergarten and reported that he had been admonished for hugging a friend who was crying and told that touch was not allowed in school. His mother, certain that the child had misunderstood the real intention of the teacher's rule, engaged him in a discussion. "I'm pretty sure she didn't mean that you couldn't touch each other; she must have meant that you couldn't hit each other or hurt each other. I think you should try again." Two days later the child came home from school and reported: "Mom, you were wrong. Matthew was crying, and I went to hug him, and the teacher yelled at me again. She said, 'You know the rule: We don't touch other children in this classroom. Keep your hands to yourself.'" The parent - an education professor - was wrong; the five-year-old was right. He had not misunderstood. Touch, even a hug for an unhappy friend, was unacceptable.

Children learn that seeking bodily pleasure is wrong and dangerous. The little girl who leans into a classmate while seated on the rug for story time is often told to move away from her neighbor. Little boys who touch little girls are apt to be labeled as sexual aggressors or predators, even at an incredibly young age, and little boys who touch each other are particularly alarming.

How can students learn to form relationships and learn ways of connecting, interacting and loving, if they are prohibited from engaging in the most human of activities - touch? The sense of separation and isolation among students is highly problematic, not only because positive touch is not allowed, but because bodies become sites of struggle and competition, not sources of support and connection. Not allowing touch can be seen as a form of dehumanization, since providing loving touch to others is one of the essentials of being human.

At the same time that children's bodies and desires must be brought under control, the teacher's own bodies and desires must be tightly regulated as well. Phelan (1997) describes the ways in which teachers' bodies become intimately connected with notions of control and classroom management. She states, "Teachers are expected to distance themselves from their students, to exercise self-control, to honor a static notion of autonomy that eliminates the possibility of intimacy with children, and to maintain a serious attitude in the classroom" (p. 87).

Leavitt and Power (1997) describe how teachers "touch children primarily to control and manipulate their bodies, to exercise their power, and much less often to express affection, tenderness, comfort, or intimacy" (p. 65). Piper and Smith (2003) describe the frustration of caregivers who must ignore what they know and believe about teaching in order to comply with "no touch" policies and interrogate the effects of the increasing surveillance imposed on teachers to make sure they have not touched children inappropriately.

What is it like to teach in a setting in which one's behavior is carefully observed to make sure that there is compliance with no touch policies? How is it possible to teach from an embodied position if one must control physical contact so carefully? Such policies instill fear, promote lack of authenticity and feel dehumanizing, driving teachers - loving, caring, affectionate humans - away from the classroom. Piper and Smith (2003) state,

> The touching of children in professional settings is no longer relaxed, or instinctive, and primarily concerned with responding to the needs of the child. It has become a negative act that requires a mind-body split of children and adults controlled more by fear than by caring.
>
> *(p. 891)*

Not being able to *teach* bodies and *have* bodies also limits classroom curricular and pedagogical choices; differentiated instruction using multiple intelligence demands that we be in our bodies.

Concerns about sexual impropriety have produced a flurry of attempts to monitor and regulate the ways in which teachers touch their students. The fear for teachers, particularly male teachers, is palpable. They are asked to never be alone with a child, to make sure someone else is present if they have to touch a child to clean them up or assist them with toileting. In an article on no touch policies by Johnson (1997), a male teacher says:

> In the school where I work, I have been told by female teachers that I often appear to be cold and uncaring toward students, but with all the court appearances, who can blame me? I do show some verbal emotion towards students, but only if there is another teacher or student in the room. I avoid body contact.
>
> *(pp. 102–103)*

The director of one day care center explains the Center's no touch policy and her enforcement of it:

> The picking-up thing, I just - I don't allow it, because that's one of those issues where you have, you know, the direct physical contact, body to body, that could be misconstrued, so I – I stop it there. (...) I'll say, "No. No holding." Or if it's one of the little kids, I might say, "OK, Steven, now you know you need to get down," and then I will privately remind the [caregiver]. "Remember, now, we don't do that. I know you're just enjoying this child. However, it could be misconstrued. It could be a problem for you."
>
> *(Johnson, 1997, p. 109)*

It is mind boggling to imagine how one could care for young children all day without touching them, but, in many settings, that is the goal and the regulation. Children in the United States are touched far less than their counterparts around the world (Zur & Nordmarken, n.d.) and although positive touch is absent in many children's lives, negative or punitive touch is easily available. Many children learn that the only way to be touched is through the use of aggression; although hitting and pushing are not sanctioned, they do result in desperately desired physical contact.

We have created a vicious circle; we are so nervous about inappropriate touch that we fail to touch children, and this lack of touch leads to ever-increasing aggressive and anti-social behavior which is responded to punitively and sometimes even with physical punishment (Piper & Smith, 2003). Although the research shows that 90% of reported cases of child abuse and neglect occur in the home, it is schools and teachers that have become tightly regulated (Finkelhor & Ormrod, 2000).

Teaching for Social Justice

What does it mean to "teach for social justice"? And what would it look like if love and "loving touch" were central to schools' missions on social justice and equity? Many educational programs now list social justice as part of their mission statement. There is not, however, a shared understanding or universally accepted definition of exactly what that means. Bree Picower (2012b) defines six elements of a social justice curriculum for elementary classrooms. Picower believes that enacting these elements can help teachers visualize social justice education and provide direct applications for curriculum and learning activities. These six elements are: (1) Self Love and Knowledge; (2) Respect for Others; (3) Issues of Social Injustice; (4) Social Movements and Social Change; (5) Awareness Raising; and (6) Social Action. Picower explains that:

by addressing these six elements of social justice education in the elementary classroom, teachers lead students to value themselves, respect the diversity of the world around them, understand how diverse people have been treated differently and often unjustly, recognize that ordinary people have worked to address such injustice, and take action themselves.

(Picower, 2012b, p. 2)

Although attention to social justice with children is often framed as helping them to recognize and address "unfairness," Picower's model extends beyond recognizing injustice to helping students develop mindsets and skill sets to be activists who can stand up for social justice. Although Picower does not directly address early childhood education, I believe that these same principles apply.

An excellent article by Caitrin Blake (2015) provides examples of the kinds of questions that can be used with students (even young ones, I would argue) that will enable deep conversations about issues of social justice.

These include asking students "Who makes decisions and who is left out?" and "Why is a given practice fair or unfair?" Hytten and Bettez (2011) believe that a primary purpose of education should "help to promote the knowledge and skills needed for thoughtful citizenship" (p. 19). And I believe it is possible to think about what it means to be a "thoughtful citizen" even in settings for very young people.

One of the most operationalized enactments of social justice has been described as "anti-bias education" (Adams, Griffin & Bell, 2007; Derman-Sparks & Edwards, 2010; Farago & Swadener, 2016; Kalin, 2002; Sapon-Shevin, 2007). Anti-bias education is rooted in the belief that in order for anyone to challenge or resist oppression, three components are necessary: individuals must recognize that something unfair, discriminatory or oppressive is taking place; must be able to name that injustice in some way; and must have active strategies for addressing that injustice.

Derman-Sparks and Edwards say that:

children cannot construct a strong self-concept or develop respect for others if they do not know how to identify and resist hurtful, stereotypical, and inaccurate messages or actions directed toward them or others. Developing the ability to think critically strengthens children's sense of self, as well as their capacity to form caring relationships with others.

(Derman-Sparks & Edwards, 2010, p. 5)

I am interested in how the attention to injustice can be fostered within a loving community with particular attention to love, touch and connection.

My own vision of social justice is one that extends beyond particular aspects of character and a focus on injustices and inequalities. My vision is an *embodied* one that asks how social justice is enacted in and through children's bodies. My vision privileges how bodies move through space and interact with one another and interrogates how love and loving touch are manifested in early childhood settings. I ask: How are children's bodies respected and treated as part of a loving community? How is love evidenced through children and adults' physical interactions? What are children taught about how they can use their words and their bodies to support justice, inclusion and equity?

How It Could Be: Early Childhood as a Beloved Community

What would a social justice orientation actively infused with love look like? The expression the "Beloved Community" was popularized by Dr. Martin Luther King Jr. as a society based on justice, equal opportunity and love of one's fellow human beings. Coretta Scott King, the founder of The King Center, explains:

> Dr. King's Beloved Community is a global vision in which all people can share in the wealth of the earth. In the Beloved Community, poverty, hunger and homelessness will not be tolerated because international standards of human decency will not allow it. Racism and all forms of discrimination, bigotry and prejudice will be replaced by an all-inclusive spirit of sisterhood and brotherhood.
>
> *(Ritterman, 2014)*

What would it look like if we envisioned early childhood settings as places and opportunities to envision and enact the Beloved Community. What would that mean for how we design and implement educational policies and practices? In a publication by the United Methodist Church (2017), Dr. Arthuree Wright describes 25 traits of the Beloved Community. I would like to speak here to what some of these might look like in an early childhood education setting, connecting conceptualizations of Beloved Community with an approach to early childhood education that is rooted in a commitment to social justice and democratic schooling and that works with a framework of explicitly anti-bias education (see Table 10.1).

Enacting the Beloved Community

I believe that the Beloved Community could be actualized in early childhood education in four ways:

1. Honoring children's bodies as a form of love
2. Touching one another thoughtfully as a form of love
3. Inclusion as a form of love
4. Social-justice oriented social skills as a form of love.

TABLE 10.1 The Beloved Community in early childhood education

Trait of the Beloved Community	What this might mean in Early Childhood Education
Offers radial hospitality to everyone; an inclusive family rather than exclusive club	Fully inclusive classrooms; all children are welcomed and belong. Hospitality would mean that inclusion goes beyond mere physical presence and includes the creation on a welcoming community.
Gathers together regularly for table fellowship, and meets the needs of everyone in the community	There are frequent and on-going efforts made to build community. This may include morning meetings, community building activities and extended times for students to talk and interact with one another. Social interaction is privileged in and of itself, not simply as a vehicle to improve academic achievement.
Recognition and affirmation, not eradication, of differences Builds increasing levels of trust and works to avoid fear of difference and others	This speaks directly to an anti-bias approach to early childhood education which eschews colorblindness in favor of helping students recognize, name and understand many kinds of differences. The desire is not to create homogeneity but to honor and build on heterogeneity. Children are helped to learn language related to differences in race, class, gender, ethnicity, language, religion, family make-up, etc.
Listens emotionally (i.e., with the heart) – fosters empathy and compassion for others Speaks truth in love, always considering ways to be compassionate with one another Acknowledges conflict or pain in order to work on difficult issues	Social skills including empathy and compassion are named and taught. Students are encouraged to develop listening and support skills and to employ these when classmates are distressed. There is explicit recognition that life can be hard, painful and unjust.
Focuses energy on removing evil forces (unjust systems), not destroying persons Unyielding persistence and unwavering commitment to justice Promotes human rights and works to create a non-racist society	A commitment to understanding, naming and discussing injustice pervades the classroom. Children are given skills in noticing and responding to inequities regarding student participation, respect and acknowledgment and develop skills in personal and social justice advocacy.

Honoring Children's Bodies as a Form of Love

If bodies were fully integrated, accepted and valued in education, then students would be taught the language of bodies. They would be encouraged to move their bodies during the day in a variety of settings. They would be taught to talk about their feelings, paying careful attention to what was happening for them internally and externally as well. Bodies would be respected as an important source of information and knowledge. "Trust your gut" would be seen as important pedagogy.

Seymour School

> Seventeen children sit in a circle on little (half-size) yoga mats with their eyes closed. Their teacher, Midge Regier, sounds a chime, and when the sound stops, they open their eyes.
>
> They take five breaths together, while holding out their hands, fingers splayed; they "blow out" their fingers, one at a time. "Why are we doing this?" asks their teacher. "To calm ourselves," they reply. Then they take quick bunny breaths, for energy, grab the sunshine with their hands and pull it in.

In chorus, they recite their yoga pledge, each line accompanied by a different yoga pose:

> Yoga makes me feel energized and powerful
> Yoga makes me feel balanced and centered
> Yoga makes me feel strong and flexible
> Yoga makes me feel calm and focused
> Yoga makes me feel peaceful and loving
> We are all connected (finger interlaced)
> Your heart and my heart are one (they point to one another). Namaste.

Midge teaches a lesson about birds and perseverance, and the children pretend to be different kinds of birds. She then links her instruction to a book about birds. After a half hour of pretending to be different kinds of bird, it is time for a meditation. The children lie on their backs, breathing quietly. Midge walks around and places a Beanie Baby on each child's stomach, so that the animal moves up and down as the child breathes. The room is quiet, and the little bodies are still. The focus is on breathing. As they close, a song is played: "Namaste."

The teacher walks around the room and puts a little lavender oil on each child's forehead. She gives each child an affirmation and tells each student she loves them. Midge says this gives her a loving connection with each child.

Teacher Midge Regier is trained in a method called Yoga Kids[2] which is growing quickly in the US. There is increasing research to support a correlation between yoga and increased academic performance, fewer discipline referrals and increases in attendance and self-esteem. Although increases in achievement are welcomed, for Midge, who teaches in a dual language school which is one of the poorest in the city, the benefits of helping students be in their bodies goes far beyond that. She explains "So much is happening in their brains when they're doing this. We're changing them inside out. We don't even begin to understand what we're doing. It's monumental."

Touching One Another Thoughtfully as a Form of Love

What would it mean to connect with our own bodies while we are teaching, and to allow students to connect with their own and others' bodies as well? As hooks (1994) asserts, we must be whole as humans in the classrooms if we are to allow others to be wholehearted as well.

While the need to protect children is certainly valid, there are other ways to do this than by making blanket no-touch policies. We can best keep children and teachers safe by making discussions about touching frequent, easy and fluid, by empowering students to make decisions about their own bodies and by opening, rather than closing, channels of communication.

Rosa Parks Elementary School

I was working in a classroom with two wonderful kindergarten teachers. There had been a recent incident in the classroom in which one little boy had grabbed the behind of a little girl. There was much upset, and the situation quickly escalated to talk of "sexual harassment" and abuse; the teachers were alarmed and tried to take charge of the situation. They gathered the students on the rug and spoke to them: "There's something very important we have to talk about. It's not okay to touch one another. You can't touch each other in this classroom. Does everyone understand?"

The children looked puzzled about what was being said. While they were being lectured about not touching, they were sitting in close proximity to one another, some of them touching and cuddling close to each other. Moreover, this didn't sound like their teachers - both of whom I had seen hug many children throughout the day.

After this conversation, I approached these teachers: "I'm wondering about what you just said to the kids," I said. "Is that really what you mean? That they shouldn't touch each other?" As we continued the conversation, they articulated quite clearly that it wasn't about touch, obviously, but about certain kinds of touch that were negative - hitting, pushing or inappropriately intrusive (grabbing underwear). I suggested spending some time engaging in activities in which they get to touch one another - in ways that are appropriate - so that we could talk to them about appropriate and inappropriate touch.

We gathered the kids and went out on the playground. We played two cooperative games: "People to People," during which students touched one another in silly ways, shaking hands, elbows and knees, and "Touch Blue," a form of human twister. There was lots of giggling and silliness. We ended by doing a singing/dancing game, in which children danced with partners and then changed partners after each round. The discussion which followed was quite different. We discussed all the wonderful ways we could touch one another and the ones that were problematic.

How do we protect our children from inappropriate touch? From invasions of their bodies and their space? By making rules: no touching, no hugging, no interaction? Or by giving them many opportunities to touch one another appropriately, to learn language about touch and feelings, and articulate: "I don't like that;" "That's too hard;" or "That makes me nervous."

Another body-friendly approach is called Peaceful Touch.[3] Begun by Hans Axelson in Stockholm in the early 1990s, the Peaceful Touch program is based on three fundamentals: (1) Touch is necessary for human growth and development; (2) That the calming hormone, oxytocin, is activated through touch; and (3) That a permission process supports healthy touch and helps establish good boundaries.

More than 300,000 students in Europe have been recipients of Peaceful Touch, in which children learn to give one another massages and to touch each other gently and respectfully, and it is institutionalized in Swedish pre-schools. An article about the program reports: "Healthy touch, which is what we'll call it here, helps foster attachment; decrease aggression, depression and anxiety; and helps children identify healthy touch so they are less vulnerable to abuse, and less likely to be prematurely sexually active" (LaPlante, 2007, p. 76). The article quotes Frances M. Carlson, author of *Essential Touch: Meeting the Needs of Young Children*, who says, "What I think we don't understand in this culture is that withholding touch from children from fear is as physically and emotionally harmful to children as harmful touch is" (Carlson, 2006). The originators of the program have adapted it for the US, including eliminating hand to skin contact and some forms of massage.

Inclusion as a Form of Love

The operationalized enactment of resistance to discrimination, marginalization and exclusion is the creation of truly inclusive settings. We teach children to see and name differences - the opposite of a "colorblindness" ideology - and we teach them how to interact with and support classmates who are different. Jowonio is an inclusive pre-school in Syracuse, New York. It was one of the first schools in the United States to include children with significant disabilities. The name Jowonio comes from the word in the Onondaga nation language which means "to set free." "The school's founders chose this name because they believed that education should be freeing minds and emotions to learn and grow, freeing individuals from stereotypes and prejudices."[4] Now, in its 50th year, Jowonio teaches specifically to goals of inclusionary, anti-bias thinking and behavior.

They state:

> We want children to learn to respond to classroom peers in helpful ways, to make choices and become independent in their work, and to maintain a strong and positive sense of themselves while adapting to the routines and demands a group setting like school requires. We hope to model non-sexist behaviors and encourage nurturing and active play in both boys and girls. We value the great diversity in our community in terms of cultures and needs and the learning opportunities this brings to us all.[5]

At Jowonio, children learn to think "inclusively" about snack, which means considering children who keep kosher, children who eat only Halal food, children with food allergies and children who can only eat soft foods or are fed through a tube. There are open discussions about how to organize snacks and eating so that everyone has their needs met, and questions are answered honestly.

Children explore how they can celebrate birthdays, understanding that not every person likes to be sung to, can eat cake or comes from a family, culture or religion that celebrates birthdays in the same way, or at all. The playground at Jowonio is designed so that all children can play, including those with limited mobility and those who use wheelchairs or walkers. Discussions of "fairness" in games deepens children's understanding of the exclusionary effects of competition and the need to design activities that provide opportunities for participation and fun for everyone.

Talking explicitly about the principles and values of inclusion are everyday occurrences. There is no attempt to ignore differences or to shame children for their natural curiosity about other children's bodies or skills. And discussions about respectful helping that maintains the dignity and agency of the person being helped are ongoing. When the school celebrated its 25th anniversary, I composed the following poem, speaking directly to the links between what children at Jowonio were learning and its extension in the wide world.

What the Children of Jowonio Know

The children of Jowonio know—not because they have been told—but because they have lived it

That there is always room for everyone—in the circle and at snack time and on the playground—and even if they have to wiggle a little to get another body in and even if they have to find a new way to do it, they can figure it out—and so it might be reasonable to assume that there's enough room for everyone in the world

The children of Jowonio know—not because they have been told—but because they have lived it

That children come in a dazzling assortment of sizes, colors and shapes, big and little and all shades of brown and beige and pink, and some walk and some use wheelchairs but everyone gets around and that same is boring—and so it might be reasonable to assume that everyone in the world could be accepted for who they are

The children of Jowonio know—not because they have been told—but because they have lived it

That there are people who talk with their mouths and people who talk with their hands and people who talk by pointing and people who tell us all we need to know with their bodies if we only listen well—and so it might be reasonable to assume that all the people of the world could learn to talk to and listen to each other

The children of Jowonio know—not because they have been told—but because they have lived it

> That we don't send people away because they're different or even because they're difficult, and that all people need support and that if people are hurting, we take the time to notice, and that words can build bridges and hugs can heal—and so it might be reasonable to assume that all the people on the planet could reach out to each other and heal the wounds and make a world fit for us all.
>
> *(Sapon-Shevin, 2010, p. 11)*

When my daughter Dalia was a young adult, she worked at Jowonio for a year, and she speaks directly to what it means to truly internalize a worldview that is inclusive and responsive. She says: "Whenever I see someone's nose running, I reach for a tissue. When I see someone's laces untied, I bend over to tie them. And when I hear people saying mean things to one another, I sometimes say, 'Can you use your kind words?'" While she acknowledges that reaching down to tie the shoelaces of a woman in the supermarket or offering a tissue to a stranger at the bank may not be socially normative, her experience at a school that genuinely lives and breathes inclusion and a commitment to social justice was transformative.

How might we see early childhood settings such as Jowonio as models for what could be? What if the world were one in which we were, as citizens, constantly alert to injustice and ill-treatment and skilled in challenging oppression and working for inclusion and justice?

Social Justice-Oriented Social Skills as a Form of Love

Early childhood education has always had the development of positive social interaction skills as one of its foci. Unlike later grades in which social and emotional development is positioned as separate from academic achievement, early childhood education has recognized young children as social beings who are learning to co-exist and interact in shared settings.

Both the research literature and the popular press are replete with lists of the social skills that young children should master during their pre-school and early childhood years.

Social skills are often categorized as relating to self-management (controlling feelings, thoughts, et,); self-awareness (recognizing feeling and thoughts); social awareness (including empathy with others and perspective-taking); responsible decision making (following rules, showing respect); and relationship skills (listening to others, offering help, resolving conflicts, etc.).[6]

However, it is important to ask what social skills are privileged for instruction, monitoring and evaluation? According to what cultural lens are social skills deemed acceptable or unacceptable? Is calling attention to injustice positive or could it be read as disrespectful and disruptive? One person's "brave" is another person's "rude." Are the social skills that are chosen for instruction and monitoring always compatible with a vision of early childhood settings as sites of social justice and democracy? I would like to propose that examining social skills' development within a context of social justice and anti-bias education might lead us to privilege different behaviors.

What would it mean, for example, not only to teach children to ask politely for a cookie, but also to notice who doesn't have a cookie and take steps to address that situation?

What would it mean to not only teach children NOT to tease (using kind words, etc.) but also to begin to develop awareness of who gets teased in their classroom and what the teasing is about (Husband, 2016; Sapon-Shevin, 2001)? Why are children teasing Matthew about putting on a dress and high heels in the dress-up corner and how can they support Matthew? What do children need to know and do to support Sarita who, newly arrived from Mexico, struggles to be understood and included in the life of the classroom?

And what are students to do in the face of genuine tragedy, inequality or pain? What happens when life isn't joyful, when children's situations are painful, and when societal inequalities are enacted in classrooms? What skills might we teach students that acknowledge that life can be painful, messy, complicated and sometimes incomprehensible? How might we re-configure social skills that are typically labeled as "manners" or "politeness" in ways that encourage collective responsibility for how everyone is treated in the class?

I believe there is a strong need to expand or re-configure what we call "social skills" to include social injustice awareness and advocacy. As Derman-Sparks and others have modeled, even very young children can become knowledgeable and active advocates for equity and inclusion.

Looking Forward

It is exciting to think that young children could experience early childhood education that is rooted in a social justice, anti-bias perspective with love at the center. And, through a focus on respecting bodies, teaching thoughtful touch, modeling full inclusion and teaching social-justice oriented social skills, children might grow to become citizens who embrace and enact diversity, justice and inclusion in their lives, and who fight for equality in all that they do. This is important work; let us move forward with love.

Notes

1 See https://www.responsiveclassroom.org.
2 See www.yogakids.com.
3 See www.peacefultouch.net.
4 See jowonio.org.
5 See jowonio.org/curriculum/.
6 See https://www.kiddiematters.com.

References

Adams, M., Bell, L.A. & Griffin, P. (Eds.). (2007). *Teaching for diversity and social justice* (2nd Ed.). New York: Routledge.

Aslanian, T.K. (2018) Embracing uncertainty: A diffractive approach to love in the context of early childhood education and care. *International Journal of Early Years Education*, 26(2), 173–185. doi:10.1080/09669760.2018.1458604

Blake, C. (2015). Teaching social justice in theory and practice. Retrieved from https://education.cuportland.edu/blog/classroom-resources/teaching-social-justice/

Campbell-Barr, V. & Varga, A.N. (2015). Developing professional early childhood educators in England and Hungary: Where has all the love gone? *European Education*, 47, 311–330.

Carlson, F.M. (2006). *Essential touch: Meeting the needs of young children* (1st Ed.). Washington, DC: National Association for the Education of Young Children.

Carlson, F.M. & Nelson, B.G. (2006). Reducing aggression with touch. *Dimensions*, 34(3), 9–15.

Cousins, S.B. (2017). Practitioners' constructions of love in early childhood education and care. *International Journal of Early Years Education*, 25(1), 16–29.

Derman-Sparks, L. & Edwards, J.O. (2010). *Anti-bias education for young children and ourselves*. New York: NAEYC.

Farago, F. & Swadener, B.B (2016). Race and gender in United States early childhood settings: Researcher reflections. In R.R. Scarlet (Ed.), *The anti-bias approach in early childhood* (3rd edition) (pp. 333–341). Mt. Victoria, AU: Pademelon Press.

Finkelhor, D. & Ormrod, R. (2000) *Characteristics of crimes against juveniles*. Bulletin. Washington, DC: US Department of Justice, Office of Justice Programs, Office of Juvenile Justice and Delinquency Prevention. Retrieved from http:///www.ncjrs.gov/pdfiles/ojjdp/179034.pdf

Hooks, b. (1994). *Teaching to transgress: Education as the practice of freedom*. New York: Routledge.

Husband, T. (2016). Ignorance is not bliss: Moving beyond colorblind perspectives and practices in education. In T. Husband (Ed.), *But I don't see color*. Rotterdam: Sense Publishers, 3–19.

Hytten, K. & Bettez, S.C. (Winter-Spring-Winter-Spring, 2011). Understanding education for social justice. *Educational Foundations*, 7–24

Johnson, R. (1997). The "No Touch" policy. In J. Tobin (Ed.), *Making a place for pleasure in early childhood education* (pp. 101–118). New Haven: Yale University Press.

Kalin, J. (2002). *Antiracist education: From theory to practice*. New York: Rowman & Littlefield. Retrieved from https://www.kiddiematters.com

LaPlante, C. (2007). The kids are all right. *Massage Therapy Journal*, 46(3), 74–81.

Leavitt, R.L. & Power, M.B. (1977). Civilizing bodies: Children in day care. In J. Tobin (Ed.), *Making a place for pleasure in early childhood education* (pp. 39–75). New Haven: Yale University Press.

Phelan, A.M. (1997). Classroom management and the erasure of teacher desire. In J. Tobin (Ed.), *Making a place for pleasure in early childhood education* (pp. 76–100). New Haven: Yale University Press.

Picower, B. (2012a). *Practice what you teach: Social justice education in the classroom and the streets*. New York: Routledge.

Picower, B. (2012b). Using their words: Six elements of social justice curriculum design for the elementary classroom. *International Journal of Multicultural Education*, 14(1), 1–17.

Piper, H. and Smith, H. (2003). 'Touch' in educational and child care settings: Dilemmas and responses. *British Educational Research Journal*, 29(6), 879–894.

Ritterman, J. (2014). The Beloved Community: Martin Luther King Jr.'s prescription for a healthy society. *Huffington Post*. Retrieved from https://www.huffingtonpost.com/jeffrey-ritterman/the-beloved-community-dr-_b_4583249.html

Sapon-Shevin, M. (2001). Making inclusion visible: Honoring the process and the struggle. *Democracy and Education*, 14(1), 24–27.

Sapon-Shevin, M. (2007). *Widening the circle: The power of inclusive classrooms*. Boston: Beacon Press.

Sapon-Shevin, M. (2009). To touch and be touched: The missing discourse of bodies in education. In S. Shapiro (Ed.), *Education and hope in troubled times: Visions of change for our children's world* (pp. 68–183). New York: Routledge.

Sapon-Shevin, M. (2010). *Because we can change the world: A practical guide to building cooperative, inclusive classroom communities* (2nd Ed.) Thousand Oaks, CA: Corwin Press.

Shapiro, S. (2002a). Toward a critical pedagogy of peace education. In G. Salomon & B. Nevo (Eds.), *Peace Education* (pp. 63–71). Mahwah, NJ: LEA.

Shapiro, S. B. (2002b). The commonality of the body: Pedagogy and peace culture. In G. Salomon & B. Nevo (Eds.), *Peace Education* (pp. 143–154). Mahwah, NJ: Lawrence Erlbaum Associates.

Shapiro, S. B. (2002c). The body: The site of common humanity. In S. Shapiro and S. Shapiro (Eds.), *Body pedagogy, politics and social change movements* (p. 35). Creskill, NJ: Hampton Press.

Silin, J. (1996). *Sex, death and the education of our children: Our passion for ignorance in the age of AIDS*. New York: Teachers College Press.

Tobin, J. (Ed.). (1997). *Making a place for pleasure in early childhood education*. New Haven: Yale University Press.

United Methodist Church (2017). *25 traits of the Beloved Community*. Retrieved from http://www.gcorr.org/25-traits-of-the-beloved-community/

Zur, O. & Nordmarken, N. (n.d.). To tough or not to touch: Exploring the myth of Prohibition on touch in psychotherapy and counseling: Clinical, ethical and legal considerations. Retrieved from https://www.zurinstitute.com/touch-in-therapy

11

SOCIAL JUSTICE IN EARLY EDUCATION AND CHILD CARE

"What Is" and "What Ought to Be?"

Marianne N. Bloch

Introduction

In a recent chapter, Shirley Kessler (2018) writes about "what is," and "what could be" with regard to the early childhood curriculum. This volume focuses on notions of democracy and social justice in early childhood curriculum(s) and in programs for young children locally, nationally, and globally. Yet—as I am just celebrating the birth of my third grandbaby, a little girl named Remi—I cannot help but think of the inequalities and inequities that are already apparent in her life, and so many others. As much as I am grateful for the good prenatal and postnatal health care her mother has had, and the likelihood that she will have "a good life," I cannot ignore the fact that the majority of the world's young children and their mothers and families have unequal and inequitable access to food, housing, and prenatal and postnatal health care. Too many, without choice, have no access to life-saving early immunizations, medicine, and early education or later schooling. How is it that our global cultural systems have been organized in such a way as to, seemingly, accept, or not to be able to "fix" the global inequities and inequalities related to young children, and their families around the world? In this chapter I use quantitative reasoning for "inequalities" that manifest themselves so clearly in statistics, and the term "inequities" to reinforce a more qualitative sense of fairness. Both concepts relate to notions and material realities of social justice/social injustice for children and families, worldwide.

In what follows, I emphasize the long history of social, economic, and political inequities (see Ladson-Billings, 2006, on the "educational debt") as well as social, political, and economic inequalities and inequities in many geographic areas within the US and across all regions of the world. I also recognize cultural/racial inequities that occur during a young child's life. These inequities start with social, geographic, economic, housing, health, and justice system policies that are unfair and discriminatory. They end with a history of multi-generational cumulative effects of policies and resulting, often, in vast, material differences in children's family and community life. The worst current example in the United States is occurring at our Southern Borders, where children's and families' rights are being abused/violated in the worst way through separation of children from families and forced incarceration of children in cages and for-profit group homes where many children have been abused.

As I go deeper into a litany of injustices, I don't want to ignore the caregivers and educators working in early education and child care settings. Whitebrook (2018) catalogued the many ways in which pay and benefits for those who take care/educate our youngest children all too often leave caregivers'/educators' families stuck at or under poverty levels. I also question the long-standing inequitable access to "higher quality" types of programs, and to the high turnover, lack of diversity among, and literal dearth of caregivers/teachers for young children who have a good background and experience in early education—especially with those from diverse gender, language, and cultural backgrounds. The lack of early childhood teachers/caregivers may be a result of low pay and benefits, as well as a gendered society that assumes "women's work" needn't be paid well (Whitebrook, 2018). Taking note of these long-standing issues and questions helps us to understand the breadth and depth of local and global injustices that have gone on way too long—and our own positions and actions.

How Do We Reconceptualize and Act on "What Is" Versus "What Ought to Be?"

As we attempt to reconceptualize democratic policies, gendered, racialized, culturally and economically unequal and unjust/unfair practices in this book, the words above are meant to illustrate the long-standing challenges that "we have not overcome" in the US, nor in our global interrelations and communities; indeed, we now are beginning to critique ourselves more—as it is obvious "we" and "I" are and am part of the problem after so many years in this type of work. Yet, I still draw on hope and love. As Luther King (1958), in my interpretation, suggested the arch of social justice is long, we should not give up hope, or ways to think anew. I am writing this chapter within this "arch of hope."

What do I Mean When I Use the Term "Social Justice"?

Throughout my career as a writer, teacher, and researcher, I, and others, have used different theoretical lenses in doing our work to look at different questions, issues, and policies (Bloch, 1992; Bloch, Holmquist, Moqvist, & Popkewitz, 2003), and today, many of us draw on a "toolbox" of diverse theories and methodologies in examining different issues. In this section, I use examples from my own and others' work to illustrate different ways we can look at the concept and practices, as well as analysis of "social justice" within early education and child care work.

An Equality and Equity Framework.

In several smaller and larger scale research projects I used statistical differences and similarities to examine ways in which disparities exist, looking for patterns and policies that would "close the gaps"; this would be closer to a social justice as equality/inequality framework. When one speaks about equal access to opportunities for good health care, nutrition, immunizations, good preschools and primary schools, I have often been hopeful that opportunity might afford a social justice purpose; after all, the majority of children and families should or ought to have equal opportunities in housing, be free of hunger, and have the opportunity to have a "good life." In work in West Africa in Senegal, the Gambia, and in Guinea, I, along with other researchers, tried to provide ways to erase obstacles to access for children to preschools and primary schools; in Guinea, for example, a country where girls have little ability to get to or get through primary school, we looked for obstacles and developed policy proposals to erase barriers (Anderson-Levitt, Bloch, & Soumare, 1998). In another example, Swadener and Bloch examined multiple reasons for why and how inequality of access to preschool occurred in Senegal and the Gambia (Swadener & Bloch, 1990; Bloch & Swadener, 2007). Policy recommendations were aimed at equality; but other recommendations focused on equity issues unfairly presenting barriers to girls more than boys.

A Reconceptualist Framework of Social Justice Focusing on Unequal Structural Power Relations.

While the equality/inequity issues are important, early childhood reconceptualists have drawn on a variety of frameworks, including those of Freire (1970), Habermas (1985), Apple (1982/1995), black and Latina feminists bell hooks (e.g., hooks, 2000) Patricia Hill Collins (2000/2008), and Gloria Anzualdua (e.g., Anzualdua, 1987; Moraga & Anzualdua, 2015) to examine unequal power relations. Questions focus on whose knowledge counts in the curriculum, and who decides. Whose knowledge is omitted from the curriculum, and why? Why are there continuing issues related to race, class, caste, and gender such as inequitable access to schools, unequal suspension/expulsion rates, and few teachers of color in many of our programs?

We need to question the stagnant policy framework that fails often to question massive inequities in our child care/early childhood and primary schools for younger (and older) children. Why are wages so low for caregiver educators of our young children, at a time when science tells us that approximately three quarters of women are in the workforce and require care/education for children as young as six weeks? Why are there "child care deserts" (almost no centers) in many urban, suburban, and rural lower income neighborhoods? What are the structural race, class, gender, and ability/disability processes that keep these inequalities and inequities in place? Why are policies made and maintained that continue incremental shifts that include some, while maintaining exclusion for so many? Intersectionality theory suggests that each "identity" and all "identities" may play a part in both internalized oppression and external discrimination and oppression. Intersectionality of structural aspects of oppression allows us to examine the specific and varied ways in which one's cultural/racial/social identities are enacted in different situations—by self and others. The maintenance of discriminatory, unequal or unfair and unjust practices forces us to identify the problems and practices, as well as posit what we/I might do to make change.

Whereas many have drawn on a "grand narrative" (class, race, gender structural oppression) to understand cultural/educational reproduction and production, as well as resistance strategies, others have used a structural perspective such as Critical Race Theory (e.g., Ladson-Billings & Tate, 1995), that incorporates a patriarchal and/or class framework to look at who benefits from our curriculum choices and whose knowledge is included/excluded. In the US the dominant early education curricular approaches draw directly from Developmentally Appropriate Practice (DAP) guidelines published by the National Association of the Education for Young Children (Copple & Bredekamp, 2009.) Many have suggested over the years that this approach privileges white middle-class or elite western children. Culturally relevant pedagogy, critical anti-bias education, or a decolonizing curriculum (Forago, Murray, & Swadener, 2017; Ladson-Billings, 1995; Ritchie & Skerrett 2014) approaches critique curricula that privilege dominant group knowledge, and reconceptualize curriculum for young children to be inclusive and more socially justice-oriented.

Nonetheless, while some have tackled policy by resistance, counter-measures, and strategic alliances with policy makers in other countries, in the USA little change has been occurring. Indeed, strategies that reinforce the importance of developmental theory and DAP as "best practice" or indicators of high "quality" have spread to other countries (Dahlberg, Moss, & Pence, 2013). These recurring practices and beliefs will be illustrated shortly in my work in two schools in the United States.

A Reconceptualist Framework Drawing on Poststructural, Feminist, and Posthuman Frameworks

O'Loughlin (2018) suggests that many reconceptualists are no longer "waiting for the revolution," but, rather, moving toward resistance and renarrativization in more locally situated contexts. Parkes, Gore, and Amosa (2010) argue that "poststructural theory can inform a productive rethinking of social justice pedagogy." Poststructural approaches to social justice pedagogy are linked to complexity, unpredictability, specificity, and the fluidity as well as the situatedness of how things happen at particular moments. Rather than an "essentialist" framing of identify, or a structural oppression explanation for why things remain the same, and a call to empower others, or to reframe the curriculum to include the knowledge of others "omitted", here the emphasis is on a "multiplicity of identifies," that are situated in particular contexts. Drawing on Foucault (1980), many poststructural perspectives look at power/knowledge relationships and their impact on cultural reasoning systems of what is "truth", the construction of "normal/abnormal" or "good/best/poor" practice. A *Common World* approach to early childhood curriculum (e.g., Ritchie & Skerrit, 2014; Katchebaw-Pacini & Nxumalo, 2018) also highlights a posthuman (Braidotti, 2013; Haraway, 1991; 2007; 2016) concept of the "nomadic subject" and human/nonhuman interaction. This allows us to look at ecological and environmental justice issues as they relate the child, family, environment, animate and inanimate.

Lastly, Deleuze and Guattari (1987) draw on the notion of "the serpent" and "lines of flight"–ever present danger, along with new openings that are unpredictable, within an "assemblage" of the capitalist machine (Bloch & Kennedy, 2014). In terms of social justice frameworks, these positions allow work (research, teaching, and resistance) to add notions of the nomad, lines of flight, unpredictability, complexity, and notions of ethics (Levinas, 1969) as we construct and listen to the other. Interrogating our ways of reasoning about how we come to think and act has proved very fruitful in renarrativizing or overturning what we understand as "truth," what is "normal" and how we and others govern ourselves through this taken-for-granted "knowledge." While it complicates the notion of "power" as owned or not, the notion of a "capitalist machine" that is a complex assemblage of discourses and/or technologies of power/knowledge, has opened up other ways to rethink social justice/injustice early childhood education/childcare policy and pedagogy. I use two similar, yet different, preschools in the US to illustrate social justice issues and ways in which different frameworks are relevant.

New Lines of Flight: Two New Schools

In 2017 and in 2018, as a retired professor, I volunteered in two local preschool programs. For different reasons, I had strong hopes that my involvement in these two programs would offer an opportunity to collaborate on policy formation, the discourses exerting pressures on schools, and to be a participant in the development of the programs—in ways that could lead to experimentation, and perhaps new lines of flight/spaces for imagination or reconceptualization. I hoped to be part of the two "start ups," and affect some of what happened. I also hoped that as an ally, partner, and co-worker in the establishment of policies, curriculum, the selection of teachers, and, through conversations and observations, I could see, but also help construct or select which pedagogical values and practices would be prioritized. After one year of working in each program, I feel that changes, while small in each, still left openings and new places for hope. I had visited in the same county over many years, as well as other schools in very different settings in the US and in diverse places around the world. In some, I had seen new approaches to pedagogy and curriculum for young children emerge; I knew locations where policies as well as practices were supportive of socially just curricula for children, their families, and their caregiver/educators (Bloch & Kim, 2012). In brief, after many years of fighting and resisting establishment pedagogies in early education, I had seen programs that showed shifts (e.g., Ritchie & Skerrett 2014), and practices that were aimed at that illusive and, still variously defined, term "socially just" curriculum (Yelland & Bentley, 2018.) In the descriptions below, and in the concluding section, I draw on the "toolbox" of theoretical frameworks outlined above, to examine and discuss the early childhood programs with which I worked.

The two schools, briefly described below, are both in one county in the Midwest US. Both programs are led by innovative leaders. I was a volunteer in both programs but considered "staff." While I describe common characteristics of both schools, there are differences, too. In the presentation and concluding section, I focus on both schools as representative of early childhood centers found in many parts of the USA currently. Both schools are characteristic of "good quality" preschools and child care centers. While there are differences that reflect persistent stratification in early childhood, my purpose is not to compare one as inferior or superior to the other, but to point out social justice/injustice aspects illustrated by both programs.

The Nature Preschool

The first school, The Nature Preschool (a pseudonym), is a new school that opened in the fall of 2018; I have been working with it since summer 2018. This school is representative of the majority of preschools in the US—which are predominately private—with fees paid by parents for part-time or full-time early education in what we call a large group early childhood center environment. The school will serve up to 300 children, though it is not that big yet. It is situated in a moderate to higher income neighborhood where other childcare and preschool programs compete for family enrollment. Full-day, full-week tuition for parents is approximately $350 per week, or $1400 per month per child. Many children attend from six weeks (when mandatory unpaid parental leave is done) on, and the early childhood learning center accepts children through age five, and has a partially state subsidized or partially publicly subsidized "4K" program for four- and five-year-olds. Teachers are paid a minimum of $15 per hour, and they may be paid by educational and experience level up to $22 per hour with partial health benefits, and additional options for some benefits. The majority of the staff are white and female, as are the majority of families and children. The curriculum is a combination of "developmentally appropriate practices" embedded in another child-centered curriculum, in this case, titled "The Project Approach" (Katz,

Chard, & Kogan, 2014). The building is new, and has good materials for children and teachers, as well as a "good" developmentally oriented outdoor/indoor environment representing what one might currently expect in a private preschool serving middle-to-upper income parents in the US today—materials not so different from those present in "high quality" preschools around the nation.

The Play and Readiness School

The second school, which here I call The Play and Readiness School (a pseudonym), is also in a new school building, though it has been remodeled from an older building, and is geographically located in what we term an urban "childcare desert," a neighborhood where very few other group child care or preschool centers exist and many families use informal family child care. It is a partially private and partially publicly subsidized school representative of fewer preschools in the USA—those that qualify for at least partial community, state, or federal subsidies for children to attend. Some parents pay fees, while most have scholarships or public subsidization for part-time or full-time early education; the center is a medium size early childhood center situated in a diverse ethnic and socio-economic neighborhood. The school is new, and serves approximately 100 young children. It offers a full-day, full-week early childhood program for children and their parents. The majority of each child's tuition is subsidized or fully covered through scholarships that cover a tuition of approximately $300 per week or $1200 per month per child. Many children attend from six weeks on, and the early childhood learning center accepts children through age five; there is a state subsidized "4K" program for four- and five-year-olds.

Similar to the first "Nature Preschool," teachers are paid a minimum of $15 per hour, and they may be paid by educational and experience level up to $22 per hour with partial health benefits, and additional options for some benefits. Here, the staff (administrators and educators) are ethnically diverse with many more male and female teachers of color than most preschools in the area. The majority of families and children are from diverse ethnic backgrounds and are from lower socio-economic backgrounds. The curriculum is a combination of "developmentally appropriate practices" embedded in a child-centered curriculum, in this case titled "The Creative Curriculum Approach" (Dodge, Colker, & Heroman, 2008). One major difference in the two schools is the size of the playground. The type of materials selected are also related to the size of the playground and different philosophies of play. The Nature Preschool has five playground areas, while The Play and Readiness Preschool has three much smaller playground areas. Both focus on natural materials, "loose parts," oriented toward child-interest, and children's "developmental opportunities" for learning in and through play.

Both preschools have followed the state "Quality" guidelines and are highly rated; both are being assessed for the public 4K programs by the Early

Childhood Rating Scale (ECERS) (Harms, Clifford, & Cryer, 2015) and child-centered philosophies oriented toward developmentally stages and norms, with some focus on literacy and numeracy assessment tools mandated for the publicly subsidized 4K programs. The Play and Readiness Preschool has more explicit curricular attention focused on "school-readiness" and attention toward literacy and numeracy "skills" than the Nature Preschool.

The Neighborhood, Families, Children, Teachers, and Programs: What "Is" and What "Ought to," or "Might" Be.

As suggested, while there are many specific differences in the schools, examining the similarities allows us to focus on broader issues of social justice/injustice represented by both schools. I draw on all theoretical toolboxes and frameworks outlined earlier below.

Access and Equity

The Nature Preschool is situated in a neighborhood where there are many preschools competing to enroll children. The Play and Readiness Preschool is situated in what I have earlier termed an urban "child care desert" in which very few children and families have easy affordable access to good preschools or child care programs (terms the schools both use to describe their programs). Both schools serve a majority of children whose parents are employed and need child care along with, ideally, good preschool education from an early age. While both schools have high tuition, The Nature Preschool has no scholarships, and only subsidies for its four-year-old 4K program from the state. The Play and Readiness Preschool families are almost entirely subsidized through private scholarship funds, or community and state and federal subsidies, including for its 4K program. In the Play and Readiness Preschool, without private scholarships, the school's families would not be able to afford to pay tuition, and the school would eventually close. Nonetheless, the high cost of tuition—whether paid through private scholarships or from parents' income—amounts to $14,400–$16,200 per year for families, a larger amount than most other nation's families pay for access to early education.

For poorer families, there is only a choice to NOT have a child attend preschool from infancy through age four when public schools offer free 4K programs, to have a scholarship, or to pay $14,400 per child per year which most families cannot afford. Even for wealthier families, $14,400 (or $16,200) per child per year is still equivalent to a year of college tuition and is considered to be a difficult expenditure. Therefore, the issues of access and equity is difficult for families in both schools, but much more complex for families in The Play and Readiness School, compounded by the school being one of the very few situated in any of the low-income neighborhoods.

Teacher Backgrounds and Income, and Benefits

Both schools pay teachers an annual salary that ranges from $28,800 (at $15/hour and a 40-hour, 12-month work schedule) to $42,240 (at $22/hour and a 40-hour, 12-month work schedule). All receive benefits related to their salaries, though at the Nature Preschool only 50% of health insurance is paid; there are only options to contribute to a retirement plan. The lower paid teachers have previous experience as assistant teachers in other programs, while the more education a teacher has, along with prior experience, the higher his/her pay. Therefore, a teacher with a master's degree might have the highest salary. In both schools, the average teacher has a two-year associate degree, and is paid approximately $30,000 (gross salary) per year. This income for a family of three or four is near the poverty level in the US. Despite both schools paying hourly minimum wage of $15 to all staff (or higher), the family income contribution is perceived as low—even for the most highly educated staff members. Is this because it is a "gendered" field, "women's work," as Whitebrook (2018) suggested? And what social justice issues does this present? It is important to note, based on my being in discussions about hiring, that leaders in both The Nature Preschool and The Play and Readiness Preschool believe that the wages they are paying are very competitive and represent good wages for early childhood educators. The wages offered by both preschools are higher than most educators/child care workers receive in most US child care/early childhood programs.

Access to Health Care

The Nature Preschool requires all children to have immunizations before coming to school, and appropriate medical care when ill. The Play and Readiness Preschool assumes parents will pick up children, despite jobs, to care for them when sick. When caring for sick children at the school was discussed, the Director said it would be too expensive to incorporate sick child care. The leader in The Nature Preschool appeared to assume *all* families have health insurance, time to care for their children at home, and sick leave policies at the parents' workplaces that will not penalize parents. The leaders of The Play and Readiness Preschool, in contrast, do not and cannot make these assumptions. They provide medical exams, require immunizations from early ages, and support for families who do not have easy or affordable access to medical, dental, or vision care for children. At the Play and Readiness Preschool, families do not have good health insurance, and caring for children when sick at home may mean parents lose valuable wages, time, even their employment, which typically has no sick leave benefits.

The Developmentally Appropriate Curricula, Environments, and Material

Both schools follow Developmentally Appropriate Practice Guidelines (DAP) set by the National Association for the Education of Young Children (NAEYC), as well as curriculum models, the Project Approach (Katz, Chard, & Kogan, 2014) and the Creative Curriculum Approach (Dodge et al., 2008) highly related to DAP guidelines set by NAEYC. They are both described as child-centered, play-based, inquiry-oriented curricula. Materials in both schools are similar though not identical, and strategies for involving children in experiential projects and activities follow children's interests, are problem-solving oriented, and focus on stages of children's development in pedagogical decisions as well as assessments of the child/children. While culturally relevant materials are present in both centers, at The Nature Preschool these are represented in books, dolls, and in a minority of program discussions, despite the insertion of a sentence into the school's "Guiding Principles." At the Play and Readiness Preschool, the staff, families and children are diverse, except that most are from low-income backgrounds.

Thus, The Nature Preschool and the Play and Readiness Preschool both draw from developmentally-oriented curriculum—DAP, The Project Approach, The Creative Curriculum—as well as assessments and quality standards, which all rest on studies of largely white middle-class families. In the Play and Readiness School, however, pedagogies also include stories, histories, and images of children and families like the children in the school. In addition, the school focuses more directly on making sure the children have skills required of primary schools aimed toward "closing the achievement gap." Staff and families' constant encouragement of children and construction of children as "with potential" counters the more dominant construction of these children as "at risk" or "deficient" and unlikely to succeed. While the norms of the curriculum prescribed favors white, middle-income children (such as those at the Nature Preschool), there seems to be more of a "culturally relevant social justice curriculum" at the Play and Readiness Preschool.

The Nature Preschool and the Play and Readiness Preschool: What "Is" and "What Ought to Be" or "Might Be"

While my descriptions of both schools are purposely brief, they are both from the same county in the US, and they are representative of some of the ways in which social justice/injustice is found in the early education/child care systems in the US. Drawing on the equality/equity framework I discussed earlier, we can examine the two schools in terms of access and affordability, access to health care, and access to time to take care of children without losing wages or jobs. Access to both the Nature Preschool and the Play and Readiness Preschool depends upon high tuition, paid for by scholarships, subsidies and/or parents' income (largely in The Nature Preschool). Families in the lower socio-economic background urban areas of the county in which both preschools have been started also have little access to schools such as The Play and Readiness Preschool (which is in a "child care desert"). Therefore, geographical inequities, based on histories of segregation schools and housing policies for poorer families, also are significant in this community, and across the nation. Teacher wages and benefits, while above the minimum in both schools, represent relatively low wages for even the best educated of the staff members.

Drawing on Critical Structural Theories on Social Justice/Injustice and Post-structural, Posthuman Theoretical Frameworks, I can question why these inequalities and inequities have occurred, *and been maintained,* over more than one century in the US. Critical race theory can be used to highlight the ways in which segregation, and slavery, have affected house ownership, housing and school policies over, according to Ladson-Billings (2006), more than 300 years. In addition, drawing on Foucault (1980), we can interrogate what truths and knowledge are considered normal or representative of best practice. From these perspectives, or lens, we can see that the norms for curriculum, standards for schools, and evaluative assessments favor dominant, largely Euro-American, or white, middle-class children and families. While changes have been made to include cultural and linguistic diversity, and equity issues in national guidelines, new additions of DAP, or the Harms et al. (2015) ECERS scale by which environmental and teaching quality are judged, rest on these largely homogeneous developmental norms. While there are exceptions, represented in part by the Play and Readiness School, the curriculum and quality standards still are not culturally relevant; they ask all children to assimilate to the "hidden" curriculum of only some.

Teacher/Educator Background and Knowledge

The staff at The Nature Preschool are also homogeneous, and, along with most parents, represent the majority white middle-class population of the community. In The Play and Readiness Preschool, by contrast, the staff and families are diverse ethnically and linguistically; children's and families' stories are brought into the curriculum, and a counter-narrative as resistance against constructing the children as "deficient" or "at risk" is purposeful and related to a socially just orientation that is the overall guiding purpose of this new program. This is an important, and strategic issue.

Community Action/Activism

The county's population is geographically segregated, too. While it is "progressive" and known for its social and educational advocacy against inequities related to class and race, clearly the inequities, or social justice/injustice issues, start with policies and practices that have been in place for a long time. The dominant white middle-class community rarely recognizes or focuses on geographical segregation, health disparities, the existence of food, or preschool or child care "deserts," or disparities in children's prenatal to high school access to care and education. As in the nation, there is recognition of the importance of disparities, but few policies or attempts to make change. Yet the community is also known to be progressive in policy and practice. The scholarships for the children in The Play and Readiness Preschool come from progressive members and organizations in the broader community. The school could not exist without that base, though this is only one school, in one neighborhood of the community.

Teacher wages and benefits, differential opportunities for parents, differences in medical opportunities for children, and the largely nationally homogeneous and developmental curriculum norms, standards, and assessments all provide a window into the broader social pattern of justice/injustice for all that is represented by patterns in these two schools.

Concluding Questions

Here I focus on who holds power, what truths and knowledge guide our practices, and ways in which past as well as current policies and practices do or do not represent socially just policy, curriculum, or an environment of hope. I use these two examples from the US from centers I have been working in myself to illustrate places where forms of social justice work is being done, and also ways certain policies and long-held beliefs of what constitutes "best practice" constrain socially just pedagogical policies and practices in both centers. While these centers are used as short case studies, they represent many of the issues discussed in earlier parts of the chapter.

As an ally to the administrators and teaching staff in each center, I must start with the question of "who am I to judge or analyze?" "Who" has the ability or right to say, "what is" or "what ought to be" or even "what might be" in a given society, or across diverse local, national, or global contexts? Second, when working as allies or in collaboration, how does resistance versus renarrativization of issues work— what if we disagree? Third, how do shifts in reasoning and policy occur, from the top, from the bottom, or through micro-level as well as macro-level change? Fourth and finally, what are *our* most hopeful strategic actions moving forward?

The maintenance of governing norms (DAP norms and guidelines representing best practice) and regulation that is both technical, instrumental, and narrow, privileges the hierarchy embodied in "white and middle-elite class" privilege. The maintenance of these norms and guidelines that favor some over others, despite critique, is an area where interrogation, reconceptualization, and action are still crucial, even after at least 25 years of critique (see Cannella, 1997; Kessler & Swadener, 1992, as two examples). However, the possibilities for alternatives are increasingly obscured by the corporate and organizational battery of measures, standards, norms, and tests used to represent the early childhood field that reinforce the governing mentalities about what constitutes quality and best practice.

There are multiple possible reasons why the critiques of yesteryear by those in the reconceptualizing early childhood group and others in the early childhood education/child care communities (e.g., see Whitebrook (2018) on teacher wages, Polakow (2018) on children in the "other America") have had small effects. Small political and pedagogical successes have led to slow and little change, and fail to address or affect change in the broader structural system of justice/injustice.

Critique and action, as well as hope, may carry us to new spaces, new ways to open up to new thought and practices. Others, in this book, and elsewhere (e.g., Bloch et al., 2018; Farago, et al., 2017; Yelland & Bentley, 2018) show that anti-bias and socially just practices are emerging in many spaces and places. I embrace the slow but hopeful shifts in thinking as well as actions. In the end, however, the continuing argument for resistance has to be laced with, perhaps, sharper inter-rogation, critique as well as resistance, and more strategic actions at both the micro- and macro- levels—locally, nationally, internationally.

The long enduring dominant practices are forceful, and *govern our souls* (Rose, 1999), as well as what we appear to accept as "truth", "knowledge", and "best practice" for "all." However, clearly, the "all" is a fabrication or a construct that serves some families and children, teachers and program directors, and organizations better than it does "others." The corporate world, as well as the broader "capitalist machine" appear to be best served by not shaking up the system or the "assemblage" of complex and multiple ways in which the global/local "system" stays together.

The Illusiveness of Social Justice in Early Education and Child Care Policy and Curriculum.

Earlier in this chapter, I played with the notion that the long arch of history bends toward social justice (King, 1958), and wonder, as we did at the 2017 Women's March in Washington, DC, "why are we still fighting this shit?" Where is the hope when the arch is so long? How can we be hopeful with incremental changes—that change little?

What can we accomplish through research and our interrogation? I believe there are small spaces for and ideas with hope. The chapters in this book represent one effort. The act of writing, and critiquing also allows me to think anew: What can I do? What should "we" be doing? How do we better attack "what is," and identify, for all children and families, "what ought to be"? Certainly, we should be erasing homelessness, hunger, health disparities, and even, given the touted importance of early education programs, disparities in access to affordable, child care and preschool education from an early age? What should or ought to be happening? By analyzing the assemblage of truths and practices that holds the "system" together, and by holding out hope for interrogation, renewed collaborations, and collection action, perhaps we can still make changes.

References

Anderson-Levitt, K., Bloch, M. N., & Soumare, A. (1998). Inside classrooms in Guinea: Girls' experiences. InM. N. Bloch, B. R. Tabachnick, & J. Beoku-Betts *Women and education in Sub-Saharan Africa: Power, opportunities, and constraints*(pp. 99–130). Boulder, CO: Lynn Reinner Press.

Apple, M. (1982/1995). *Education and power* (2nd Ed.). New York: Routledge Press.

Anzualdua, G. (1987). *Borderlands/La Frontera*. San Francisco: Aunt Lute Books.

Bloch, M. N. (1992). Critical perspectives on the historical relationship between child development and early education research. In S. Kessler & E. B. Swadener (Eds.) *Reconceptualizing the early childhood curriculum: Beginning the dialogue* (pp. 3–20). New York: Teachers College Press.

Bloch, M. N. & Kennedy, D. (2014). The assemblage: Global speak, research, policy, childhood, and hope. *International review of qualitative research*, 17(1), 15–38.

Bloch, M. N. & Kim, K. (2012). Governing young children's learning through educational reform: A poststructural analysis of discourses of best practice, standards, and quality. In S. Steinberg & G. S. Cannella (Eds.), *Critical qualitative research reader* (pp. 257–275). New York: Peter Lang.

Bloch, M. N., Holmquist, K., Moqvist, I.,& Popkewitz, T. S. (Eds.) (2003). *Governing children, families, and education: Restructuring the welfare state*. New York: Palgrave Press.

Bloch, M. N., Swadener, B. B., & Cannella, G. S. (2018) (Eds.). *Reconceptualizing early childhood education and care: Critical questions, new imaginaries, and social activism* (2nd ed.). New York: Peter Lang.

Bloch, M. N. & Swadener, B.B. (2007). "Education for all": Social inclusions and exclusions: introduction and critical reflections. *International Journal of Educational Policy, Research, and Practice: Reconceptualizing Childhood Studies*, 7(1), 1–12.

Braidotti, R. (2013). *The posthuman*. Cambridge, UK: Polity Press.

Cannella, G. S. (1997). *Deconstructing early childhood education: Social justice and revolution*. New York: Peter Lang.

Collins, P. H. (2000/2008). *Black feminist thought: Knowledge, consciousness, and the politics of empowerment* (2nd/3rd Eds.). New York: Routledge.

Copple, C. & Bredekamp, S. (2009). *Developmentally appropriate practice in early childhood programs—serving children from birth through age 8* (3rd ed.). Washington, DC: National Association for the Education of Young Children.

Dahlberg, G., Moss, P., & Pence, A. (2013). *Beyond quality in early education and care: Languages of evaluation* (3rd ed.). London: Routledge.

Deleuze, G. & Guattari, F. (1987). *A thousand plateaus*. Minneapolis, MN: The University of Minnesota Press.

Dodge, D. T., Colker, L. J., & Heroman, C. (2008). *The creative curriculum for preschool* (College Edition). Washington, DC: Teaching Strategies.

Farago, F., Murray, C., & Swadener, B. (Eds.) (2017). Special issue on anti-bias early childhood education introduction. *International Critical Childhood Policy Studies Journal*, 1 (6), 1–6.

Foucault, M. (1980). *Power/Knowledge: Selected interviews & other writings 1972–1977*. (Ed. C. Gordon). New York: Pantheon Press.

Freire, P. (1970). *Pedagogy of the oppressed* (2nd ed.). New York: Continuum.

Habermas, J. (1985). *Theory and the communicative action* (Vol. 1 and 2). New York: Beacon Press.

Harms, T., Clifford, R., & Cryer, D. (2015). *Early children environmental rating scale (ECERS)* (3rd ed.). New York: Teachers College Press.

Haraway, D. (1991). *Simians, cyborgs, and women: The reinvention of nature.* New York: Routledge Press.

Haraway, D. (2007). *When species meet.* Minneapolis, MN: University of Minnesota Press.

Haraway, D. J. (2016). *Staying with the trouble.* Durham and London: Duke University Press.

hooks, b. (2000). *Feminism is for everybody: Passionate politics.* Cambridge, MA: South End Press.

Katchebaw-Pacini, V. & Nxumalo, F. (2018). Posthumanist imaginaries for decolonizing childhood praxis. In M.N. Bloch, B.B. Swadener, & G.S. Cannella (Eds.), *Reconceptualizing early childhood education and care: Critical questions, new imaginaries, and social activism* (2nd Ed.) (pp. 216–228). New York: Peter Lang.

Katz, L., Chard, S., & Kogan, Y. (2014). *Engaging children's minds: The project approach.* (3rd ed.). New York: Praeger Press.

Kessler, S. (2018) Reconceptualizing the early childhood curriculum: An unaddressed topic. In M.N. Bloch, B.B. Swadener, & G.S. Cannella (Eds.), *Reconceptualizing early childhood education and care: Critical questions, new imaginaries, and social activism* (2nd ed.) (pp. 35–46). New York: Peter Lang.

Kessler, S. & Swadener, B.B. (1992). *Reconceptualizing the early childhood curriculum: Beginning the dialogue.* New York: Teachers College Press.

King, M. L. (1958). King delivers "Nonviolence and Racial Justice" at Friends General Conference in Cape May, New Jersey Event, June 27, 1958.

Ladson-Billings, G. (1995/2009). *The dreamkeepers: Successful teachers of African-American children* (2nd Ed.). New York: Jossey Bass.

Ladson-Billings, G. (2006). From the achievement gap to the education debt: Understanding achievement in U.S. schools. *Educational Researcher,* 35(7), 3–12. (Originally presented as the Presidential Address at the Annual Meeting of the American Educational Research Association, San Francisco, April 2006).

Ladson-Billings, G. & TateIV, W. F. (1995.) Toward a critical race theory of education. *Teachers College Record,* 97(1), 47–68.

Levinas, E. (1969). *Totality and infinity: An essay on exteriority.* Pittsburgh, PA: Duquesne University Press.

Moraga, C. & Anzualdua, G. (2015). *This bridge called my back: Writings by radical women of color* (4th ed.). Albany, NY: Persephone Press.

National Institute for Early Education Research (NIEER) (2017). Growing disparities in enrolment, investments, and quality: 2002–2017. The state of preschool 2017. Retrieved from http://nieer.org/wp-content/uploads/2019/02/State-of-Preschool-2017-Full-2-13-19_reduced.pdf

O'Loughlin, M. (2018). Still waiting for the revolution. In M.N. Bloch, B.B. Swadener, & G.S. Cannella (Eds.), *Reconceptualizing early childhood education and care: Critical questions, new imaginaries, and social activism* (2nd ed.) (pp. 68–80). New York: Peter Lang.

Parkes, R. J., Gore, J. M., & Arnosa, W. (2010). After poststructuralism: Rethinking the discourse of social justice pedagogy. In T. Chapman, & N. Hobbel (Eds.), *Social justice pedagogy across the curriculum: The practice of freedom.* New York: Routledge

Polakow, V. (2018). None for you: Children's capabilities and rights in profoundly unequal times. In M.N. Bloch, B.B. Swadener, & G.S. Cannella (Eds.), *Reconceptualizing early childhood education and care: Critical questions, new imaginaries, and social activism* (2nd ed.) (pp. 247–260). New York: Peter Lang.

Ritchie, J. and Skerrett, M. (2014). *Early childhood education in Aotearoa New Zealand.* New York: Palgrave Pivot Press.

Rose, N. (1999). *Governing the soul: The shaping of the private self* (2nd ed.). London: Free Association Press.

Swadener, B.B. & Bloch, M. (1990). Pre-primary policies and realities: Senegal and The Gambia, 1988–1990. Project Report, 1–32.

Whitebrook, M. (2018). Durable inequalities among ECE teachers in the US. Plenary Session. Presented at the 26th International Reconceptualizing Early Childhood Education Conference, Copenhagen, Denmark, October 18, 2018; also see http://cscce.berkeley.edu/at-the-wage-floor/ (retrieved March 30, 2019).

Yelland, N. & Bentley, D. F. (2018). *Found in translation: Connecting reconceptualist thinking with early childhood practices.* London: Routledge.

12

EQUALITY AND DEMOCRATIC EDUCATION EVALUATION

A Way Forward for Teachers[1]

Shirley A. Kessler

A Look Back

Almost 90 years ago in the 1930s the faculty at Teachers College, Columbia University, New York believed they faced a national emergency. In 1940 the faculty published this statement:

> Europe and much of Asia are under the domination of ruthless, military dictatorships. It can no longer be in doubt that the present world crisis constitutes a threat of the most serious character to the United States and to the democratic way of life.
>
> *(Teachers College Faculty, 1940)*

The faculty were also troubled by several events within the US that threatened democratic values in the 1930s. For example, Henry Ford, one of the nation's largest automobile manufacturers, and a known anti-Semite, published his views in *The Dearborn Independent*, which he owned, claiming that a vast Jewish conspiracy was infecting America (Public Broadcasting System, n.d.). Hitler was inspired by Ford's technological innovations, particularly the assembly line method of manufacturing he developed as well as his writings, and in 1939 awarded Ford the Grand Cross of the German Eagle.

Other factors must have alarmed the Teachers College faculty. For example, the weekly broadcasts of a Father Charles Coughlin in the 1930s, listened to by one-third of the nation, had a tremendous influence on Depression-era America (Social Security History, 2018) and included attacks on prominent Jewish figures, that many people considered evidence of anti-Semitism. Also of concern to the faculty must have been the pronouncements of the American First committee founded in 1940. Its most famous spokesman, Charles Lindbergh, known for his nonstop flight across the Atlantic, visited Germany in 1939. Impressed with Germany's military might, he thought that no nation could defeat it. He wrote that the Western nations, "can have peace and security only so long as we band together to preserve that most priceless possession, our inheritance and European blood" (Lindbergh, 1939). Hermann Goering awarded Lindberg the Service Cross of the German Eagle in 1938.

Likewise alarming to the Teachers College faculty must have been the presence of America Nazis demonstrating throughout the State of New York in the 1930s, orchestrated by the German-American Bund, the fastest growing American version of the German Nazi Party. The Bund rally at New York's Madison Square Garden in February 1939 was attended by approximately 22,000 "hate-spewing American Nazis" (Sander, 2017).

Threats to democracy from abroad and within the US prompted the Teachers College faculty to develop a manifesto that they hoped would start a conversation about the meaning of democracy and the relationship between those beliefs and education. This manifesto, the "Creed of Democracy," was signed by 137 members of the faculty (Appendix A). A few of the core principles are cited below. The Creed begins, We believe in and will endeavor to make a democracy which":

- respects the personality of every individual, whatever his origin or present states;
- does not tolerate an enduring social stratification based on birth, race, religion, or wealth, inherited or otherwise acquired;
- maintains human rights to be more important than property rights;
- renews its strength by continued education as to its meanings and purposes.

(Teachers College Faculty, 1940)

The Creed was presented orally at a mass meaning and later distributed in pamphlet form to students and printed in educational journals, including *the Journal of the National Educational Association*. A poster highlighting key points in the manifesto was printed and displayed.

Current Realities

Educators today face a similar crisis. Democracy is under threat in the US and around the world (Abramowitz, 2018). This same situation existed in Europe between the two world wars, when demagogues took over political parties that had been mainstream. Democracies no longer end with a bang – a revolution or military coup – but with a whimper – the slow steady weakening of critical institutions, such as the judiciary and freedom of the press, as well as the gradual erosion of long-standing political norms (Levitsky & Ziblatt, 2018), such as the expectation in the US that candidates for public office release their tax returns. Today, democracies wither at the hands of insiders who gain power initially through elections, as in Russia, the Philippines, Turkey, Venezuela, Ecuador, Hungary, Nicaragua, Sri Lanka, Ukraine, Poland, and Peru (Levitsky & Ziblatt, 2018). At the time of this writing Brazil can be added to this list. Furthermore, right-wind political parties and groups have become more vocal and visible in the US, France, Germany, and elsewhere reminding many familiar with the history of Fascism how fragile democracies are in the face of unrelenting attacks on its institutions, such as the free press, and political processes, such as the separation of powers in the US.

This loss of democratic values is seen by some as related to neoliberal political theory, that, at the very least, advocates lower corporate and personal taxation, a thinning of the welfare net, the weakening of trade unions; deregulation of the business community, and the privatization of publicly owned industries and companies (Coates, 2017), including the privatization of public education in the US. Neoliberalism promotes a kind of hyper-individualism that undermines the development of strong community ties, feelings of concern for others, debates about the common good, and democratically oriented associations (Chomsky, 2017; Giroux, 2018). In addition to undermining mutual solidarity and support, neoliberal policies marginalize democratic education and foster the treatment of students as "human capital."

Students as Human Capital

The influences of neoliberal policies on education are numerous. Business models have been adopted where schools are run like businesses (Apple, 2001); the bottom line is student achievement (not profit), measured by tests that lack validity and reliability when administered to young children (Berliner, 2015; Urban & Swadener, 2016). Competition between schools is regarded as necessary to progress. Under neoliberal views of education lies a vision of students as human capital, "students as future workers … [who] must be given the requisite skills and dispositions to compete efficiently and effectively" (Apple, 2001, p. 38). This metaphor, students as human capital, highlights one widely accepted purpose of schooling, the need for students to learn job-related skills, but neglects to emphasize that, historically, other purposes have been articulated, such as the need to promote the understanding and commitment to democratic ideals and processes.

In addition, neoliberal governing policies have had a tremendous influence on school practice and a curriculum planning process that excludes the voices of parents and children, a process that undermines a democratic education (Gutmann, 1987). The identification and articulation of specific job skills has dominated discourse as to the goals and objectives of the curriculum and education evaluation. The metaphor of "production" can describe the current view of curriculum development and evaluation practices held by business-oriented interests (Kliebard, 1975). In this sense, metaphor is not just a "fancy literary device" (Kliebard, personal communication, 1980), but a fundamental way to organize thoughts and generate new ways of understanding (Kessler, 1991). Using the metaphor of production, one would view schools as factories. Students are the raw material who are run through an assembly-line process (the curriculum) where they are shaped and molded to design specifications and emerge as a finished product. This product is then examined and tested to determine if the manufacturing process has been successful or if it needs adjustment.[2] In contrast, the metaphor of "growth views the curriculum as a greenhouse ... where students will grow and develop to their fullest potential under the care of a wise and patient gardener" (Kliebard, 1975, p. 84). The metaphor of "travel" describes the curriculum as "a route over which students will travel under the guide of an experienced guide and companion" (Kliebard, 1975, p. 85). What is highlighted when students are viewed as raw material and/or as human capital and the way to accomplish one's vision of the good life (Kessler, 2018), a vision that, in this case, embodies economic competition between nations? What alternatives to this view are hidden or obscured? Further, applying an ethical standard to this metaphor, one must ask, "Is it good or just to regard students as raw material or human capital, the means to an end? Is it fair?" I think not. The metaphor of production can be applied to the view of the learner, the recommended curriculum and the assessment practices developed by the Organization for Economic Cooperation and Development (OECD).

The Organization for Economic Cooperation and Development

As you may know, the Organization for Economic Cooperation and Development (OECD) is an intergovernmental economic organization with 36-member countries, founded in 1961 to stimulate economic progress and world trade. It is a forum of countries describing themselves as committed to democracy and the market economy, providing a platform to compare policy experiences, seeking answers to common problems, identifying good practices and coordinating domestic and international policies of its members.

The testing initiatives of the OECD, the Program for International Student Assessment (PISA) and the International Early Learning Study (IELS), sometimes called "Baby PISA," exemplify the influence of corporate interests on education and the use of students as human capital (OECD, 2018b; OECD, 2018c).[3] Currently, OECD tests 15-year-olds to determine the extent to which the countries they represent have the human capital to be competitive in the global economy. Furthermore, OECD, with impetus from business communities, has set forth a set of competencies in a document called, "Program Definition and Selection of Competencies" (DeCeCo) (OECD, 2018c). According to DeCeCo, students should be able to achieve specific competencies in order to boost productivity and market competitiveness, minimize unemployment, and develop an adaptive qualified labor force. The competencies are: use tools interactively (e.g., language, technology), interact in heterogeneous groups, and act autonomously (OECD,

2018c). Thus, OECD's has extended its reach into the realm of curriculum planning – determining what knowledge is of most worth (the primary question in curriculum planning) for children all over the world to possess to make nations economically competitive. This action should alarm us all. If the curriculum represents a vision of "the good life," or a utopian vision (Kessler, 2018), and I think it does, we must examine and judge the vision held by OECD. Does the good life consist primarily of countries competing for economic prosperity on the backs of students? What other aspects of the good life are left out? I suggest we educators articulate our own vision of the good life if we move forward in developing a "manifesto" of our own.

Furthermore, OECD's latest initiative is to test children between 4.5 and 5.5 years of age in a program now called The International Early Learning and Child-Well-being Study (IELS), the purpose of which is "to identify key factors that drive or hinder the development of early learning" (OECD, 2018a). How should educators respond to these impositions by OECD that have hijacked curriculum development and education evaluation to suit its own narrow needs and interests? Should we develop a manifesto like the Teachers College faculty did in the late 1930s? If so, how would we go about it? What would it look like? What would we do with it?

Numerous critiques have been set forth regarding PISA/IELS. Experts cite problems with the design and implementation of the tests. Others criticize the program by drawing upon questions of philosophy. Still others criticize the program from a political point of view.

Technical Critiques of PISA and IELS

Bob Stake, former director of the Center for Instructional Research and Curriculum Evaluation (CIRCE) at the University of Illinois and an early proponent of case study methodology in research and evaluation (Stake, 2004), cited several problems with PISA, when I interviewed him in April 2018 (Stake, personal communication). He pointed out that OECD has spent absolutely no money on validation. He was quite adamant on this point, "Not a single penny," he emphasized. David Berliner agrees, pointing out that most tests (of 15-year-olds) can measure achievement reliably, but the national scores have substantial validity problems when used to predicting a nation's future economic growth (Berliner, 2015). Others point out the well-established fact that there is low reliability of results in standardized test with young children (Urban & Swadener, 2016). Yet, OECD proceeds as if its testing policies and procedures were meaningful.

Another fault lies in the way such assessments are used (Berliner, 2015; Stake, 2018, personal communication). As in the parable of the blind man and the elephant, if one were blind, he/she could learn about one part of the elephant, such as its tail, by touch for example, but could never understand the whole. "PISA is quite like the elephant," Berliner states.

> There are so many facets to this enormous and ambitious program, and each facet could be the object of study for years. And even were those many studies of the various facets of PISA competently completed, we are still not likely to have a good grip on the whole.
>
> *(Berliner, 2015)*

Yet OECD assumes that the tests results of a few thousand students can accurately describe a school system of a nation and suggest its failings.

David Berliner makes another important point. Out-of-school factors greatly influence test scores of students. He asks, "how do … national educational policies, school level variables, and a myriad of out-of-school factors influence in-school achievement and interact with one another to influence PISA test scores?" (Berliner, 2015). This argument reminds me of another comment made by Bob Stake in the late 1970s when I interviewed for a research assistantship at CIRCE. He said, "We don't evaluate students here, we evaluate the curriculum." Today I wonder: What if OECD evaluated the out-of-school experiences of students in various locales, or the "curriculum of the community," if you will? This curriculum would not be viewed as a "course of study," the most common definition of curriculum. Instead, the out-of-school experiences of children in the home and in the community would be examined, including the political and economic contexts of those experiences. Recently, Berliner emphasized this point in an interview published in *The Washington Post* (Strauss, 2018). He claimed that three factors alone – family income, level of parental education, and the percentage of single-parent households in a community – could predict with great accuracy the performance on standardized tests of students, results that are used by that community to judge its schools. As he puts it, "Although demographics may not be destiny for an individual, it is the best predictor of a school's outcomes – *independent of that school's teachers, administrators and curriculum!*" This argument is supported by the results of PISA tests given in Australia in 2003 (Perry & McConney, 2010). Researchers found that an increase in the mean SES (socio-economic status) of a school is associated with significant increases in students' academic achievement. As they put it, "In the Australian case, the socio-economic composition of the school matters greatly in terms of students' academic performance" (p. 1). Wouldn't a study of the SES of students in their neighborhoods and communities address the stated purpose of IELS, to identify key factors that "drive or hinder the development of early learning" (OECD, 2018c)? And wouldn't recognition of this relationship lead to different solutions?

Philosophical Critiques of PISA and IELS

Philosophical critiques claim, as Urban and Swadener (2016) point out, that very important questions are not asked in the IELS, such as the purpose of early childhood education and care. In addition, they argue, larger and more ambitious goals, such as promoting democracy, citizenship, and children's civil rights, are not addressed in the IELS. This argument was also made by educators who signed on to an op-ed in *The Guardian* in 2014. They pointed out that PISA addresses the economic goals of education, but fails to measure other educational objectives, such as physical, moral, civic, and artistic development (The Guardian, 2014).

Political Critiques of PISA/IELS

Turning now to the political-oriented critique of PISA and IELS, I again refer to remarks made by Bob Stake. When I asked him what he thought of PISA, he immediately said, "I'm against it." When I asked why, he replied, "For the same reason I'm against any kind of testing. Any comparison and description [of] individuals leave some less strong and disenfranchised; [these are the ones] who don't win." On this view, testing establishes political relationships of power and authority. Furthermore, signatories to the op-ed I mentioned earlier point to the fact that OECD has no mandate like that of UN organizations, such as UNESCO or UNICEF, where there is an agreed upon goal to improve education and the lives of children around the world. Yet, OECD has assumed the power to shape educational policy, with no debate about the necessity or limitations of its goals (The Guardian, 2014).

Bureaucratic Evaluation

It might be helpful to view the OECD testing program as an example of what the late Barry MacDonald calls "bureaucratic evaluation," contrasted with "democratic evaluation." Bureaucratic evaluation serves government agencies and offers information which enables them to accomplish their policy objectives (MacDonald, 1977). Thus, bureaucratic evaluation serves the interests of political structures and individuals and groups and, therefore, cannot be regarded as objective or neutral. In strong language, MacDonald describes evaluation as not just an enterprise of questionable social worth, but a form of *political action* (my italics). As he put it,

> Unless we can ... solve the fundamental issues raised by the widespread acknowledgement that evaluation is a significant form of political action, then I doubt very much whether the kind of activity in which I and many

others throughout the Western hemisphere are presently engaged can survive as a defensible social role.

(MacDonald, 1978)

Whose interests are served by the OECD testing program? The interests of the OECD as an institution, the interests of the companies that manufacture the testing instruments, and individuals who depend on the OECD for gainful employment. Stake remarked that a former student of his, whom I will call James, graduated with a doctorate in education evaluation from the University of Illinois and went to work in Paris for OECD. "He was in charge of the whole thing. I love James, but I don't like what he is doing." When I asked how someone whose training in education evaluation that advocated case study methodology and qualitative research methods could engage in developing and implementing PISA, Stake replied, "It [the program] didn't take. The doctoral program was not fully developed at that time." Then he added, "It was a career decision."

This comment recalled statements made by Michael Apple (2001) who maintains that the move to the right in education policy, what he calls "conservative modernization," is not a unitary movement, but exists as a coalition of groups and individuals. Neoliberal policies in education exert the largest influence, he writes, but another part of this coalition is comprised of technical experts and educational professionals, "a faction of the professional new middle class that gains its own mobility within the state and within the economy based on the use of technical expertise" (p. 57). He continues, "They are experts in efficiency, management, testing and accountability; they provide the technical expertise to put in place the policies of conservative modernization. Their own mobility *depends* on [its] expansion …" (p. 58).

I wonder if educational professionals whose research points to best practices that raise test scores are unwittingly supporting current policies, though they may have liberal leanings. I recall a remark made by one of Apple's students, the late Lanny Beyer (Beyer, 1981, personal communication) who claimed that most educational research simply "moves the furniture around in a classroom," that is, offers ways to make small improvements in curriculum and pedagogy, but fails to address the elephant in the room – the structures of inequality, such as poverty-stricken neighborhoods, that account for students' experiences of the schooling and student achievement. I wonder about my own research. Does my work simply move the furniture around? Whose interests are served by the work that I do? This is a question we all must ask ourselves.

Democratic Evaluation

In contrast to bureaucratic evaluation, MacDonald advocates democratic evaluation. "Democratic evolution is an information service to the community about the characteristics of an educational programme" (MacDonald, 1977, p. 226). It recognizes a plurality of values and acts as a broker in exchanges of information between different groups. Bob Stake writes, "The democratic evaluator seeks to serve the public and others remote from power, not those in political, economic, and academic control" (Stake, 2004, p. 201). House and Howe (1999) agree and view democratic evaluators as facilitators of information and debate (p. 202). The OECD testing projects, PISA and IELS, contrast sharply with the basic tenets of democratic evaluation. They do not serve those remote from power, nor do they foster the exchange of information between groups. Further problematic is that PISA/IELS further the entrenched interests of elites for control of educational structures, including the curriculum, that undermine democratic education and democratic values in the US and elsewhere.

Reconceptualization

Another point I want to emphasize was made by William Pinar who first coined the term "reconceptualists" in his well-known work in curriculum theory called *Curriculum Theorizing: The Reconceptualist* (Pinar, 1975). Contributors to this edited collection offer alternatives to the "technical-rational" approach to curriculum planning that focuses on goals, objectives, pedagogy and outcomes, in a linear fashion. I and others thought the idea of "reconceptualizing" should be applied to our organization, and so it was in 1991. Pinar admonished us that to reconceptualize was simply the first step in promoting educational change. To stop there, he claimed, was irresponsible (Cannella, 1977). He strongly suggests that researchers point to a way forward or propose possible solutions to identified problems.

Inclusive Approaches to Education Evaluation

Heeding Pinar's directive, I found several alternatives to the current approach to education evaluation exemplified by PISA/IELS, that embody principles of democratic evaluation. One approach advocates the collection of many kinds of information, such as student self-assessments, teacher observations, interviews, portfolios, and school reviews by outside experts, including the results of town meetings (Meier & Koestner, 2017). Katrin Macha (2018) describes ways in which researchers can identify the views of children and use them to improve education programs.

The Alliance for Excellence in Education (2018) suggests ten principles for building a high-quality system of assessment. One suggestion, number seven, states: "Include meaningful, ongoing input and collaboration from local communities and diverse stakeholders in the development and continuous improvement of the system." Further, the concept of "competent systems" (Urban, Vandenbroeck, Van Laere, Lazzari, & Peeters, 2012) requires that linkages exist between various stakeholders in an education endeavor, such as policy makers, administrators, teachers, and parents, another example of a more democratic approach to education evaluation.

Finally, one approach to improving education worldwide invokes the idea, "Educational Diplomacy." Education diplomats do not represent states or countries but represent learners. As diplomats, educators acquire specific skills "to bridge understanding, solve education challenges, and promote transformative agendas that ensure equitable and inclusive, quality education" (Murphy, 2018, p. 3). As such, education diplomats engage in information gathering, reach certain objectives via negotiation, achieve agreement between diverse participants, and focus on building long-term relationships (Hone, 2018, p. 8). What if we acted like education diplomats? How would that change our work to influence OECD and policy makers in our individual countries? This type of action might require us to "reconceptualize reconceptualization," by committing ourselves to *praxis*, combining our thoughts with action in the political arena, requiring us to move into new territory and try on different roles (Bloch, Diaz, Jipson, Kessler, & Lysack, 2019).

A Way Forward for Teachers

How can we convince the OECD and other policy makers to agree to more democratic forms of curriculum development and education evaluation that are more humane and just? If we view the OECD projects as political endeavors, even as forms of "political action" (MacDonald, 1978), we must act in the political arena to bring about change. However, to act politically I believe we educators must think carefully about who we are. What are the core values and beliefs that influence our work? What if we created a position paper, or manifesto, like that published by the Teachers College faculty in 1940, that would state our basic principles and beliefs as to what democracy means to us and its relationship to curriculum development and education evaluation? What if we created a poster that summarized those beliefs and posted it in school hallways and classrooms?

Another way forward would be to view such a manifesto as a political platform, like that developed by political parties. For those of us interested in professional organizations taking a political stand, we could begin by suggesting topics or issues to guide our work in creating such a platform. Issues could include curriculum and evaluation, educational funding, environmental justice, children's rights, inclusion, the rights of indigenous peoples and members of the LGBTQ community, immigration, teacher education, and so forth. What if we educators used such a document to create coalitions with likeminded groups, such as members of professional associations like the Association of Childhood Education International (ACEI) and the National Association of Early Childhood Education (NAEYC) revising the document as we go along? What if we worked with international organizations such as

UNICEF and UNESCO to influence educational policies, curriculum development, and evaluation practices related to programs for young children? UN documents such as "Sustainable Development Goals" (UN, 2018), that includes ending poverty and hunger, and providing a quality education for all, as well as the UN "Declaration of the Rights of the Child" (UN, 1990) could inform and inspire us. "The Creed of Democracy" could also provide many ideas as to what a manifesto could include.

With such a platform in hand we could approach organizations in our respective countries, as well as policy makers, and advocate, agitate, and maybe even march to advance our political agenda. We might even consider engaging in an uprising like that successfully carried out recently in Norway, where teachers, family members, teacher educators and others, through protests and sit-ins, managed to stop the standardization and testing of language skills in all programs for 5-year-olds (Eide, n.d.). I believe that acting in the political arena is the only way to create meaningful educational change in curriculum development and evaluation practices in early childhood education and care programs throughout the world.

Notes

1   This paper was originally presented at the 26th International Reconceptualizing Early Childhood Education (RECE) Conference, Copenhagen, Denmark, October 18, 2018. I am grateful to Janice Jipson and Dory Lightfoot for reading an earlier draft of this paper.
2   Recently, this metaphor was referred to as the "factory model," characterized by teacher-centered classrooms that privilege memorization and recall. See Nurenberg (2019).
3   Most OECD members are high-income economies with a very high Human Development Index and are regarded as developed countries. As of 2017, the OECD member states collectively comprised 62.2% of global nominal GDP and 42.8% of global GDP at purchasing power parity. OECD is an official United Nations observer.

Appendix A: A Creed of Democracy

We believe in and will endeavor to make a democracy which
1—extends into every realm of human association;
2—respects the personality of every individual, whatever his origin or present status;
3—insures to all a sense of security;
4—protects the weak and cares for the needy that they may maintain their self-respect;
5—develops in all a sense of belongingness;
6—protects every individual against exploitation by special privilege or power;
7—believes in the improvability of all men;
8—has for its social aim the maximum development of each individual;

9—assumes that the maximum development possible to each individual is for the best interest of all;

10—provides an opportunity for each and every individual to make the best of such natural gifts as he has and encourages him to do so;

11—furnishes an environment in which every individual can be and is stimulated to exert himself to develop his own unique personality, limited only by the similar rights of others;

12—assumes that adults are capable of being influenced by reason;

13—appeals to reason rather than force to secure its ends;

14—permits no armed force that is not under public control;

15—implies that a person becomes free and effective by exercising self-restraint rather than by having restraint imposed upon him by external authority;

16—imposes only such regulation as is judged by society to be necessary for safeguarding the rights of others;

17—assumes that all persons have equal rights to life, liberty, and the pursuit of happiness;

18—guarantees that rights and opportunities accorded to one shall be accorded to all;

19—insures standards of living in which every individual can retain his own self-respect and unabashed make his peculiar contribution to the society in which he lives;

20—does not tolerate an enduring social stratification based on birth, race, religion, or wealth, inherited or otherwise acquired;

21—recognizes a desire on the part of people to govern themselves and a willingness to assume responsibility for doing so;

22—holds that government derives its powers solely from the consent of the governed;

23—tests the validity of government by its effort and success in promoting the welfare of human beings;

24—lays on individuals an obligation to share actively and with informed intelligence in formulating general public policies;

25—requires that the responsibilities and activities of citizenship be generally held to be among the highest duties of man;

26—holds that men deserve no better government than they exert themselves to obtain;

27—believes that the decisions concerning public policies made by the pooled judgment of the maximum number of interested and informed individuals are in the long run the wisest;

28—weighs all votes equally;

29—has faith that an individual grows best and most by actively and intelligently exercising his right to share in making decisions on public policy;

30—permits, encourages, and facilitates access to information necessary to the making of wise decisions on public policies;

31—provides free education from the beginnings of formal schooling as long as it may be profitable to society for each industrious individual to continue;

32—attempts a general diffusion among the people of the ideals, knowledge, standards of conduct, and spirit of fair play which promote a sense of equality;

33—permits the unhampered expression of everyone's opinions on public policy;

34—guarantees the right of free expression of opinions on all matters, subject to reasonable libel laws;

35—implies that all who are bound by decisions of broad public policy should have an opportunity to share in making them;

36—demands that minorities live in accord with the decisions of the majority, but accords the right to agitate peacefully for the change of such decisions;

37—exercises tolerance to others without sacrificing the strength of conviction favoring different notions and practices;

38—accepts representative government as an economy necessitated by the size of the population;

39—delegates responsibility to individuals chosen by the people for their peculiar competence in defined areas of action, but retains the right to withdraw this authority;

40—develops a steadily increasing sense of obligation to a constantly enlarging social group;

41—induces a willingness to sacrifice personal comforts for the recognized general welfare;

42—stimulates a hope of constant betterment and provides means which the ambitious and earnest may use;

43—encourages constant reappraisal of things as they are and stimulates a hope that leads to action for their betterment in the future;

44—uses peaceful means for promoting and bringing about change;

45—holds that the fundamental civil liberties may not be impaired even by majorities;

46—permits unrestrained association and assembly for the promotion of public welfare by peaceful means;

47—recognizes and protects the right of individuals to associate themselves for the promotion of their own interests in any ways that are not incompatible with the general welfare;

48—grants the right to labor at work of one's own choosing, provided it does not interfere with the interests of society;

49—guarantees the right to enjoy the fruits of one's honest labor and to use them without molestation after paying a part proportionate to wealth or income to the cost of necessary government and general welfare;

50—encourages individual initiative and private enterprise in so far as they are compatible with the public weal;

51—maintains human rights to be more important than property rights;

52—so regulates the natural resources of the country as to preserve them for the widest use for the welfare of all the people;

53—insures freedom of movement;

54—guarantees a legal assumption of innocence until proof of guilt, definite charges before arrest and detention, and open and speedy trial before a jury of peers, with protection of rights by the court and by competent counsel;

55—guarantees freedom from persecution by those in authority;

56—provides that no individual be deprived of life, liberty, or property without due process of law;

57—permits worship according to the dictates of one's conscience;

58—separates state and church;

59—provides such security, freedom, opportunity, and justice for all of its members that they will.

60—renews its strength by continued education as to its meanings and purposes.

References

Abramowitz, M. J. (2018). Freedom in the world 2018: Democracy in crisis. Retrieved from https://freedomhouse.org/sites/default/files

Alliance for Excellence in Education (2018). *10 principles for building a high-quality system of assessment*. Washington, DC:Author.

Apple, M.W. (2001). *Educating the "right" way: Markets, standards, god, and inequality*. New York: Routledge.

Berliner, D.C. (2015). The many facets of PISA. *Teachers College Record*, 117(1), 1–20. Retrieved from http://www.tcrecord.org

Bloch, M., Diaz, M., Jipson, J., Kessler, S.A., & Lysak, M. (2019). Crossing over: Exploring the evolution and political possibilities of RECE. Paper Presented at the 28th annual Reconceptualizing Early Childhood Education Conference, Las Cruses, Mexico.

Cannella, G.S. (1977). *Deconstructing early childhood education: Social justice and revolution*. New York: Peter Lang.

Chomsky, N. (2017) Neoliberalism is destroying our democracy. Interviewed by L. Christopher, June 2. Retrieved from https://chomsky.info/06022017/

Coates, D. (2017). Democratic primaries in the shadow of neoliberalism. *Huffington Post*, May. Retrieved from https://www.huffingtonpost.com/david-coates/democratic-prima ries-in-t_b_10018638.html

Eide, K. (n.d.). *In Norway there is a kindergarten uprising…*Oslo: Emancipation Solutions Group AS.

Giroux, H.A. (2018). Neoliberal fascism and the twilight of the social. *Truthout*, October 5. Retrieved from https://truthout.org/series/public-intellectual/

Gutmann, A. (1987). *Democratic education*. Princeton, NJ: Princeton University Press.

Hone, K. (2018). Education and diplomats: A changing world demands our attention. *Childhood Education*, 9(43), 4–9.

House, E.R., & Howe, K.R. (1999). *Values in evaluation and social research*. Thousand Oaks, CA: Sage.

Kessler, S.A. (1991). Early childhood education as development: Critique of the metaphor. *Early Education and Development*, 2(2), 137–152.

Kessler, S.A. (2018). Reconceptualizing the early childhood curriculum: An unaddressed topic. In M. Bloch, B. B. Swadener, & G. Cannella (Eds.),*Reconceptualizing early childhood education and care – a reader: Critical questions, new imaginaries & social activism* (2nd ed.) (pp. 35–45). New York: Peter Lang.

Kliebard, H. M. (1975). Metaphorical roots of curriculum design. In W. Pinar (Ed.), *Curriculum theorizing: The reconceptualists* (pp. 84–85). Berkeley: McCutchan.

Levitsky, S., & Ziblatt, D. (2018). *How democracies die*. New York: Crown.

Lindbergh, C. (1939). Our race is our nation: Aviation, geography and race. *Readers Digest*, November. Retrieved from www.landoverbaptist.net/showthread.php?t=30612

MacDonald, B. (1977). A political classification of evaluation studies. In D. Hamilton, D. Jenkins, C. King, B. MacDonald, & M. Parlett (Eds.), *Beyond the numbers game* (pp. 224–227). London: Macmillan.

MacDonald, B. (1978). Democracy and evaluation. Paper presented at the University of Alberta Faculty of Education, Edmonton, October 17. Retrieved from https://www.uea.ac.uk/documents/4059364/4410085/MacDonald-1979-

Meier, D., & Koestner, M. (2017). *Beyond testing: Seven assessments of students and schools more effective than standardized tests*. New York: Teachers College Press.

Macha, K. (2018). Do children have a voice in the ECEC system? Looking for ways to include the children's views within the system. Paper presented at the 27th International Reconceptualizing Early Childhood Education Conference, Copenhagen, Denmark, October.

Murphy, Y. (2018). Education diplomacy: The two sides of innovation. *Childhood Education*, 94(3), 3.

Nurenberg, C. (2019). Want to Scrap the "Factory Model" classroom? Mind these common pitfalls. *Education Week*, March.

OECD (2018a). What is PISA? Retrieved from http://www.oecd.org/pisa/aboutpisa/

OECD (2018b). The International Early Learning and Child Well-being Study – The Study. Retrieved from www.oecd.org

OECD (2018c). Definition and Selection of Competencies (DeSeCo). Retrieved from http://www.org/education/school/definitionandselectionofcomop etenciesdesecokills-beyone-s

Perry, L., & McConney, A. (2010). Does SES of the school matter? An examination of socioeconomic status and student achievement using PISA 2003. *Teachers College Record, 112*(4), 1137–1162. Retrieved from http://wwwtrecord.org

Pinar, W. (Ed.). (1975). *Curriculum theorizing: The reconceptualists*. Berkeley: McCutchan.

Public Broadcasting System (n.d.). Ford's anti-Semitism. Retrieved from https://www.pbs.org/wgbh/americanexperience/features/henryford-antisemitism

Sander, G.F. (2017). When Nazis filled Madison Square Garden. *Politico*, August. Retrieved from https://politico.com/magazine/story2017/08/23/nazi-german-america n-bund-rally-madison-square-garden-215522

Social Security History (2018). Father Charles E. Coughlin. Retrieved from https://www.ssa.gov/history/cough.html

Stake, R.E. (2004). *Standards-based & responsive evaluation*. Thousand Oaks, CA: Sage.

Strauss, V. (2018). Education professor: My students asked me who I would vote for. Here's what I told them. *The Washington Post*, October 25. Retrieved from https://www.washingtonpost.com/education/2018/10/22/education-professor-my-students-a sked-who-i-would-vote-heres-what-i-told-them/?utm_term=

Teachers College Faculty (1940). A manifesto on democracy and education in the current crisis. *Teachers College Record*, 42(2), 99–115. Retrieved from http://www.tcrecord.org

The Guardian (2014). OECD and PISA test are damaging education worldwide – academics. May 25. Retrieved from www.theguardian.com.

United Nations (1990) Declaration of the rights of the child. Retrieved from https://unicef.org/malaysia/1959-Declaration-of-the-Rights-of-the-Child

United Nations (2018) The sustainable development goals report 2018. Retrieved from https://unstats.un.org/sdgs/report/2018/overview/

Urban, M., & Swadener, B.B. (2016). Democratic accountability and contextualized systematic evaluation. A comment on the OECD initiative to launch an international early learning study (IELS). *International Critical Childhood Policy Studies*, 5(1), 6–18. Also available at receinternational.org

Urban, M., Vandenbroeck, M., Van Laere, K., Lazzari, A., & Peeters, J. (2012). Towards competent systems in early childhood education and care: Implications for policy and practice. *European Journal of Education*, 47(4), 508.

AFTERWORD

William Ayers

After thirty-six hours of labor—bone-deep exhaustion tempered with fluttery exhilaration and raw ecstasy—our oldest son splashed into the world on a shimmering wave of blood and goo in our fifth-floor walk-up. The midwife wiped him dry and swaddled him in a fresh blanket before handing him to his mother, who, crying joyfully, held him to her breast.

Can you picture the scene?

OK, so who was teaching who how to nurse?

True, his mom was prepared—she'd read a lot, talked with experienced friends, and joined La Leche League. But the newborn was also prepared, naturally and in his own way, and he knew some things she didn't know: hold me here, he seemed to say, change sides now, more please, oops, too much. He was five minutes old, and he was already displaying his remarkable agency, engaging his mother in a fledgling dialogue that would evolve and deepen and last a lifetime.

It's real life, and this newborn (like others) has the capacity to express a few primal preferences and desires and understandings right from the start. And if that's true, how much more can a five-year-old or a fifteen-year-old bring?

Practices, in or out of school, that assume any human being is a blank slate passively awaiting instruction is wrong in both senses: they're incorrect, and they're ethically compromised. The challenge for teachers and parents and youth workers—and for all of us—is to recognize the agency that we know is there in this three-dimensional child, and to unlock the wisdom in every situation—in the room, on the street, in the community.

In a dazzling comic strip (*New Yorker;* 9/27/93), the legendary author Maurice Sendak strolls through the woods with his friend and fellow artist Art Spiegelman discussing their work and arguing about the marketing of children's books. When

Spiegelman argues that he wants to protect kids from books like his own *Maus*, Sendak asserts that *kids know everything*, and that while people act as if childhood is all quaint and succulent, like Peter Pan, in fact "childhood is deep and rich. It's vital, mysterious and profound. I remember my own childhood vividly ... I knew terrible things. But I knew I mustn't let adults know I knew ... It would scare them."

Educating for Social Justice in Early Childhood is a gathering of a propulsive group of authors who are not scared to embrace children as three-dimensional beings with hearts and minds and bodies and experiences that must somehow be taken into account. These authors ask a vital question—What kind of a person is a child?—and offer a dialectical response: a child is a whole human being with full human rights, and simultaneously, a child is a special human being with different needs and worthy of unique attentiveness, compassion, and considerations. They hold this contradiction in their minds as they explore what it means to take a deep dive into the meaning-making perspectives of young children, to face them honestly and authentically, to listen closely and to see them as vital participants in our shared world—personal, familial, social—and to note that notions of fairness and compassion come naturally to them. Whether in the borderlands of the US Southwest, the cities of the Northeast or in Australia, these scholars affirm that children have something to say, and an impulse to act.

I came to teaching from an odd direction: I was a student caught up in the civil rights struggle and the early stirrings of anti-war sentiment, when I committed my first act of civil disobedience, sitting in at the offices of the local draft board. Thirty-nine of us were charged with trespassing that day and carted off to county jail where I learned about a freedom school in town from a fellow protester. Intrigued, I went made a visit as soon as I was released. What I found was enchanting and captivating, a little utopian dream called the Children's Community—"an experiment in freedom and integration"—housed in a shabby church basement. All I saw was color and laughter and life. I was hooked—I'd walked out of jail and into my first teaching job, and from that day until this teaching has been linked for me to the persistent longing for freedom, and the never-ending quest for justice.

Most days were like that first one—pockets of calm, eclectic projects and fleeting efforts in every corner, laughter and tears and a current of wildness that could ignite in a heartbeat, sending a rollicking handful of roughnecks harum-scarum around the room. I believed that most schools tried to break and control kids, enacting some cleaned up kind of Calvinism, beating the hell out of them for their own good. I embraced, then, whole-heartedly a contrary idea: kids are naturally good and will blossom beautifully if raised in freedom. A little Rousseau, a little Thoreau, a little Ashton-Warner, a little A.S. Neill.

Experience, experience, experience. We wanted the kids to think, to be bold and adventurous, and so we pushed each other to be bold and to think ourselves. Trips became a big-letter statement about the centrality of first-hand experience as adventure and investigation and learning. Whenever a kid expressed an interest in anything—the weird, the bizarre, the intriguing, the surprising—off we'd go to have a look. We went to the hospital to visit a mother who worked as a nurse's aide, and to the county jail to visit Tony's uncle. We didn't know how to stop or where. Experience, experience, we said. Go further.

The urgency of "going further" is even more stark today: catastrophic capitalist environmental collapse, endless war, racism resurgent and white supremacy entrenched, an abiding crisis in the possibility of participatory democracy, and more. There are countless examples of teachers today taking that mandate seriously, none more playful and profound than Jeanne Marie Iorio and Clifton S. Tanabe's account of the "Out and About" project in Australia (Chapter 11), an effort to build relationships between human beings and the earth by regularly exploring the nearby beach and reflecting on the symbiotic connections. Go further, go deeper.

On a field trip to the local fire house with a group of preschoolers, four-year-old Caitlin asked our tour guide, Jimmy, when there would be a woman firefighter at the station. Jimmy exploded in derisive laughter: "A woman!" he said. "I hope never. Women can't do this work. The neighborhood will burn down." Caitlin was outraged: "That's not fair!" Back at school Caitlin wrote a protest letter to the mayor: Women can do anything! she said. And then she organized her classmates and their parents to write letters too. We made the local news! Years later Caitlin wrote her college essay on this event and noted that kids are natural activists. In Chapter 6, Lacey Peters offers powerful evidence affirming Caitlin's point.

I came to believe that the chief function of most schools was to make kids docile and obedient. For many students the experience of schooling was easily summed up: Nothing of real importance is a part of classroom life, nothing is connected to anything else, nothing is pursued to its furthest limits, nothing is ever undertaken with investment or courage, and nothing of lasting value is ever accomplished. Too many schools seemed to celebrate ignorance in an odd way, insisting that matters of real importance to children be banned (too controversial, or just diversionary). Most schools seemed to fetishize rules, control, standardization, conformity, facts, and order, rather than honoring, say, freedom, divergence, variation, creativity, novelty, flexibility, improvisation, and uniqueness. We asked the serious questions: What's the evidence? How do we know? Whose viewpoint is privileged and whose left out? What are the alternatives, the connections, the resistance, the patterns, the causes? Where are things headed? Why? Who cares? In Chapter 9, Mariana Souto-Manning, Gail Buffalo, and Ayesha Rabadi-Rao challenge the idea that access is an adequate response to injustice, and illustrate the ways in which white supremacy—unstated, invisible until uncovered—is the default setting in early childhood education.

In my lifetime young people have risen up to challenge and change the world again and again, from Little Rock to Birmingham, Soweto to Tiananmen,

Palestine to Chiapas, Wounded Knee to Cairo. It's always the youth who reject taken-for-granted injustices—I always remember that the average age of a person escaping slavery in 1850 was seventeen—and in this moment it's young people who are providing the insight and inspiration as catalysts, activists, and organizers.

The activism of the Black Lives Matter movement today—angry and loving—not only illustrates the brilliance and clarity of young people, but also flies in the face of popular currency that children and youth are passive and disengaged, or less competent and less thoughtful, less wise but more dangerous than adults. Dana Frantz Bentley and Betty Chan's classroom stories and Lacey Peters' research challenge that popular myth directly. The continuing reality of young people as social actors stands in opposition to official policies of silencing, suppressing, searching, expelling and punishing youth, depriving them of an education and denying their right to be heard. Inspired by the courage and determination of Ferguson youth, young people across the nation exercised their stubborn agency and walked out of schools, marched on police stations and city halls, sat-in, died-in, blocked highways and bridges—becoming a fresh, searing force for equality, racial justice, and dignity.

With their radical impulse to revolt, a spirit of hopefulness and possibility, their laser-like insights into the flaws in the world they've inherited and the hypocrisies of the adult world, youth are propelled to break the rules, link arms, and re-imagine their futures. They look at the *status quo* as unnatural and immoral—a state of emergency for the downtrodden, the marginalized, the exploited and oppressed.

Education for free people is powered by a particularly precious and fragile ideal: *every human being is of infinite and incalculable value*, each a work in progress and a force in motion, each a unique intellectual, emotional, physical, spiritual, moral, and creative force, each of us born equal in dignity and rights, each endowed with reason and conscience and agency, each deserving a dedicated place in a community of solidarity as well as a vital sense of brotherhood and sisterhood, recognition and respect. And here we embrace another fundamental contradiction: each is the one of one, and each of us is at the same time one of the many; we are entirely unique and we are radically the same. Holding onto that contradiction and noting that basic ethic and spirit, we recognize that the fullest development of each individual—given the tremendous range of ability and the delicious stew of race, ethnicity, points of origin, and background—is the necessary condition for the full development of the entire community, and, conversely, that the fullest development of all is essential for the full development of each.

It starts at the beginning.

INDEX